European Foreign Policy Making toward the Mediterranean

EUROPE IN TRANSITION: THE NYU EUROPEAN STUDIES SERIES

The Marshall Plan: Fifty Years After
  Edited by Martin Schain

Europe at the Polls: The European Elections of 1999
  Edited by Pascal Perrineau, Gérard Grunberg, and Colette Ysmal

Unions, Immigration, and Internationalization: New Challenges and Changing Coalitions in the United States and France
  By Leah Haus

Shadows Over Europe: The Development and Impact of the Extreme Right in Western Europe
  Edited by Martin Schain, Aristide Zolberg, and Patrick Hossay

Defending Europe: The EU, NATO and the Quest for European Autonomy
  Edited by Joylon Howorth and John T. S. Keeler

The Lega Nord and Contemporary Politics in Italy
  By Thomas W. Gold

Germans or Foreigners? Attitudes toward Ethnic Minorities in Post-Reunification Germany
  Edited by Richard Alba and Peter Schmidt

Germany on the Road to Normalcy? Politics and Policies of the First Red-Green Federal Government
  Edited by Werner Reutter

The Politics of Language: Essays on Languages, State and Society
  Edited by Tony Judt and Denis Lacorne

Realigning Interests: Crisis and Credibility in European Monetary Integration
  By Michele Chang

The Impact of Radical Right-Wing Parties in West European Democracies
  By Michelle Hale Williams

European Foreign Policy Making toward the Mediterranean
  By Federica Bicchi

European Foreign Policy Making toward the Mediterranean

Federica Bicchi

palgrave
macmillan

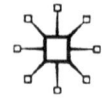

EUROPEAN FOREIGN POLICY MAKING TOWARD THE MEDITERRANEAN
© Federica Bicchi, 2007.

All rights reserved. No part of this book may be used or reproduced in any manner whatsoever without written permission except in the case of brief quotations embodied in critical articles or reviews.

First published in 2007 by
PALGRAVE MACMILLAN™
175 Fifth Avenue, New York, N.Y. 10010 and
Houndmills, Basingstoke, Hampshire, England RG21 6XS
Companies and representatives throughout the world.

PALGRAVE MACMILLAN is the global academic imprint of the Palgrave Macmillan division of St. Martin's Press, LLC and of Palgrave Macmillan Ltd. Macmillan® is a registered trademark in the United States, United Kingdom and other countries. Palgrave is a registered trademark in the European Union and other countries.

ISBN-13: 978–1–4039–6864–7
ISBN-10: 1–4039–6864–0

Library of Congress Cataloging-in-Publication Data

Bicchi, Federica.
    European foreign policy making toward the Mediterranean / by Federica Bicchi.
        p. cm. — (Europe in transition : NYU EU studies)
    Includes bibliographical references and index.
    ISBN 1–4039–6864–0 (alk. paper)
      1. European Union countries—Foreign relations—Mediterranean Region. 2. Mediterranean Region—Foreign relations—European Union countries. 3. European Union countries—Foreign relations—Arab countries. 4. Arab countries—Foreign relations—European Union countries. I. Title. II. Series.

JZ1570.A545B53 2007
341.242'2091822—dc22   2006031107

A catalogue record for this book is available from the British Library.

Design by Newgen Imaging Systems (P) Ltd., Chennai, India.

First edition: July 2007
10 9 8 7 6 5 4 3 2

Printed in the United States of America.

Contents

List of Illustrations — vii

Acknowledgments — ix

Introduction — 1

1 European Foreign Policy Making in Search of a Theory — 9

2 The Euro-Mediterranean Relations from 1957 to 1972: When No Tailored European Foreign Policy Existed — 43

3 Inventing the Mediterranean: From the Global Mediterranean Policy to the Euro-Arab Dialogue — 63

4 The Partition of the Mediterranean — 111

5 The New Post–Cold War Activism — 129

Conclusions — 181

Notes — 193

References — 217

Index — 243

List of Illustrations

Tables

2.1	Legal Basis of Agreements between the EEC and Mediterranean Countries, 1957–1972	49
2.2	Timing of Agreements between the EEC and Mediterranean Countries, 1957–1972	53
3.1	Trade of EEC Countries with Mediterranean Countries	76
3.2	Supply of Oil for OECD Europe	77
3.3	Agreements between the EEC and the Mediterranean Nonmembers	105
5.1	Germany, Stock of Foreign Population from the Mediterranean	135
5.2	France, Stock of Foreign Population from the Mediterranean	135
5.3	Italy, Stock of Foreign Population from the Mediterranean	136
5.4	Spain, Stock of Foreign Population from the Mediterranean	136
5.5	Spanish Diplomats Covering Key Posts on the Mediterranean, 1989–1995	160
5.6	Agreements between the EC and the Mediterranean Partners	173

Figures

I.1	The *Pars Destruens* and the *Pars Construens* of European Foreign Policy Making toward the Mediterranean	4
1.1	Three Views on EU Policy Making	14
3.1	Number of Terror Attacks Attributed to Arab-Palestinian Terrorists, 1968–1974	70
3.2	Number of Publications on the Subject of Energy and Oil, 1971–1975	79

Acknowledgments

One of the many things I learned during the writing of this book is that good research is dependent on the help of other people. I would like to thank all those who made this research possible, though only a few can be mentioned here. First, I am grateful to Thomas Risse, whose advice has always been the best one could hope for: intellectually stimulating and farsighted. A number of scholars were not only kind enough to comment on various drafts, but also taught me how to do good research. I am indebted to Emanuel Adler, Christopher Hill, Leonardo Morlino, Jean Blondel, Barry Buzan, Maurizio Cotta, Raffaella Del Sarto, Richard Gillespie, Margot Light, Mary Martin, Michelle Pace, Daniela Pioppi, Ghassan Salamé, Martin Schain, Karen Smith, Daniel Verdier and three anonymous (and very fair) reviewers. My heartfelt appreciation also goes to others who commented on the research project, draft chapters, and the papers presented on various occasions. My special thanks to the participants in the Staff Research Seminar of the Department of International Relations of LSE.

Several public officials took pains to explain to me "how reality works" and I am most grateful for that, especially to those who commented on the draft chapters. To all of them I guaranteed complete anonymity, but a few, who have become good friends along the way, deserve an open mention for also helping out with the practicalities of research: Cristina Ravaglia (Italian Ministry of Foreign Affairs), Francesco Settembri (European Commission), and Liborio Stellino (Italian Ministry of Foreign Affairs). Editorial support was generously provided by Martina Langer, whose standards of efficiency I can never match.

This research was made possible only due to the financial support received from several sources: the European University Institute in Florence (Italy), the Italian National Research Council (CNR), an Erasmus grant from the European Union, the Salvador de Madariaga

Foundation, the Rotary International Foundation, the University of Siena, and the Department of International Relations of LSE. I am grateful to the Center for European Studies of New York University, the Centre for the Analysis of Political Change (CIRCAP) of the University of Siena, and the Department of International Relations of LSE for providing an inspiring environment during the time I have spent there.

The book is dedicated to Andrew, whose patience was at times severely tested, but who has been a source of happiness throughout the numerous drafts of this book.

Introduction

Fifty years of EC/EU relations with its southern Mediterranean neighbors have produced a picture of extremes. Two bursts of EC/EU activity punctuate long periods of neglect. In the first 15 years of its existence, the EC/EU expressed only "accidental" interest in its southern neighbors (Hager 1974, 231) and in Eurospeak there was no Mediterranean to talk about. In 1972, a conceptual revolution occurred, leading to the first European Economic Community (EEC) initiative defining the Mediterranean as a relatively homogenous region. This initiative, under the name of the Global Mediterranean Policy, was followed shortly afterward by the Euro-Arab Dialogue. Yet this activism ran out of steam by the mid-1970s and was followed by another long period of negligible activity. Interest was rekindled at the end of the cold war, when the EU launched the Renovated Mediterranean Policy and then the Euro-Mediterranean Partnership. Currently, the region is also part of the new European Neighbourhood Policy, although this too, could run out of momentum.

What explains this stop-start pattern of two periods of intense negotiations and activism, interspersed by near total neglect? There are cases of collective policy making, in which policies change incrementally, slowly embracing a more or less coherent set of principles. There are other cases, to which the EC/EU Mediterranean policy appears to belong, characterized by "long periods of stability and short periods of dramatic reversals" (Baumgartner and Jones 1991, 1044). In these cases policy initiatives lead to significant innovation, not only in the format, but also in the principles governing the action, and the result is a paradigmatic policy change (Howlett and Ramesh 1995, 184ff.).

Cases of paradigmatic policy change are particularly intriguing, as they force us to consider the reasons behind such changes and the type of "mechanisms" by which they take place. What brings about innovation in European foreign policy? Why do member states and EC/EU institutions agree upon a policy initiative that upsets the previous pattern of EC/EU external relations? These questions, in turn, beget other questions. Echoing the debate about national agenda setting, one can pose the following questions: "How does an issue come to be viewed as an important and appropriate subject of attention?" (Cobb and Elder 1972, 12). How is the EC/EU agenda defined? Who are the actors most likely to act as catalysts of change? What are the dynamics of decision making that are most likely to deliver agreement on innovative change?

Put another way: *how, when, and why does the EC/EU formulate a new foreign policy initiative?* What are the structural conditions? Who are the key actors? What are the main processes through which European foreign policy making occurs? These questions lie at the core of this research.

My dependent variable, that is, what I shall be explaining in this volume, is the adoption of a European foreign policy initiative toward the Mediterranean.[1] In empirical terms, I will analyze why the EC/EU decides to upset and upgrade established patterns of relations with Mediterranean nonmember countries. I will adhere to the EC/EU official definition of "Mediterranean," meaning the countries that border the Mediterranean, and which are not EC/EU members. This group has changed over time as the EC/EU has enlarged and some Mediterranean countries are now termed southern European countries.[2] To be specific, I define European foreign policy (EFP) as that body of declarations, decisions, and actions, that are made by the use of all the instruments that the EC/EU has at its disposal, that are decided at the EC/EU level, and conducted in its name toward a country or an area outside its borders.[3] Thus this analysis covers more than European Political Cooperation (EPC) and its post-Maastricht successor, the Common Foreign and Security Policy (CFSP).[4] My understanding of the EFP also includes external economic relations, development policy instruments, migration issues, as well as the gray area that has developed as a consequence of the EU third pillar (collaboration on matters related to police and judicial cooperation, and so on). However, I will consider the member states' national foreign policies separately insofar as they are not conducted in the name of the EC/EU.[5]

What I will show is that EFP making is first and foremost an *ideational* process, involving member states and EC/EU institutions. A collective policy toward the Mediterranean has developed as member states and EC/EU institutions have crafted new understandings of Euro-Mediterranean relations and forged new initiatives based on them. For this ideational shift to occur and turn into a policy initiative, this research will demonstrate that it was necessary for three conditions to be in place.

The first condition is the opening of a "policy window" or a window of opportunity.[6] More precisely, I suggest that member states have been more likely to look positively upon a joint Mediterranean initiative when they have experienced "cognitive uncertainty" as to what must be done at their national level about challenges that originate from the region. When new issues have arisen (such as terrorism in the 1970s and migration in the 1990s), then policy makers have faced a novel situation and they have "puzzled" about policy making.[7] They have thus been forced to consider new interpretations and policy solutions. It was only when a majority of member states have experienced cognitive uncertainty about the Mediterranean (i.e., when national policy makers "did not know" what to do about it), then they have been available to discuss the Mediterranean at the EC/EU level. This is the type of policy window this research explores.

The second condition for the existence of EFP is the presence of a policy entrepreneur. Whereas the policy window expresses a set of background conditions, the policy entrepreneur adds an agential element to the picture. I will show that the most effective policy entrepreneurship has come from a member state, or from a coalition of actors guided by a member state. I will elaborate on the type of entrepreneurship that a member state provides and on what inspires it to act. I will suggest that entrepreneurs might act as "believers," driven by the strength of their convictions, or as "brokers," with a desire to secure a positive outcome to the process but flexible as to the content of the end product. I will suggest that while much of the literature has focused on entrepreneurs as "believers," there is a lot to be gained from looking at entrepreneurial states as "brokers." In this connection, I will argue that the range of motivations that push a member state into action is in fact very broad, and nonmaterial goals figure predominantly among the triggers of entrepreneurial action.

Once a policy window exists and a policy entrepreneur acts on it, the third factor that leads to the development of European foreign policy making is the interaction among member states and EC/EU institutions. The third condition in my argument is that policy making in the EC/EU is based on the common definition of ideas, while articulating problems in common terms and suggesting common solutions. Member states, together with EC/EU institutions, compare, evaluate and discuss different interpretations of the issues at stake. They put forward potential solutions and endeavor to back these up with appeals to facts and evidence. They thus create common knowledge, which then acts as a reference framework within which bargaining can follow. This process of cognitive interaction consists of "framing"[8] the new challenges and piecing together separate ideational streams into a narrative that defines the problem and its solutions at the EC/EU level.

How do these three conditions logically combine in the formulation of a European foreign policy initiative? What does the simultaneous presence of a policy window and a policy entrepreneur, followed by a debate, entail? This cognitive-ideational approach to EFP making can be said to comprise two components, a *pars destruens* and a *pars construens* (see figure I.1).

First, newly perceived security challenges appear on the horizon of the foreign policy priorities of member states and create uncertainty about policy relevant knowledge (which I call "cognitive uncertainty"). Previously established ways of thinking about, in this case, relations with the Mediterranean nonmembers are challenged by new debates at the national level, an evolving international environment, and more generally by a perceived mismatch between the "previous way of doing things" and developments on the ground (Florini 1996, 378).

Second, on this fertile soil, member states engage in a debate at the European level about how to deal with Mediterranean nonmembers, thus developing a common ideational frame that serves as the basis for a common European initiative. However, the debate at the European level does not flow automatically. It needs to be activated, and member

Pars destruens

Policy Window: Newly Perceived Security Challenges Create Cognitive Uncertainty

Policy Entrepreneur: A Member State Promotes a European Foreign Policy Initiative

Member States and EC/EU Institutions Develop a Common Ideational Frame

EFP Initiative toward the Mediterranean Nonmembers

Pars construens

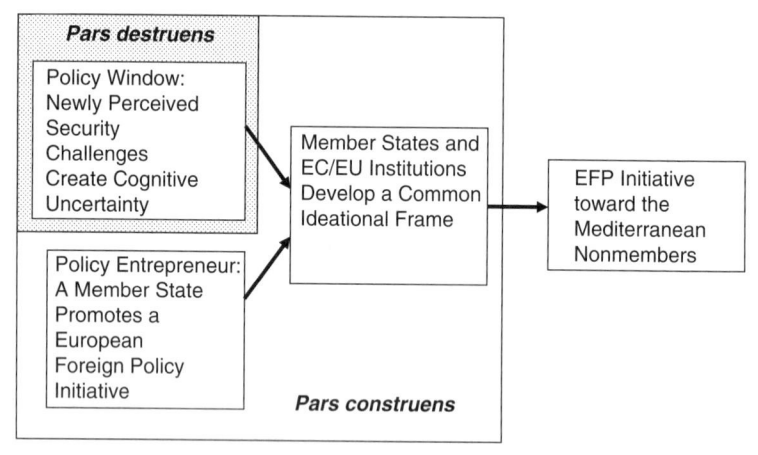

Figure I.1 The *Pars Destruens* and the *Pars Construens* of European Foreign Policy Making toward the Mediterranean

states are the principal, most effective catalysts for this. There are thus two interrelated processes at stake in this second, *construens* component. On one hand, there is a member state that promotes the formulation of a European initiative. On the other hand, the definition of a common understanding unfolds in the interaction between *all* member states and EC/EU institutions.

In a broader perspective, there are three ways in which this process might interest the reader. The first way to look at it (and to read this book) is as a process of deconstruction of national preferences and of the definition of common European principles, based on interlocking arenas.[9] To ensure that the EFP process is made possible, previous national preferences that excluded a European initiative must be challenged, set aside, and replaced with a willingness to "shop around" for policy ideas. When national preferences are in flux, a period of potential transformation opens up. In other words, European integration can potentially flow from uncertainty of preferences. While politicians are more likely to turn first to the domestic arena to tackle the problem, the European arena might offer a complementary forum and an alternative arena for problem solving. Domestic elements are crucial in explaining why member states are interested in participating in a European process, but the outcome cannot be understood without taking into account the link between national arenas and the EC/EU. Interlocking arenas affect preference formation.

Second, this book reads as a response to the structure-agency dilemma. Since the famous article by Wendt (1987), international relations theories have struggled to address how to treat the existence of parts that are embedded within a whole. Following the call to conceptualize structures as conditions for action (e.g., Patomäki and Wight 2000, 230–231), this research imports concepts from Policy Analysis to offer an answer. The simultaneous presence of a policy window (the structural context) and of a policy entrepreneur (the agent) is the condition necessary to spark a debate and a process of framing which in turn will lead to European foreign policy making. This follows the path opened by Carlsnaes, who imported into Foreign Policy Analysis and to International Relations in general the morphogenetic approach of Archer (1995), according to which social analysis should focus on the *longue durée*.[10] By accounting for 50 years of Euro-Mediterranean relations, this book adopts a similar view, offering an analysis of the process of co-constitution of agency and structure across time.

Finally, and most importantly, this book aims to contribute to two different debates about the role of ideas and about the motives and consequences of the actions of states. The central role in the process, which I will describe, is the crafting of new ideas and the crucial importance of what policy actors believe, and believe they know in the evolution of both political perception and policy solutions. As such this book helps to further the debate about the role of ideas in international relations (Finnemore and Sikkink 1998; Wendt 1999). It also places the action of national entrepreneurs in a new light, stressing the scope for member states' entrepreneurial actions to have supranational effects. In other words, I aim to break down the stark theoretical dilemma, according to which either member states pursue limited integration, or supranational actors purse supranational outcomes. I suggest instead that the analysis of member states' role is more complicated and more open ended than liberal intergovernmentalism (e.g., Moravcsik 1998) would have it. My aim here is to put forward an "analytical rescue" of member states[11] and of their actions in European integration processes. What I am pointing at is a new way of understanding European integration, namely as a collective creation of knowledge that brings member states closer together as they struggle to cognitively address multiple challenges with the aim of policy formulation. This framework is ideational, because of the emphasis on ideational and cognitive processes, and at the same time it is intergovernmental, because of the role played by member states. Hence I adopt the label of ideational intergovernmentalism to describe it.

It is fair to mention at the start the limitation of this research. The conceptual approach focuses on macroconditions and there is little room for microanalyses. Admittedly, the cognitive processes that I examine do have microfoundations, but it was not possible to explore them in this research. The focus will thus remain on macro processes, generally referring to states or to national representatives, to the European Commission (hereafter referred to as the Commission) or to specific Commissioners, but little effort is taken to delve into the individual level of knowledge formation or to inter- and intra-group dynamics that play a crucial role in it. That is the subject for another analysis.

A few words should also be mentioned about the method adopted to gather the empirical evidence in this book. Primary sources have been used whenever possible, but this was not always the case. Policy documents, both from ministries of Foreign Affairs and EC/EU institutions, have been analyzed, although the archives for the early 1970s have opened only in very few countries. Hence I have relied on the information for this period on French Archives and EEC Archives, which are relatively easy to access. To compensate for the limited access to official documents for this period, I have devoted special attention to gray materials and newspapers. Moreover, both for the 1970s and the 1990s, I have carried out a number (around 70) of semi-structured and off the record interviews in Brussels, London, Madrid, Paris, Rome, and part of which will be quoted in the following chapters. To all interviewees I guaranteed complete anonymity, which unfortunately for the reader prevents me from quoting their names. I will also present some statistical analysis for specific issues, such as economic relations and migration flows. Otherwise, I have relied on secondary sources to put interviews into context and to analyze broad historical trends. At times this was a choice of necessity, given the broad time span (1957–2007) covered in this research.

Chapter 1 sets out the main tenets of the argument, contrasting them with prevailing positions in International Relations and European Studies. The empirical analysis is divided into sections that describe the low and high points of EFP making toward the Mediterranean. Chapter 2 deals with "time zero" of EFP toward the Mediterranean before the first initiatives were formulated, while chapter 3 covers the period when the Mediterranean was officially "invented" through the Global Mediterranean Policy and Euro-Arab Dialogue. Chapter 4 presents a case of "dogs that did not bark," namely the lack of a policy window matched with a low-key attempt at policy entrepreneurship by the Commission, and the consequential absence of EFP. Chapter 5 examines the second period of activism, and how the pattern shown in the 1970s is repeated, though in a more complex configuration, in the aftermath of the cold war. It analyzes the processes leading to the formulation of the Renovated Mediterranean Policy, of the Euro-Mediterranean Partnership and, for what is possible at the moment of writing, of the European Neighbourhood Policy. The conclusions come back to the broad questions sketched here and summarize the answers provided by the empirical findings, and draw general remarks about the implications for future research.

CHAPTER 1

European Foreign Policy Making in Search of a Theory

Introduction

The aim of this book is to understand how, when, and why the EC/EU launches a foreign policy initiative toward a third party such as the Mediterranean nonmember countries. The type of change I focus on is paradigmatic policy change (Hall 1993; Howlett and Ramesh 1995, 184), policy innovation and "policy setting," understood as a middle way between history making decisions, such as treaties and constitutional changes, and decisions setting the details of a policy (Peterson and Bomberg 1999, 5ff.).

The primary argument of this book is that EFP formulation is first and foremost an ideational process in which member states and EC/EU institutions converge toward a common definition of problems, policy solutions and the EC/EU's role in them. Such a process takes place under three conditions. First, there needs to be an open policy window defined as a situation of cognitive uncertainty, namely uncertainty about how to interpret social reality. When new issues arise on national agendas, national policy makers ponder about how to address them and are available to discuss new interpretations and policy solutions at the EC/EU level. Second, for this availability to turn into an active debate leading to policy making, a policy entrepreneur is required, and member states tend to be the most effective policy entrepreneurs in European foreign policy making toward the Mediterranean. Entrepreneurs can act out of the strength of their convictions (as "believers") or they might broadly aim for policy change (as "brokers"), with little specification about policy details. The latter group is most relevant for the analysis of EFP toward the Mediterranean. Finally, the third factor leading to European foreign policy making is the cognitive interaction among member states and EC/EU institutions. Member states, together with EC/EU institutions, develop common knowledge about the new challenges by framing the issues at stake and by piecing together separate ideational streams into a narrative that defines the problem and its solutions at the EC/EU level. Whereas the first condition represents the *pars destruens* of the process of EFP formulation, the second two conditions constitute its *pars construens*, through which a new EFP initiative toward the Mediterranean is agreed.

This chapter lays out the theoretical argument in greater detail, and it is organized as follows. First, I will summarize current debates on European integration theories and where my own approach, which I label ideational intergovernmentalism, fits into the existing literature. EFP, as I conceive it, is part of the European integration process, despite being a somewhat special case within the broader set of EC/EU policies. I then turn to the analysis of the three conditions that make up my argument. In the second section, I address the definition of the policy window and explore the type of window represented by cognitive uncertainty, and the consequences this uncertainty entails. In the third section, I analyze the issue of policy entrepreneurship, and how it can be reconceptualized so as to capture a broader range of possibilities and their potential consequences. In the fourth section, the account will turn to cognitive interaction and to the framing of common knowledge on which EFP initiatives are based. The concluding section puts forward a few analytical considerations about the process of EFP making as sketched out in this chapter and about the epistemological relevance of the overall argument of this book.

Contemporary Approaches to European Integration

In the past 15 years, studies of European integration have increased not only in number and quality, but also in the range of disciplinary backgrounds they have drawn from. Whereas this has brought new and intriguing theoretical disputes to the EC/EU empirical evidence, the change has not yet fully come to fruition for scholars and students in terms of a wider set of alternative understandings of EC/EU policy making. In this section, I suggest that, despite new insights from International Relations, Comparative Politics, and from literature on global governance and Policy Analysis, there remain two alternative explanations of EU policy making, one rooted in a rationalist process of utility maximizers and another that emphasizes the indirect socialization of national representatives. They depict, however, an unnecessary small set of possibilities. The argument I present aims at striking a middle route, which conceives of states as uncertainty minimizers and EU policy making as an active process of knowledge definition with the aim of policy formulation.

As Pollack put it (2005, 357), the study of European integration has been transformed by scholars from three broad disciplinary backgrounds that have undertaken the analysis of the EU. Researchers from the International Relations perspective have cast the EU in the framework of the debate between rational choice and constructivism. The liberal intergovernmentalist approach championed by Moravcsik (1997, 1998, 1999) spelled out a rationalist approach to European integration, which provoked a constructivist reply, aimed at reinterpreting neofunctionalism in a constructivist perspective (Sandholtz and Sweet Stone 1998; Christiansen et al. 2001; Risse 2004). Most notably, constructivists have stressed the crucial importance of ideational factors in the analysis of international relations, while liberal intergovernmentalists and scholars who are inspired by rational choice paradigms sit uneasily on this issue, stressing at the same time the importance of economic advantages and of reputational status of negotiating states. Comparative Politics has come in to strengthen the rationalist (and materialist) side of the debate, from a different disciplinary angle. As Hix has suggested, (1994) the EU as a system is not too different from domestic politics, for instance, in the United States and therefore outcomes in the EU can be analyzed as an institutional power game (Tsebelis 1994; Pollack 1997; Franchino 2000; Thomson and Hosli 2006). In this view, actors negotiate in a strategic manner, along the lines of what rational choicers have called bargaining (Scharpf 1988; Schneider and Cedermann 1994) and opposite to what constructivists have labeled arguing (Risse 2000).

The dispute between rational choice and constructivism across International Relations and Comparative Politics has been complemented by the accounts of authors who start from a Governance approach and from Policy Analysis. The former have aimed at including a broader set of formal and informal actors, cutting across different levels of the EU system, from the local to the European (Jachtenfuchs 2001; Marks et al. 1996; Hooghe and Marks 2001). Such an approach has been notably important in the analysis of European foreign policy, where it has fostered a "global governance" agenda (Knodt 2004; Lavenex 2004; Rosamond 2005). Policy Analysis offers yet another starting point to the study of the EU, which by definition contributes to the examination of policy making in the EU (Richardson 2005; Anderson and Eliassen 2001; Peterson and Bomberg 1999). I believe that it offers a fresh look at EU agenda setting and decision making. The framework adopted in this book in fact elaborates on an argument presented by Kingdon (1984/95), which proposes that a policy initiative occurs as a result of the simultaneous presence of a window of opportunity and a policy entrepreneur, who will profit from it. Using a Policy Analysis approach emphasizes how EFP is formulated, rather than focusing on the existence of such a thing as a "European foreign policy" or on the character of the EU as an international actor.

So, how does this plethora of approaches account for EU policy making? Simplifying for the sake of clarity, the variety of perspectives boils down to two main alternative views on policy making processes within the EU: a rationalist view and a constructivist one. They express two different rationales of policy setting in the EU.

The rationalist explanation takes its cue from two-level games, one game being at the domestic level and one taking place among states (Putnam 1988). Rational, goal-oriented national representatives negotiate in a strategic manner on the basis of preformed preferences with the aim of approximating as much as possible their preferred outcome within a given set of institutional constraints (Moravcsik 1998; Thomson and Hosli 2006, 7). States are thus central actors, and they are considered to be effective in both assembling domestic interests and representing them consistently over a period of time in international negotiations. Big member states are particularly important in determining the final outcome, as relative power is crucial in the definition of where, on the Pareto frontier, negotiations end. Negotiations are not however simply zero-sum games and tend instead to approximate positive-sum games (Moravcsik 2001, 238). Negotiations centre squarely on bargaining, although in a cooperative and more sophisticated environment than crude neorealist interpretations of international affairs would have it. In this perspective, while the main reason for EU policy making consists of domestically formed states' preferences, the main actors are states' representatives and the main negotiating style is bargaining.

Whereas the emphasis is on rational actors, it does not follow that they will succeed in keeping everything under control, and it is about this aspect that the debate is most lively in the rationalist literature. Most of the authors agree that member states do not operate in the perfect informational environment and the situation is likely to generate a momentum of its own. How much momentum is a matter of debate. According to many, national representatives are aware of limitations to what they can do, and tend to factor them into their preferences and negotiating strategies. This is the case, for instance, with the delegation of powers to the Commission and to other supranational bodies, as member states try to limit the drift from the original outcome of negotiations, although in doing so they may create yet another set of problems (Majone 2001; Pollack 2003; Franchino 2000). Schimmelfennig pushes the argument further, stating that, in a "community environment," a rationalist stage of preference formation is followed by a constructivist stage of international interaction (2003, 284–285). Actors using community values thus change outcomes, but their policy preferences are not affected by the interaction.

Despite variations, therefore, the sequence of EU policy making according to this literature starts from member states' domestically formed preferences and ends in the interaction among them, with supranational actors playing a subsidiary role in terms of lowering transaction costs.

A constructivist explanation of EU policy making reverses this sequence. Integration advances precisely because of the consequences of interaction on member states' interests (Checkel 1999).[1] The general understanding is that actors, such as national governments, are affected by EU social norms in which they are embedded, and these norms not only regulate behavior, but also constitute their identities and interests, and therefore their preferences (Risse 2004, 163). Therefore, EU policy making is grounded in the accumulation of positive experiences of cooperation, which seep into the preference pattern of participating states and open the way to future integration. Cooperation among member states develops into trust and a habit of coordination, which other actors are able to exploit and turn into specific instances of policy making. One of these other actors is the European Commission (e.g., Garrett and Weingast 1993; Cram 1994; Laffan 1997; Smith 1999), but policy networks and epistemic communities (e.g., Radaelli 1999) can also fill that role, and so can lower layers of the Council hierarchy, such as the Committee of Permanent Representatives (COREPER) (e.g., Lewis 1998). The process that then develops among key participants, variously characterized as arguing (Risse 2000), persuasion (Checkel 2001), or communicative action (Niemann 2004), consists of a process by which actors engage in a genuine process of "truth-seeking." In a social perspective inspired by constructivism, therefore, the main reason for EU policy making lies in the dynamics of socialization, the main actors tend to be all but the highest ranking national representatives, and the main negotiating style is closely related to arguing.

Unlike rationalist approaches, the issue within this literature is not how much of an impact do unintended consequences have on participating actors (the answer is a lot), but how does such a change happen. Some contributions, especially drawing on traditional versions of neofunctionalism, stress the relevance of the structural conditions in the form of the socialization process taking place in the background. This is the case with the shift of loyalties emphasized by early neofunctionalists (e.g., Haas 1958). Similarly, analyses of EFP by Smith (Smith 1998) and by Øhrgaard (1997) suggest that the tight network of diplomats gathering in the Political Committee (POCO) develops a dynamics of its own, leading to foreign policy cooperation in areas previously unforeseen. Øhrgaard specifies that the momentum develops in spite of the de facto absence of the Commission and its entrepreneurial skills in the CFSP framework. Others highlight the importance of agential elements in propelling the process forward. These can take the shape of a persuader/persuadee division of labor (e.g., Checkel 1997, 2001), mainly executed among national representatives, or in the actions of other nonnational players, as highlighted by part of the literature on "global governance." Still, the agential analysis is generally set against a strong structural background, an aspect that at times casts this literature in relatively passive tones.

A constructivist account of EU policy making stresses the ideational side of the story and makes full use of the variety of actors indicated by neofunctionalism and global governance approaches. Moreover, it turns the rationalist explanation round, by describing an indirect process through which socialization affects actors' interests and preferences.

Figure 1.1 summarizes the contrast between these two views. It also sets them alongside the one I am going to put forward, which is more

	Rationale for EU Policy Making	Main Entrepreneurial Actors	Nature of Negotiations
Rational Choice	Member States' Preferences	Member States	Bargaining
Constructivism	Socialization, Habit	Commission, Policy Networks, COREPER, and so on.	Arguing
Idealist Intergovernmentalism	Cognitive Uncertainty	Member States	Framing

Figure 1.1 Three Views on EU Policy Making

specific and relies on assumptions that tend to overlap with constructivist ones, while focusing on issues generally raised by rationalist accounts.

The approach I propose in this book, and which I will develop in this chapter, aims to pursue a middle path between these two competing visions. I term it ideational intergovernmentalism for the parallel emphasis it puts on ideational processes and on states. The rationale for EU policy making consists of member states' need to address cognitive uncertainty; the main actors promoting a European process are states and the gist of negotiations is the attempt to "frame" new knowledge with the aim of using it to formulate policy.

States are conceived as uncertainty minimizers, meaning that national representatives need to address new challenges with novel policy solutions. In other words, there exist situations in which they do not know what is going on, but they need to be in charge and be seen in control of policy developments. Routinely repeated sets of actions do not solve the problems any longer and thus national policy makers experience cognitive uncertainty about how to interpret and react to social events. Widespread cognitive uncertainty across member states creates a window of opportunity to discuss common problems at the European level. A member state or a coalition of member states is a particularly effective way to kick-start this debate and promote a process of EU policy making, as member states are capable of bringing urgency to the debate, feeding information into it, and adding a political flavor to the endeavor in a manner that the Commission and other actors have not (yet) been able to. The nature of the negotiations that ensue is first and foremost ideational and, more precisely, cognitive. The first step toward EU policy making is the definition of a common knowledge that contributes to understanding common challenges and, second to that, responding to them in a common way. Member states and EU institutions "piece together" information, data, and cognitive schemata (such as cause and effect relations), in a joint attempt to achieve an interpretation of events able to resonate with their own domestic experiences. On that basis, they define the role of the EU in responding to those events.

My starting point is thus opposite to rational choice, and it is complementary but does not overlap with the social-constructivist one. Uncertainty features in rationalist accounts. They acknowledge that actors need to see "through the fog created by the uncertainty of the future" (Kirzner 1997, 51), and "good" information is scarce.[2] Three aspects of uncertainty are relevant to rational actors: uncertainty about others' preferences, about others' actions and about the consequences of actions in general (Koremenos, Lipson, and Snidal 2001, 778–779). In this view, uncertainty affects strategies for interaction, most notably in the case of the EU because of credibility problems (Moravcsik 1998, 485–486; Pollack 2003, 63; Franchino 2000).[3] But it does not alter the manner in which actors form their preferences: they try to minimize consequences and "make do" with what information they have. Crucially, from my point of view, uncertainty does not lead to social interaction beyond a basic exchange of information. As the Bayesian learning model describes,[4] actors can exchange information but there is no "ready means by which an agent learns from other agents" (Breen 1999, 472). Interpretations, cognitive schemata and more substantial forms of knowledge than information are elaborated in solitude. Although uncertainty is thus acknowledged, it has consequences on strategies for interaction but not on preference formation, and it is socially "thin."[5] According to a rational choice perspective, reasons for EU policy making lie elsewhere.

The constructivist approach is complementary to the notion of cognitive uncertainty, but it heavily discounts its existence. It is easier to conceptualize cognitive uncertainty within a constructivist environment, as it encompasses the possibility that uncertainty is not only about others' preferences, but also about the decision maker's own preferences and the meaning of information more generally. The past tends to be ambiguous, knowledge is context dependent and the link between means and ends, causes and effects, policies and activities is tenuous at best. Uncertainty then highlights the relevance of the social context and of interaction for the definition of personal preferences. The problem with constructivist accounts, in my opinion, is that they depict uncertainty as a rare phenomenon. There is logic to that. As Wendt put it, culture and ideational structures tend to be self-fulfilling prophecies that once in place tend to reproduce themselves (Wendt 1999, 339). Social norms and relational networks permeate decision makers' environment to the point where it seems improbable that their minds could just go blank. Change is usually portrayed as taking place incrementally, rather than as a breakdown in the cognitive structure within which states act. States' identities are "always in process, always contested, always an accomplishment of practice" (Wendt 1999, 340), but the whole point of the process is that it is gradual and evolutionary, with all the fluidity of a moving balance in which equilibrium is maintained even as states learn from, react to and elaborate on encounters with significant others (Wendt 1999, 341).

In a nutshell, according to rationalists, uncertainty exists, but has few consequences in terms of policy making. According to constructivists, uncertainty potentially has huge consequences, but it hardly ever happens. In both accounts, therefore, reasons for EU policy making must be sought elsewhere. In my view, as I shall explore in the next section, uncertainty is a fundamental condition of politics and it has substantial consequences on policy making in the EU.

The type of entrepreneurship I shall explore falls between the two paths proposed by rationalists and constructivists. My primary aim here is to break the apparently stark alternative between, on the one hand, a portrait of self-interested states fostering their own preferences, and, on the other, a picture in which every other actor apart from high ranking national officials is involved in triggering supranational outcomes. I suggest watering down the intrinsically normative content of policy entrepreneurship and to turn the issue into a more empirical question. Both in the rationalist and in the constructivist vein, entrepreneurs are motivated by a strong set of beliefs. Whether it is customary to interpret states in a liberal intergovernmental perspective as goal-oriented, such a conception is actually very similar to the constructivist one, which sees actors such as the Commission as norm-oriented. Norm entrepreneurs are "agents having strong notions about appropriate or desirable behavior" (Finnemore and Sikkink 1998, 896), whose aim is to convince actors and more specifically states to embrace new norms. Similarly, epistemic communities (Haas 1992, 2), and advocacy coalitions (Sabatier and Jenkins-Smith 1993, 5) are brought together by a common set of beliefs and a common policy endeavor. These concepts, which have all been used to explain EU policy making, limit the range of possible entrepreneurial behavior to one motivated by the specific content of the policy proposal. The explanation for the entrepreneur's action and its impact becomes teleological, in the constructivist as in the liberal intergovernmentalist descriptions of entrepreneurial behavior.[6]

The apparent alternative between two views on entrepreneurship in the EU thus is not very stark and makes it hard to understand logically why actors other than member states should not be considered self-interested, or why national representatives by definition do not foster supranational outcomes. The route I am going to take explores the role of member states as entrepreneurs with a rather light normative baggage ("brokers"), which trigger supranational outcomes. Admittedly, it is an approach that does not take full stock of the suggestions offered by the literature on global governance about the full range of actors involved in EFP making, but aims instead at an "analytical rescue" of member states' role in the EU.[7]

In terms of the nature of negotiations in the EU policy making process, my aim is to cut the issue transversally. Whereas rationalist and constructivist accounts focus on different modes of interaction, I aim instead to address how, within the EU setting, negotiations address cognitive issues and transform information into knowledge. The gist of the debate about arguing and bargaining (e.g., Elster 1995; Risse 2000; Schimmelfennig 2001; Erikson and Fossum 2000; Payne 2001; see also Kratochwill 1989; Fearon and Wendt 2002; Müller 2004) has hinged on different logics of action, namely what actors aim to achieve in negotiations and how they go about it. In both cases, cognitive aspects of negotiations are addressed but not fully resolved. Bargaining logics assumes that there is a common language among participants, for instance within the EU environment, which allows actors to communicate in spite of potentially very different worldviews. Thus actors exchange information, while its elaboration into knowledge is done at the domestic level. In a constructivist perspective, arguing instead entails making claims of factual truth or normative validity, with the aim to convince. There are two aspects to the constructivist take on this, though. On the one hand, all actors are expected to be open to change their minds, and the result of the interaction does affects them all, if only unintentionally. On the other hand, there is a de facto division of labor between persuaders and persuadees, which goes against the idea of all actors being equally involved. The tendency to resolve this constructivist dilemma in the latter direction is for instance clear in Checkel (1997, 2001) or in Niemann (2004).

While rationalists thus discount the relevance of common knowledge born out of social interaction, constructivists address cognitive aspects but explore one specific possibility, namely the interaction between a norm entrepreneur and the surrounding audience. My aim is to develop on the constructivist interest for thick social interaction and develop its cognitive component, while at the same time watering down the tight distinction between persuader and persuadees. Cognitive interaction is part of arguing because it aims at defining (though not uncovering) the "truth," but it is also the basis for bargaining, as actors must refer to common cognitive ground in order to make negotiations possible. Cognitive interaction aims at establishing a common cognitive framework, if it is not already there, and such a framework underpins and accompanies all types of negotiations. As knowledge is a form of power (Adler and Bernstein 2005; Haas 1992, 2), cognitive interaction under conditions of uncertainty thus defines a particular form of negotiation, compatible but not fully overlapping with "arguing" and "bargaining."

The approach I am going to sketch in the next few sections, and which is going to inform the empirical analysis that follows, thus combines and complements several of the arguments existent in the literature with the purpose of broadening the range of options for explaining EFP making and, more generally, policy making in the EU. I will explore cognitive uncertainty as a policy window that is particularly useful as a starting point for interaction at the EU level. I will analyze how member states behave as policy entrepreneurs *and* foster supranational outcomes. I will focus on cognitive aspects of negotiations within the EU. Having thus indicated where in the literature I see my approach, it is now time to turn to specify these points more in detail, and with more reference to the empirical material to come.

Cognitive Uncertainty as a Policy Window

The first condition for an EFP initiative toward the Mediterranean is the existence of a policy window for such a change to take place. Policy windows, or windows of opportunities, are "opportunities for action on given initiatives" (Kingdon 1984/95, 166). Politicians, lobby groups, activists and whoever has a stake in politics all compete to promote policy proposals in a maelstrom of ideas and initiatives. Their chances of being successful rest, not only on their efforts, but depend on the "right" time for a policy proposal to be advanced. Policy promoters paddle like "surfers waiting for a big wave" (Kingdon 1984/95, 165), which presents them with the passing, sometimes only fleeting, chance to launch their endeavor. Policy windows are a confluence of environmental conditions favoring the rise of a particular issue on the political agenda at any given moment. As such, they also represent a "stimulus for action" (Zaharidis 1999).

The concept of a policy window is basically a metaphor for highlighting the importance of background conditions for entrepreneurial action, and as such draws on the debate about structure and agency in International Relations. This debate, which emphasizes the importance and interconnectedness of both elements,[8] has added important insights into the analysis of EFP (Hill 2003; Carlsnaes 1994). Patomäki and Wight have suggested conceptualizing structures as "conditions for action," or "structural contexts" in which social action takes place and on which it depends (2000, 230–231). The concept of a policy window is useful exactly in this perspective, as it brings into focus this set of "conditions for action," which are inextricably related to the possibility for action (and to the consequences of action) on the part of the policy entrepreneur.

The question thus becomes what specifically, as opposed to generally, constitutes a policy window for EFP making, and how to recognize one if we see it. I argue that a crucial type of policy window is cognitive uncertainty, namely uncertainty about how to interpret social reality. As Heclo put it, "[p]olicy-making is a form of collective puzzlement on society's behalf; it entails both deciding and knowing" (1974, 305). One key reason why member states are prepared to discuss a topic at the European level is that they "puzzle" and they need to find new ways to address domestic issues. EU policy making, and more specifically EFP making, is thus a form of "collective puzzlement" that leads to new policy understandings.

Cognitive uncertainty occurs when patterns of domestic politics are shaken, for instance by the perception of a new challenge. In the case of Euro-Mediterranean relations, there have been substantial examples when European national policy makers have had to confront new and unprecedented issues. A typical case, which I am going to examine in chapter 5, was that of Italy and Spain turning from emigration to immigration countries. Traditionally, both countries had sent people abroad for centuries, including as recently as during the post–World War II economic boom. When the tide started to reverse in the 1980s, and the two countries begun to see more immigrants arriving than emigrants leaving, it caught both society and policy makers off guard. The visible presence of immigrants in the streets, in the job market, as subjects of the welfare state, constituted an issue that could not be addressed with previous mental maps or policy means. It fostered a sense of emergency in Italian and Spanish societies that put national policy makers under pressure to understand and control the new phenomenon. Migration climbed up the political agenda and affected political relations between governments and citizens, as well as among political parties. In that situation, national policy makers clearly faced cognitive uncertainty. They were not sure about the nature of the problem, or the key factors that were fuelling uneasiness in the society (job competition? cultural differences?), or about the policies that "would work." The problem was thus at the national, domestic level, although it extended beyond Italian and Spanish borders.

Challenges originating from outside national borders can thus have a disruptive impact on national interests, as they challenge engrained policy preferences. Policy makers' first response is to ignore the challenges and/or reiterate traditional policy responses. But this is not always possible. "Cognitive beliefs about the world are constantly tested by actual events. While failures and surprises can be reinterpreted so that they do not contradict existing norms and beliefs, they also create pressures that can lead to a reevaluation and modification of the culture"

(Berger 1996, 326). When it is not clear what happened or why it happened, it is impossible to quickly attach a routine interpretation to an event. "The complexity of, and change in, the environment often overpower our cognitive capacity" (March and Olsen 1988, 343). When this is the case, policies must be adapted, amended, or revised. The problem is how to go about this.

Cognitive uncertainty is therefore composed of two main parts: what exactly is uncertain, and how would it be possible to address it. The first component is the cognitive breakdown. There is a fundamental difference between, on the one hand, information, and, on the other, knowledge. Information is generally understood as data that contributes to meaning by reducing ambiguity and equivocality. Knowledge is more complex, as it entails the interpretation of information in the form of "cause and effect" relationships, as well as "means and ends" propositions (Huber 1991, 89). Therefore, acquisition of information and interpretation of information are two different phenomena (Dekker and Hansén 2004, 217–218). Cognitive uncertainty as defined here is uncertainty about the *interpretation* of information. It is thus something deeper than the lack of available data on a given issue. Provision of "good," reliable information is obviously important, as underlined by the rationalist literature. However, not only the assessment about quality and reliability of information is a different matter from the raw data, but also the process by which information is turned into mental maps able to guide policy makers through a process of problem solving is a more sophisticated phenomenon than the gathering of empirical evidence.

A very neat example of the difference between uncertainty about information and uncertainty about knowledge is offered by the 9/11 report by the National Commission chaired by Kean and Hamilton in the US. Before Pearl Harbor, the U.S. government knew that a Japanese attack loomed ahead, but it did not know where the strike would occur or how to prevent it. It was "excruciating uncertainty,"[9] but there were no doubts who the enemy was, and it was possible to speculate (if wrongly) on probabilities. Before 9/11, on the contrary, there was uncertainty within the U.S. government about "whether [al Qaeda] was just a new and especially venomous version of the ordinary terrorist threat [. . .] or was radically new, posing a threat beyond any yet experienced" (2004, 343). It was thus not clear who the enemy was and what kind of enemy it was, thus preventing any serious attempt at addressing the issue and speculating about potentially effective actions. When the attacks were made, policy makers could not evade the issue any longer and had to address cognitive uncertainty about al Qaeda and how to counter it.

The second aspect of cognitive uncertainty is that it triggers social interaction. The principle of social validation, which supports individual interpretations of events, is necessary to provide the cognizant with crucial reference points, which in turn lead to appropriate and "correct" policy measures. In their search for solutions to domestically experienced policy challenges, national policy makers are therefore "cognitively motivated" (Checkel 2001, 10) to shop around for fresh ideas. They need interpretations of the social process and advice about likely consequences of various courses of action (Haas 1992, 4, 15). In their effort to "articulate" new meaning out of "extant cultural raw materials or linguistic resources" (Weldes 1996, 284), national policy makers will thus operate through a series of social relations capable of producing meaning, even if this might lead to apparently dysfunctional outcomes. They will be prepared to consider new concepts and new narratives provided by trusted partners. In the example of Italy and Spain facing immigration, the two countries were keen to know what traditional immigration countries, especially those that belonged to the EC/EU, thought about the phenomenon. "[I]mitating similar individuals is one of the simplest and most effective cognitive heuristics in the calculation of utilities" (Elkins and Simmons 2005, 45; cf. Merton 1957). Social psychology and organizational theory have shown the way in which individuals tend to be dependent on others to understand the consequences of actions (Bandura 1977) and take "the values or standards of other individuals and groups as a comparative frame of reference" for shaping their behavior and evaluations (Merton 1957, 234). Therefore, policy makers experiencing cognitive uncertainty will be open and motivated to exchange ideas with reference groups in order to reconstitute an understanding of social reality. Cognitive uncertainty constitutes a policy window because it disposes national policy makers to discuss an issue at the European level, as they search for appropriate solutions.

It could be argued that, defined in these terms, cognitive uncertainty is indeed a rare phenomenon. However, as long as the agent is granted a degree of autonomy (Adler and Bernstein 2005, 296), the possibility for genuine uncertainty exists as part of the fabric of agential choice. As some constructivist scholars have come to recognize, there are several cases in which agents might not be fully socialized or their socialization might still leave space for dilemmas. One case is, for instance, when social norms clash (e.g., Cortell and Davis 2005). Other such cases are the perception of an external shock (e.g., Avant 2000, 48; see also Farrell 2001), of policy failures (e.g., Levy 1994, 305) or "the newness of an issue" (Checkel 2001, 562). These novel or critical situations impact the way in which information is processed, making it possible for new frames to emerge and new interests to be defined (Legro 2000, 424).[10]

One such case, in my opinion, is represented by processes of politicization and securitization, a perspective that has been used in this research. The approach has been articulated by the so-called Copenhagen school (Buzan 1991; Wæver et al. 1993; Buzan et al. 1998). It argues that "any public issue can be located on the spectrum ranging from nonpoliticized (meaning the state does not deal with it and it is not in any other way made an issue of public debate and decision) through politicized (meaning the issue is part of public policy, requiring government decision and resource allocations or, more rarely, some other form of communal governance) to securitized (meaning the issue is presented as an existential threat, requiring emergency measures and justifying actions outside the normal bounds of political procedure). [. . .] Depending on circumstances, any issue can end up on any part of the spectrum" (Buzan et al. 1998, 24). Issues thus enter and exit not only the arena of politics, but also the security arena.[11] Therefore, there are three key segments (or arenas) on the continuum expressing the relationship between an issue and how it is addressed by a collectivity: a private sphere, a political sphere,[12] and a security arena. The last one could also be distinguished between high and low security, following a distinction going back to Wolfers (1962, 150).

My suggestion is that whenever an issue moves from the private to the political, from the political to the security, or from the private straight into the security arena, national policy makers experience cognitive uncertainty,[13] as debate among societal actors throws up new responsibilities and new challenges. As discussed in chapter 3, for instance, the birth of modern terrorism and particularly of Arab-Palestinian terrorism in the late 1960s at first remained an issue only for private actors such as airlines to address. It escalated to the political arena when European interests (European citizens, European locations, and so on) were targeted, and it was securitized as an emergency issue that required extraordinary measures with the attacks in München at the Olympic Games in 1972. I shall argue that both moves created cognitive uncertainty among policy makers.

The case of politicization and securitization is particularly important for Euro-Mediterranean relations because, as most of the literature agrees, the Europeans tend to see the Mediterranean through security lenses.[14] Rather than as a marketplace for economic opportunities, the prevalent view in Europe is that the Mediterranean is the origin of political and security issues with the potential to affect European domestic environments negatively. This does not necessarily reflect in the formulation of security responses. On the contrary, as we shall see, the standard solution offered by the EC/EU has been predominantly economic in nature. Still, the main frames for interpreting the Mediterranean are embedded in political and security visions.

What are the indicators of cognitive uncertainty that I am going to look for in the empirical evidence of EFP making toward the Mediterranean? The denotation of a concept signifying absence is by definition elusive, although occasionally possible.[15] Policy makers are unlikely to trumpet their lack of knowledge and to issue that all very useful—for analytical purposes—press release in which they declare their incompetence. What we might see is a quick sequence of contradictory reforms or an increase in the public debate about certain issues, analyzing both causes and effects, and potential solutions. It is in fact relatively easier to focus on indicators of successful politicization or securitization, in the form of: (1) a discourse that assigns an issue to a specific arena on the continuum; (2) a series of authoritative decisions that translate the discourse into practice. As it is the interpretation that defines a political or security issue as such, discourse constitutes the basis for the definition of collective matters (cf. Searle 1995; Waever 1995; Buzan, Waever, et al. 1998). In case of a "silent" process (cf. Huysmans 2006), new laws, directives or administrative measures are all powerful indicators of authoritative decisions being taken on the basis of a widespread consensus not articulated into an open discourse.

In general terms, the focus of the empirical analysis will be on the perceptions of national policy makers as the key aggregators of societal demands, and the main providers of authoritative decisions, as well as of policy formulation. I will argue that change in perceptions among national policy makers occurs when there is evidence of a change in domestic (including official) debates and a change in authoritative decisions. Material trends such as data on economic relations will be analyzed only inasmuch as they are directly related to domestic debates, authoritative decisions and perceptions of national policy makers, or to emphasize the discrepancy between material trends and perceptions.

To sum up the broader meaning of this section on cognitive uncertainty, my suggestion is that cognitive uncertainty is a fundamental feature of social reality. Alongside the assumption of bounded rationality goes an assumption of individuals' bounded *cognition*, and their limited capacity to be always up to speed in the flow of information that permeates social lives. Individuals not only learn, enact and transform social scripts; they also puzzle, wonder, and panic about their absence.

States and more generally actors are not only power and wealth pursuers, but also "uncertainty reducers" (Haas 1992, 4). As Mitzen put it (2006), the thick layer of routine that characterizes daily life is aimed in fact at fencing off ontological insecurity, which is the most fundamental form of uncertainty. Therefore, the whole set of social norms, which is described by constructivism, should be interpreted as a layer that can break off at moments of crisis, revealing the chaos and chasm beneath. My focus here is on the cognitive aspects that characterize that crisis and most specifically on how policy makers' knowledge breaks down and how they manage to reconstitute it.

An Intervening Variable: Divergent Patterns of Priorities among Allies

My argument so far has not distinguished among policy makers' responses to cognitive uncertainty: when politicization or securitization occurs, they will puzzle and look for new ideas. But it is hard to imagine a situation in which very different states will view the same problem in the same way. Even allies will differ in their perceptions of the nature and significance of new challenges, so it is important to assess how different perceptions could affect the behavior of member states, and thus the opening of the policy window and the readiness of EC/EU member states to discuss new ideas.

There are two main relationships which impinge on European member states, which, as we are going to see in the empirical chapters, are most likely to matter in this regard. The first is the transatlantic relationship, as the United States constitutes one corner of the triangle which also comprises the EC/EU and the Mediterranean. The second relevant relationship refers to the North/South split among member states. Mediterranean issues are traditionally a concern more of southern European countries than of northern European ones, although they are by no means natural allies of their Mediterranean neighbors. Even though my focus will remain on intra-European dynamics, both these relationships represent potential cleavages that separate member states' views and perceptions of challenges that originate in the Mediterranean.

In the transatlantic relationship, Mediterranean politics might be infused by a U.S. view which interprets events differently from the one on which EC/EU member states converge. The presence of the United States as an actor in the Mediterranean has been of paramount importance since the Suez crisis in 1956. Its role and influence on EFP making raise broad issues of cooperation and conflict among member states. What happens if member states disagree with the United States? Is agreement with the United States a precondition for intra-European cooperation? This issue, which would require a research of its own, is addressed here as an intervening factor. The focus here is on conditions that lead to EFP formulation and in this sense potential disagreements between transatlantic partners could influence the behavior of member states.

Similarly, if there is little agreement within the EC/EU about the Mediterranean, it is most likely that the dividing line coincides with a North/South split. Southern European countries tend to be most sensitive to Mediterranean affairs while northern European countries might have other priorities linked to a different historical pattern of relationship. This split is particularly sensitive in the area of aid provision—the traditional policy answer supported by the southern Europeans and disbursed in the main by northern Europeans. Thus questions for policy analysis might be: under which conditions would northern European countries be more available to analyze Mediterranean challenges and possibly provide the material means to support common policy solutions? When are southern European countries most interested in cooperating among themselves to attract the attention of northern European countries toward the Mediterranean?

The issue of divergent patterns of priorities across Western countries has been researched predominantly from a realist point of view, although it has generated a wide variety of opinions among scholars. This variety also produces two opposite predictions as to the consequence of such differences: on the one hand the outcome is convergence, on the other divergence. According to hegemonic stability theory (Gilpin 1987; Gowa 1994), the main difference lies between the hegemon and the rest of the states in a system. In this light, European states would converge, "bandwagon" and follow the U.S. policy stand in the expectation of profits and easy gains. The U.S. approach to the Mediterranean would thus dictate the European approach to the area. On a minor scale, the southern Europeans would have several advantages in following the stance of their richer northern neighbors.

Alternatively, in a more classical realist interpretation, European countries would "balance" against the power of the United States or, in the absence of a hegemon, against other powerful countries, such as Germany and the United Kingdom, by adopting a different policy stance (Waltz 1979; Walt 1985). Therefore, the U.S. approach to the region would be countered by a different approach by European states. Or the position assumed by Germany and the United Kingdom toward the Mediterranean would be defied by southern European countries, both possibilities leading to divergence. The debate is too well known to review it here.[16] The common characteristic of both approaches, however, is that the triggering factor is power: the power of the hegemon that allows allies to reap significant economies of scale, or the power of one alliance threatening other countries.

Yet, it is worth scrutinizing more closely the rationale for states' behavior, from which it is possible to conclude that it is not the relative power of the actors which makes a difference, but rather the profile of their political concerns. The list of priorities and responsibilities of public authorities, as defined in the previous section, delineates a country's understanding of international relations and more specifically of relations with a certain area. I suggest that whether states choose to cooperate or clash will be influenced by how they regard the geopolitical terrain at the same historical moment, and the challenge presented by particular issues. Competing political visions, rather than competitive political power will determine whether the policy window opens wide or shrinks dramatically.

My hypothesis is that clashes of interpretation within the two key relationships I have described contribute at first to cement divergences across crucial relationships, as they have the effect of further deepening cognitive uncertainty amongst member states and emphasizing the relative importance of perceived challenges. Indirectly, they thus promote cooperation among similarly minded actors in order to overcome a perceived uncertainty and provide a common viable solution. A different agenda in foreign policy between the European countries and the United States is likely to prod member states to group together to defend "the European view." Given the nature of the EC/EU, divergences between northern and southern Europeans promote the quest for a political compromise that reconciles different priority rankings. Therefore, divergences might paradoxically enhance initially the degree of exchange and coordination among states.

Such harmony may, however, not last long. Early support for cooperation is bound sooner or later to give way to substantial obstacles when states get down to the specifics and discuss a prospective solution. Whereas divergences push states together into early exchanges of views, ultimately they damage the chances of finding common lasting solutions, and a way out of uncertainty. The persistent opposition of the United States or the lack of commitment of northern European countries are of themselves additional and permanent sources of uncertainty, which throw into doubt every solution concocted. Thus, in the long run, cracks in the relationships will reduce the basis for any substantial compromise on the principles and the content of cooperation. This issue would require more in-depth analysis than is possible here. I will limit myself to the following argument: Whenever divergences emerge in the transatlantic relationship or across the northern/southern split within the EC/EU, they will affect the opening of a policy window. At first, they will increase the dimensions of the policy window, whereas in the middle to long term the policy window will tend to close more abruptly or to display fundamental weaknesses, thus making the development of a substantial proposal most likely to fail.

Policy Entrepreneurship

Policy windows which open as a result of cognitive uncertainty help us to understand how an EFP initiative is formulated, but the opportunity represented by a policy window requires the presence of a policy entrepreneur in order to go anywhere. The policy window indicates a favorable structural setting for a policy initiative, but agency is necessary to convert such a setting into active policy formulation.

In general terms, therefore, the category of policy entrepreneurship introduces an agential element by expressing the concept of actors promoting substantial change.[17] The key elements defining a policy entrepreneur are the desire for, activism toward, and commitment to, change. Policy entrepreneurs are catalysts for policy innovation (King and Roberts 1987), they seek to "initiate dynamic policy change" (Mintrom 1997, 739) in order to "change the direction and flow of politics" (Schneider and Teske 1992, 737). Policy entrepreneurs organize networks of people and spend time and resources to support new visions and initiatives in a given policy sector (Giuliani 1998; Kingdon 1984/95, 122). Their entrepreneurship is on a substantial scale, rallying support for a watershed in policy direction of a policy, not just tinkering at the edges. The novel idea can be copied from another environment so long as it introduces a widely recognized disjuncture with previous standard procedures.

There are several ways to characterize entrepreneurial agents. I will focus on the notion of "brokers," meaning actors who have a stake in a positive outcome to negotiations and a preferred direction of change, but are open to discuss the content of the policy proposal. Most of the literature tends instead to characterize entrepreneurs as "true believers," in the form of actors believing in their proposal's rightness, with little flexibility to change it. This approach is implicit in the notions of norm entrepreneurship, epistemic communities and advocacy coalitions, as well as in liberal intergovernmentalism and in its analysis of states' entrepreneurship, as suggested earlier. There are however reasons to broaden the analysis of entrepreneurship to include brokerage. Not only does it help to refine the analysis of policy entrepreneurship in the EU, but it also allows us to explore other types of interaction sparked by the policy entrepreneur, including the possibility that the entrepreneurial broker gets the debate under way with a proposal, but the final content of the proposal is defined during interaction in a collective process, as we will see in the following section.

Brokers "influence the process by helping the parties to help themselves" (Young 1999, 807).[18] Brokers have more of an idea of the kind of change that is required and the steps to achieve it, but do not necessarily hold the monopoly of action, information and knowledge, or of concrete policy ideas. The entrepreneurial broker sparks interaction and strives to keep the debate going, but is open and liable to interaction's consequences (and to be persuaded) as much as other actors. Brokers see their goal as policy change, but their methods are less evangelical and their proposals are more susceptible to modification by partners' suggestions than believers would have it. Whereas the main action performed by a "believer" is promoting set policy goals, the bulk of the broker's activism is directed toward negotiation and mediation. Both types of actors perform a set of actions such as drafting proposals, but the emphasis in brokerage entrepreneurial behavior is on process rather than goals. Moreover, a broker differs from an entrepreneurial believer in the degree of openness to changes in the proposal put forward. A broker is more flexible on the content of proposals while showing the same continued commitment to change.

The original connotation of policy entrepreneurship by Kingdon was, in fact, closer to brokerage than to what he calls "advocacy." He suggested that "brokers" negotiate between people and contribute to match or "couple" problems with solutions, rather than focus on pushing for their preferred proposal to be adopted as advocates do (Kingdon 1984/95, 183). The origins of policy ideas are "less important than the processes of mutation and recombination that occur as ideas continuously confront one another and are refined until they are ready to enter a serious decision stage" (Kingdon 1984/95, 124). There are thus two main activities conducted by the policy entrepreneur: "softening up" the policy community, to prepare the ground for a policy proposal (Kingdon 1984/95, 127–131) and "coupling" problems, solutions and political forces through extensive negotiations

(Kingdon 1984/95, 181–182, 205). The second activity is particularly important to catalyze policy change.

In the end, the question about "believers" versus "brokers" is first and foremost an empirical one. We evaluate from the empirical evidence the type of entrepreneur who is active at a given moment in time. At the same time, the possible existence of "brokers" has theoretical consequences, because it highlights a different path to policy change than the one described so far in the various strands of the literature. Introducing an element of flexibility and of indeterminacy in the process contributes to explaining the existence of outcomes that had not been advocated at the outset by any specific actor.

Who are the potential policy entrepreneurs in EU policy making and can they be defined in terms of brokerage? The "classical" debate among scholars of European integration has taken the form of a "Commission vs. member states" confrontation, thus focusing on who are the actors that behave entrepreneurially, more than on the type of entrepreneurship they provide. In the supranational/neofunctionalist account of how supranational institutions affect European integration, the Commission tends to be depicted as a "believer" in maximizing European integration, although it has at times to revert to "brokerage" because of the opposition its action encounters. In the global governance literature, the range is broader, but it tends to exclude national policy makers and focus on policy advocates/believers. In the intergovernmental and especially liberal intergovernmentalist view, it is an entrepreneurial member state that performs all kinds of entrepreneurial actions, but it is unlikely to compromise on its entrepreneurial goals.

The intensity of this debate contributes to identify roughly four ways of analyzing entrepreneurship in the EC/EU. The two main views on actors identified by the literature on European integration focus on member states, on the one hand, and the Commission and more generally supranational institutions and policy networks, on the other. The entrepreneurial nature of the two can however be characterized in two different ways, I suggest, according to how flexible the entrepreneur is prepared to be in seeking their ideal outcome. On the one hand, actors can be seen as entrepreneurial believers, whose main activity is to promote their own set of values and policy beliefs. The Commission would fit the bill because of its prointegrationist stance, while member states would behave as believers when they push for a rigid interpretation of their national interests. From another perspective, whenever the emphasis of the entrepreneur's activity falls on mediation in negotiations, then it is more appropriate to characterize entrepreneurial agents as "brokers," to reflect their willingness to compromise and negotiate the content of proposals, and their susceptibility to interaction with other agents.

Whereas brokerage can apply to both the Commission/policy network set of actors, my analysis of Euro-Mediterranean relations will focus mainly on member states, and more precisely on entrepreneurship provided by one member state or by a coalition of actors led by a member state. A state behaves as a broker when, in cases of underspecified national interest (in terms of policy content), it aims to foster policy change and negotiations by favoring interaction and debate, rather than zero-sum games. This would be the case of a member state which acts on the opening of a policy window, converting it into a concrete policy process by engaging in debate, by putting proposals forward, and also, and especially, by providing coordination and momentum to the debate. The entrepreneurial action might also develop with a member state creating first a coalition of supportive actors and then, together with them, promoting change through debate and mediation.

Predominance of states' entrepreneurship is not a necessity, though. Once again, I argue that, in the case under examination here, it will tend to be an empirical regularity that might in the near future be disconfirmed. The empirical analysis of Euro-Mediterranean relations will show that the Commission has entrepreneurial potential, but it has not yet managed to turn it into a consistent role in EFP making, at least for the Mediterranean case. As I will stress, there are structural deficiencies as well as conjunctural obstacles to an entrepreneurial Commission, but neither are insurmountable. My hypothesis is that, in the history of EFP toward the Mediterranean *so far*, member states are more likely to be the entrepreneurial agents of change.

The range of motivations that brings a member state to act as a broker, and therefore to have strong but not rigidly defined reasons to promote change is potentially boundless. According to Kingdon, policy entrepreneurs can be motivated for instance by their "ideology," but also other motivations including personal interests, such as the protection of bureaucratic turfs, or the fact that some entrepreneurs "like the game" (1984/95, 123). Other, more targeted to EFP, reasons might encompass for instance prestige, quest for external recognition, or instrumental behavior. Here too, the issue needs to be determined empirically

One key aspect is, however, that the range of potential reasons includes not only material, but also and especially ideational motivations. According to liberal intergovernmentalism, for instance, the focus is on material gains. Entrepreneurs make an investment, which is expected to reap material benefits, typically economic benefits, which are the main concern of governments in European negotiations. Yet for entrepreneurs ideational gains might be equally, if not more, important than material ones. A whole range of reasons, from prestige to altruism, might in fact prod governments to pursue interaction within the EC/EU. As we shall see in the case of EFP toward the Mediterranean, entrepreneurial states actively seek recognition on the part of their fellow member states for their role and position in international politics. My point here is that the analysis of entrepreneurship not only needs to distinguish between actors and types of entrepreneurial behavior, but also according to the nature of their interests.

The emphasis on ideational aspects marks one key difference between liberal intergovernmentalism and the ideational intergovernmentalist approach that I advocate, while the possible supranational consequences of state entrepreneurship is another. The emphasis on ideational reasons for entrepreneurial behavior could be read in several ways. In a realist perspective, the quest for international recognition is linked to a desire for prestige. In a constructivist account, it fits rather as part of identity politics of member states within the EC/EU. The liberal intergovernmental approach, however, finds it more difficult to accommodate ideational aspects, which admittedly trigger foreign policy cooperation in the form of geopolitical considerations and ideology (Moravcsik 1998, 478). Interestingly, therefore, brokerage because of ideational motivations implies that it is possible to reinterpret realism in a constructivist way for the case of EFP. Whereas liberal intergovernmentalism suggests a pattern of state behavior that approximates realism, it does so by radically changing the emphasis on the reasons behind such behavior, namely by introducing material, economic motivations. It thus predicts a recurrent behavioral pattern (states act as policy entrepreneurs in the EC/EU), but what I suggest are for the wrong reasons. By keeping the emphasis on ideational aspects, such as in ideational intergovernmentalism, it is instead possible to be more precise not only about states' behavioral pattern as policy entrepreneurs, but also about the reasons behind it, as well as the potential consequences.

The second aspect on which my analysis of entrepreneurial states differs from liberal intergovernmentalism is that brokerage on the part of member states can lead to supranational consequences. According to the liberal intergovernmentalist interpretation of states' entrepreneurship, the integration process cannot go "out of hand" during the interaction among EC/EU policy makers (or can do so only at the margins). It is a process that runs on predictable lines, and European integration thus remains under the control of fully sovereign and fully independent member states. I suggest, on the contrary, that national interests, and more generally the motivations of the entrepreneurial state not only may vary, but they are not the only factor affecting the final outcome of negotiations. The final result is open ended, because motivations of the entrepreneurial states are not fixed and there is no teleological link between the entrepreneurial state's motivation, the entrepreneur's behavior, and the interaction process triggered by the entrepreneur. While it might lead nowhere, the process might also acquire a dynamic of its own, potentially along the lines of the "communauté d'information, de vue, d'action" analysis of de Schoutheete (1980), and take on supranational characteristics. While I will explore these issues further later on in the book and most importantly in the Conclusions, it is important at this stage to understand the potential consequences in terms of the broader picture of European integration of the type of entrepreneurship that I describe.

This emphasis on "brokerage" is consistent with the possibility of cognitive uncertainty. While I do not discard the chance that the agent is fully cognizant, the possibility of cognitive uncertainty suggests a knowledge gap or asymmetry: the entrepreneur might be *more* knowledgeable than the other participants or considered to be so. At the same time the agent's knowledge is always liable to change. Moreover, the distinction between "believers" and "brokers" is important because it serves to highlight the fact that there is an analytical and empirical difference between policy entrepreneurship and the interaction process that it sparks. As we shall see when addressing cognitive interaction, the entrepreneur is not master of the process, which instead displays a logic of its own.

So who are these "entrepreneurial states?" It is important to clarify this question. As it has long since been established (Hill 2003), reference to states is shorthand for individuals that act in the name of states. In this case, the expression principally refers to individual policy makers that have the authority to formulate and implement foreign policy in the EC/EU member states. It thus includes politicians, but also and especially the diplomats in charge of drafting foreign policy proposals, chairing or participating in meetings about foreign policy, and implementing the decisions taken. In the making of EFP, this generally includes foreign affairs officials detached to Brussels, but also the high ranking diplomats and politicians who shuttle to and fro the capitals of member states. In a sense, this research is a study of foreign policy making elites, comprising politicians in governments and parliaments as well as diplomats in Ministries of Foreign Affairs and, in some cases, officials in other relevant national ministries. When I analyze the Commission, the whole hierarchy is included, although the General Directorates (DGs) in charge of external relations are particularly under scrutiny here. Similar considerations apply for the other EC/EU institutions.[19]

One personal aspect of policy entrepreneurship, in contrast to the macroapproach adopted here, which I should mention is the relationship between the policy entrepreneur and the policy window on which the success of the entrepreneur's action depends. To what extent is cognitive uncertainty consciously recognized or orchestrated by the policy entrepreneur, rather than being just a post hoc scholarly rationalization? The policy entrepreneur might or might not consciously recognize cognitive uncertainty and the existence of a policy window. Kingdon is ambiguous on this point: the policy entrepreneur is rationally coupling the various streams and at the same time "has a sense" for riding the wave of opportunity (1984/95, 181; see also Zaharidis 1999). The whiff of opportunism contained in the idea of the entrepreneur exploiting uncertainty and the chance for change is diminished by the fact that a policy entrepreneur requires feedback from her target audiences in order to promote change. Therefore, my position is that policy entrepreneurs might sense the existence of a favorable setting, but they might also miss it and try to promote policy change when no window of opportunity exists. The identification of the policy window relies on a set of indicators that only appear clearly in a *post hoc* analysis.[20]

To sum up what has been said so far about entrepreneurship, the second key factor in EFP making (and the first component of the *pars construens*) is the existence of a member state ready to act as an entrepreneur or, more specifically, as a "broker" to spark a debate about the Mediterranean at the EC/EU level (or to build up a coalition of actors and then spark a debate). Taking advantage of what the policy entrepreneur perceives as a widespread situation of cognitive uncertainty, the entrepreneur puts forward proposals for change, stirs up debate and offers crucial mediation, with the aim of shifting the level of discussion from the national to the European level, up to the point when not only the issue of Euro-Mediterranean relations reaches the EC/EU agenda, but also EC/EU foreign policy makers reach a positive agreement about what to do about it. How the debate at the EC/EU level unfolds represents the third part of the framework I am going to describe (and the second component of the *pars construens*).

Cognitive Interaction and Framing

This section is about interaction. I have so far described a context in which member states, having perceived new challenges originating from the Mediterranean, are looking for ideas about how to interpret them and are thus potentially available to discuss the Mediterranean at the European level. I have then introduced the concept of the policy entrepreneur, in the form of a broker with an interest in the adoption of a European initiative and the intention to commit resources to that goal. The simultaneous presence of a policy window and a policy entrepreneur along these lines leads to an interaction process among member states which represents the basis of a new EFP initiative. The manner in which this occurs is by addressing the cognitive foundations of Euro-Mediterranean relations, in other words what European actors *know* about Mediterranean affairs and by defining the role of the EC/EU in them. I define this process as cognitive interaction, meaning interaction in (re)constructing cognitive templates for policy making.

Therefore, cognitive interaction is synonymous with framing and frame construction. According to Rein and Schön, a frame is "a way of selecting, organizing, interpretating, and making sense of a complex reality to provide guideposts for knowing, analyzing, persuading, and acting" (1993, 146). A frame "provides conceptual coherence, a direction for action, a basis for persuasion, and a framework for the collection and analysis of data—order, action, rhetoric, and analysis" (1993, 153). It is a perspective from which to make sense of the world. A typical example was the cold war "frame," which pointed to a problem and its causes, offered moral judgments and recommended a policy solution (Entman 1993, 52). As such, frames can be equaled to paradigms as Kuhn defined them, or to mental structures and worldviews (Rein and Schön 1993, 147), or to narratives, offering a plot to interpret events (Kaplan 1993). Frames can also be defined in a similar way to policy discourses, in the form of "an ensemble of ideas, concepts, and categories through which meaning is given to phenomena" (Hajer 1993, 45).

There are several approaches to framing that can be used to express the dynamics of cognitive interaction. A frequently used one is the stage approach. Blumer (1971) has described the classical sequence of the "cycle of definition," which consists of the emergence of a social problem, its legitimation, the mobilization of action, the formation of an official plan, and the implementation of such a plan. Spector and Kitsuse (1977) describe a process which begins with a group of actors defining a condition as harmful and creating a public issue over the matter. An official organization then recognizes the legitimacy of the controversy and proposes a solution. The debate then centers on alternative solutions, as groups advocate their preferred outcomes. Similarly, Vertzberger described information processing as involving three interrelated stages: (1) information is gathered and interpreted; (2) alternative courses of action are derived; (3) the preferred alternative is implemented or at least becomes institutionally embedded (1989, 7).

Kingdon has criticized the stage approach, pointing instead in the direction of a series of *parallel* processes through which ideas come together into a meaningful framework. "Focusing events" draw public attention to given issues, constituting a sense of crisis. Simultaneously but unrelatedly, ideas float around in a "primeval soup." They bump into one another, some survive, some die out, and some survive in a form quite different from their origins (1984/95, 131). Those that survive tend to reflect certain criteria for survival, ranging from technical feasibility to value acceptability. The process of making sense of this messy reality is thus in Kingdon less a matter of stages, than the outcome of a piecemeal and contingent approach. Ideas gradually turn into policy options, but there is little sequencing or even rationale beyond some necessary criteria that ideas tend to reflect.

Entman (1993) has adopted a similar point of view, based on the key components, rather than on a sequence of events. He has identified the relevant parts of an argument: a definition of the problem, an identification of its causes, a moral evaluation of the situation, and a policy recommendation.

Elaborating on Kingdon and Entman, it is possible to imagine that the framing of EFP relations toward the Mediterranean would involve other features as well. A substantial part of debates about EFP tends in fact to centre on identifying the target countries. Moreover, as in every complex organization, especially one with relatively few consolidated traditions, the topic of "who should do what" is central to the definition of policy alternatives, with different actors and different DGs contesting the territory. Finally, the framing process is likely to take place not only within the central EC/EU forum, broadly defined, but also on the edges, among two or more of its members. Contrary to the impression that part of the EU literature seems to convey, interactions among member countries take place not only in the formal EC/EU gatherings, but also outside of them and often with a view to coordinating positions prior to formal gatherings. This phenomenon has obviously increased since the relaunch of the EC in the 1990s, but it remains underresearched. Still, as I will show especially in chapter 5, bilateral and multilateral meetings among member states' representatives are part of the cognitive interaction process, they impact upon EC/EU meetings and thus they play a role in framing issues in EFP. Diplomatic meetings, joint seminars, exchange of information outside the COREU system, phone contacts, personal relations, participation in nongovernmental gatherings in other member states, are all channels through which cognitive interaction takes place and eventually crystallizes at the EC/EU level.

The point here is, in my opinion, to acknowledge the benefits of a staged approach, while finding a way to overcome its limitations. On the one hand, there are a set of background conditions that affect the scope and depth of the framing process and of cognitive interaction. Without cognitive uncertainty, there would be little need for member states to shop around for ideas. Without a policy entrepreneur, in the style of a "broker," there would be little momentum to the process or little scope for interaction beyond the persuader-persuadee relationship. At the same time, the piecemeal approach described by Kingdon is particularly useful because it eschews any determinism in the way interaction unfolds on the basis of these two background conditions. How a frame is constructed is less a matter of a rational decision-making system and more of an ad hoc process, in which some actors push some ideas, participants try them on for size (Kingdon 1984/95, 124, 127–128), and eventually a frame that "makes sense" is developed.

The final process of cognitive interaction, as I see it, thus does not follow any specific order. Rather, it is a collective effort at "piecing together" cognitive parts of the puzzle. Like a giant jigsaw in which the picture emerges only piecemeal and slowly, it can start from one corner of the puzzle and proceed from there, but it is more likely to build on "islands of pieces" that are consequently put together. The process of cognitive interaction thus amounts to finding and "piecing together" new ideational elements into a frame. Clearly, I am starting from a situation in which previous cognitive frames have already lost much of their legitimacy and in that sense at least there is a sequence to the process. Cognitive uncertainty expresses the idea that previous frames of knowing are unsatisfactory, and prior preferences dispensed with and laid open to being reshaped. But the point here is that after that, framing tends to be random and jagged depending on the contingent developments of the debate and on the entrepreneur's efforts. Cognitive interaction thus contributes to rebuilding frames through "piecing together" and it represents a core moment of the *pars construens* in the process that I propose.

The complexity of the process suggests features which all deserve treatment in their own right. This is not possible here, as it would complicate an already multifaceted approach to the analysis of EFP toward the Mediterranean. However, what is important is that the process of cognitive interaction and frame construction that I have described centers on the early stages of negotiations, which deserve attention as they are crucial in molding a new shared frame for EFP initiatives.

The emphasis on the contingency of the process does not amount to saying that there is no recurrent pattern in the content of the proposal. The emphasis in this research is on the process leading up to the adoption of an EFP initiative toward the Mediterranean, whereas the analysis of the specific content that initiatives take veers beyond what is possible to address here. Regularities, however, will appear and I would like to mention a few of them, while leaving the analysis to be tackled elsewhere.[21] In the case of the European framing of Euro-Mediterranean relations, the definition of the problem and its causes has tended to be predominantly in terms of security, while the policy response has been in terms of economics. As we shall see, a leitmotiv of EFP toward the Mediterranean is the connection that policy actors make between, on the one hand, the Mediterranean as a political/security issue and, on the other, an EC/EU role in dealing with this issue through economic development. In particular, political momentum and the articulation of political and security challenges tend to belong to member states' representatives, whereas the articulation of the economic details is mainly taken up by the Commission. Initiatives promoted by the Commission alone have generally lacked the political clout to deliver innovation. At the same time, the economic component tends to stick to the prevailing economic doctrine of the time. Therefore, at times of Keynesianism and state intervention, the emphasis is on Mediterranean *states*, while in the 1990s liberalization and a private sector perspective prevail. In another respect, frames about Euro-Mediterranean relations tend to embody a regional component. The EC/EU has approached its southern neighborhood with an inbuilt drive toward region building. There are not many examples of EFP toward the Mediterranean, but those that do exist involve the notion that EFP should contribute to "create a region" on the southern border of the EC/EU.[22]

The potential consequences of cognitive interaction and framing are far-reaching, in terms of the debate about interaction and preference formation within the EU. Cognitive interaction, leading to the definition of a common frame for Euro-Mediterranean relations, involves the initial deconstruction of national preferences and their subsequent joint reformulation at the European level. Without implying or going into the impact of reconstructed preferences on member state foreign policies, as my focus is predominantly on the European level, the analysis here looks at the way interaction within the EC/EU can supplement the interpretation of national preferences. As such this approach complements and reinforces the constructivist perspective of the importance of social interaction to preference formation. As I see it, cognitive interaction implies a "thick" understanding of social interaction, matching the "thick" approach to uncertainty defined earlier. The common process of policy formulation implies the convergence of actors on a set of common ideas on which to rely for future policy initiatives. Knowledge for policy making thus affects the way actors relate to the outside world by informing the actors' worldviews and preferences (Muller 1995).

Moreover, this account of interaction within the EC/EU makes it possible to think of entrepreneurship by a member state as having potentially the same consequences as entrepreneurship on the part of the Commission. The supranational/neofunctionalist perspective and the liberal intergovernmentalist approach fundamentally agree that supranational (and unintended, according to liberal intergovernmentalism) consequences occur because of the Commission's efforts to steer European integration in that direction. In my opinion, member states' entrepreneurship can also similarly lead to convergence and further integration, albeit from a different route. As national representatives and EC/EU institutions develop common views on a set of issues, the shared new principles are bound to become part and parcel of the parallel process of national preference reconstruction. Although the final outcome might be divergence (e.g., Héritier and Knill 2000), the process is also capable of delivering convergence and it offers us an alternative explanation of why and how this might occur. My point here is that, as Moravcsik forcefully put it, member states do have the resources to act as entrepreneurs, but differently from liberal intergovernmentalism, I believe that the cognitive consequences of member states' entrepreneurial action are "thick" and potentially conducive to further integration. The supranational vision could thus be rescued by a cognitive analysis which allows us to reevaluate the independent momentum created in negotiations about European integration.

Conclusions

The approach defined in this chapter has suggested a way to analyze how, when, and why the EC/EU launches an initiative of foreign policy toward a third party such as the Mediterranean nonmember countries.

More specifically, it has centered on cases of innovative change in EFP making. It has stressed the relevance of background conditions, of policy entrepreneurs and of the interaction process that takes place in the early stages of EC/EU negotiations.

I have labeled this approach ideational intergovernmentalism, with the emphasis on the cognitive-ideational qualifier more than on the intergovernmentalist part, and intergovernmental ideationalism might serve equally well as a label. What matters is that it is a cognitive approach, exploring much of the knowledge basis of EFP making, although it remains at a macro level, without exploring the microfoundations of cognitive processes. It aims at reinterpreting several of the themes generally connected with rational choice approaches, and more specifically with liberal intergovernmentalism, in a constructivist perspective, thus expanding the range of arguments addressing European integration.

The main suggestion is that cognitive uncertainty, which is associated with deconstructed national preferences, represents a powerful starting point for a process of EFP making among European partners. It offers an alternative rationale to those put forward by rationalist and constructivist explanation, opening up new research avenues. From this point of view, European integration springs not from the attempt to achieve (mainly material) gains, nor because of an indirect and passive process of socialization, but from national policy makers' active quest for meaning and knowledge in their daily lives. The manner in which the process then develops is dependent on a policy entrepreneur taking the lead. Among the several ways in which this might happen, I have suggested that there is room to analyze member states' entrepreneurship in a less deterministic light, through the notion of brokerage. There are national policy entrepreneurs that aim for change without being too specific about the details of policy change. Their motivations, which are a matter for empirical analysis, could potentially be not only very broad, but also defined in terms of ideas rather than material economic gains. The simultaneous presence of cognitive uncertainty and a broker would foster a specific type of interaction, based on framing cognitive aspects of the problematique under scrutiny. Cognitive interaction led by a broker maintains a degree of leeway that potentially can lead to supranational outcomes, thus contradicting the well established argument that national entrepreneurs deliver limited or no supranational consequences.

The broader meaning of the approach I am advocating is that social reality is a "thick," contingent process. Through cognitive uncertainty, brokerage and cognitive interaction, I have in fact introduced a substantial degree of indeterminacy in the process of EFP making. Policy initiatives start because of a challenge to established preferences and their formulation unfolds because of motivations, and through patterns that need to be empirically assessed. My intention is to take constructivism "seriously," in the sense of analyzing how key processes in the broader picture of European integration are socially constructed. Instead of following several of the typical constructivist themes in European studies, I aim to bring the challenge into the camp of rational choice and more specifically to that of liberal intergovernmentalism. I am thus going to address and depict processes that belong to the latter literature more than to the former. But the goal is to show that rationality, power politics, national interests, all matter, as rationalists would expect, but the way they are defined is socially contingent. Much of the account I am going to offer of EFP making toward the Mediterranean thus might resemble a traditional story of intergovernmental clashes and might look as if it could be explained by rationalist approaches. My point, however, is that rationalist, liberal intergovernmentalist and realist explanations might be right, but when they are, they are so for the wrong reasons, as the way in which states' behavior comes about and unfolds is socially defined and impossible to understand without considering ideational elements.

Two final remarks on the type of explanation that I am aiming to provide: First, instead of testing one theory against the other, or one set of hypotheses against the other, I am going to "try out" the ideational intergovernmental approach I have defined in this chapter and see how far it will carry the analysis. A more scientific and rigorous way of doing research would recommend drawing more specific hypotheses and contrasting them with alternative ones, while providing a well-built operationalization of all concepts encompassed. It would also make it impossible to focus on the big picture as I aim to do. My goal is to explore alternative ways of analyzing European integration and EFP more particularly, rather than to claim to be the last word on EU policy making.

Moreover, a policy window, a policy entrepreneur and cognitive interaction, as defined in this chapter, represent necessary conditions, rather than sufficient ones. In other words, they are factors that are present whenever an EFP initiative toward the Mediterranean is launched. They represent crucial elements and regularities in the process of formulating and developing every EFP initiative for the Mediterranean. If even one of them is missing, then there is no EFP initiative. However, I am not trying to contend that they are all that EFP initiatives toward the Mediterranean are about. Their existence is not sufficient for the EC/EU to agree on collective policies in the region. A myriad of contingent elements might play an important role in one case but not in another. I fully agree with Sartori that sufficient conditions in the form of "causes," which automatically trigger events regardless of the historical context, do not really belong to the realm of social sciences (Sartori 1970). What follows is thus an exploratory, critical analysis of how EFP initiatives came about in the Mediterranean case, rather than the ultimate explanation for why they did.

CHAPTER 2

The Euro-Mediterranean Relations from 1957 to 1972: When No Tailored European Foreign Policy Existed

Introduction

Between 1957 and 1972, the EEC "lacked a policy framework to organize and structure" Euro-Mediterranean relations (Ginsberg 1989, 119–120) and the Mediterranean nonmembers ranked low on the EEC agenda. The EEC seemingly tackled problems as they arose, without an agreed overall conception (Shlaim 1976, 80). Although during its early years the EEC did sign several agreements with its Mediterranean neighbors, these agreements were uncoordinated and did not derive from a common core of principles and related actions. The result was a "patchwork" of agreements (Gomez 1998, 134). Each problem was examined individually and was given a different solution. This chapter analyzes this "year zero" of the European foreign policy toward the Mediterranean, that is, the period before the EEC elaborated and launched any consistent initiative toward the Mediterranean.

This period is interesting for several reasons. First, the analysis of this period is revealing in terms of what it suggests for the conditions for EFP formulation. As there was no EFP initiative toward the whole Mediterranean, I expect to find none or only a small part of the conditions I hypothesized in chapter 1. As we shall see, neither a policy window nor a policy entrepreneur existed during this period. The policy window was absent as the time span was marked by the substantial status quo of the cold war, with no new security or political challenges to attract the attention of European countries. Moreover, no policy entrepreneur stood out to push for a common approach to the Mediterranean. Therefore, what will be analyzed in this chapter is a case of "dogs that did not bark" for reasons consistent with the model outlined in chapter 1 and in a way that is similar (though not identical) to the evidence in chapter 4 on the 1980s.

The analysis of this period is rewarding for another reason, namely that it allows us to fully appreciate the changes which take place later on. Although no policy was agreed for the Mediterranean as such,[1] several bilateral agreements were signed. In 15 years, the EEC regulated at least the most important aspects of trade with the majority of the Mediterranean nonmembers. While the timing and content of the agreements differed widely we can distinguish between a first group of agreements, which were diverse in content and a second, post-1967, more homogenous group. The first group was composed of two early and substantial agreements with Greece (1961) and Turkey (1963), which were shortly afterward followed by nondescript agreements with Israel (1964) and Lebanon (1965). Between 1965 and 1967 there were no negotiations, as the EEC plunged into the "empty chair" crisis. Contacts then resumed, leading to a group of agreements which occupied a middle ground between the two previous clusters. The difference in time and content thus gave birth to a "pyramid of privileges"[2] by which the EEC afforded a more preferential treatment to some countries while neglecting others. It was this situation that the Global Mediterranean Policy in 1972, in addressing the region as a whole, was aiming to redress, as we shall see in the next chapter.

Therefore, the empirical evidence shown in this chapter will show how the simultaneous absence of a policy window and of a policy entrepreneur prevented the Mediterranean from climbing up the EEC agenda, and undermined the formation of a coherent policy for the region, leaving only the scattered pieces of bilateral relations. This does not mean that there was no advance in terms of EFP. The mere idea of a foreign policy at the European level was highly controversial during this period. However, the Rome Treaty had put in place the key pieces of the external economic relations' architecture, much of which is still in place today (Macleod et al. 1996, 367–385). EEC relations with the rest of the world were sketched out in terms of economic agreements, and the Mediterranean was no different in this respect.

The chapter is organized as follows. First, I will outline the international context of the time, which was characterized by the predominance of the cold war. Second, I will analyze the dynamics among actors that led to the adoption of this scattered set of economic agreements. I will then conclude by examining the agreements signed, in terms of timing and content.

The Cold War and the Mediterranean

No policy window opened during the period under consideration. There was no change in Europeans' foreign policy priorities concerning relations with the Mediterranean, and no shifts in their security perceptions. The cold war's relentless grip on member states' agendas spanned the early days of the EEC well into the 1960s and left very little room for the perception of new challenges or for the redefinition of Europe's role in international politics. The struggle against the Soviet Union absorbed all the attention of Western countries, and left no leeway in the case of the Mediterranean. The United States determined the main political guidelines, while European member states contributed to the plan drafted by the United States. This was especially the case up to the mid-1960s and the bilateral agreements with Greece and Turkey are a good example of the application of cold war logic to Euro-Mediterranean relations. In the second half of the 1960s, as the cold war lost part of its urgency, the Europeans were still not interested in the Mediterranean area, as their reading of Euro-Mediterranean relations remained largely anchored to a cold war interpretation. Nonetheless, the second group of agreements between the EEC and the Mediterranean nonmembers, concluded between 1969 and 1972, is at least indirectly linked to the relenting grasp of the cold war.

The Mediterranean was indeed one of the main battle lines during the cold war and the conflicting fronts were well established by the time of the EEC creation. After an early indirect confrontation about Greece and Turkey, which led to the U.S. adoption of the Truman doctrine in 1947, the Soviet Union managed to conclude in the late 1950s an ambiguous alliance with the growing Arab radical movements, thus expanding its influence in all Arab countries. Soviet influence was "at a peak during the heyday of Arab radicalism during the 1960s" (Yapp 1996, 413). For their part, the United States by the time of Suez (1956) had definitely superseded European powers, by undertaking the direct leadership of the region that it previously shared with Great Britain and France. Both the United States and the Soviet Union got enmeshed into supporting local regimes, according to the key tenets of "competitive coexistence" that prevailed at the global level (Di Nolfo 1994, 899). While avoiding direct confrontation and escalation of local conflicts into international wars, the superpowers struggled with an endless series of international crises (Spiegel 1992).

The strategy for the Mediterranean arena that the United States adopted and shared with its European allies was primarily negative (Yapp 1996, 413) and characterized the whole period under examination. It mainly focused on countering Soviet expansion while at the same time keeping the Western bloc united under U.S. leadership in the fight against communism (Brown 1984, 176). According to U.S. secretary of state, Foster Dulles, Marx himself could have described the situation, as the Arabs looked like desperate masses of people ready to embrace a radical ideology. The way would have been paved for communism to conquer both leaders and the masses in the Middle East. The rise of radical nationalist movements, which fought for liberation from Western domination, and popular upheaval against corrupt regimes, sounded like the prelude to revolution and the establishment of communist regimes in the region. U.S. administrations in fact tended to identify Arab nationalism with communism (Kaufman 1996, 27), and as Arab nationalism thrived in reaction to European colonialism, the United States insisted that European colonial powers sever links with former or current colonies and withdraw from Middle East politics as a way of defusing what it saw as the communist threat in the region.

The Six largely embraced this perspective, their activities reflecting their support for the United States fight against communism. Already under pressure from the cold war in Europe and the menace of Soviet expansion in the Middle East, the European states maintained the cold war as their top priority in the Mediterranean. Even the nationalistic regime of General de Gaulle in France was not in a position to alter this situation. Therefore, not only did the Europeans adopt a low profile in the Mediterranean to avoid any threat of confrontation, but also the first phase of agreements between the EEC and Greece, Turkey, Israel, and Lebanon reflect an environment dominated by the security concerns of the cold war. The need to stabilize Greece and Turkey was widely felt in Europe and the prospect of EEC membership for these countries, albeit in the long run, offered immediate advantages in terms of consolidating democracy and furthering economic and political development. This perspective shared by the two candidate countries and the European member states, extended to the United States as well.[3] NATO membership and security concerns were the main reasons behind the first two association agreements signed by the EEC with Greece and Turkey (Loeff 1973, 102).[4] The convergence of views between the United States and the European states also affected the substance of the agreements. As described in detail later, both accords aimed at full membership, though Turkey's path was longer than Greece's. The carrot of eventual membership served a double purpose, as it constituted the strongest binding link through a constant check on the domestic conditions of the countries concerned, and at the same time was compatible with international regulations about trade set out in the GATT regime.

Strong solidarity within the cold war alliance played a role also in determining agreements with Israel and Lebanon. In the case of Israel, the cold war led to the postponement of the agreement. Israel had asked for negotiations on an agreement as early as October 1958 (Minerbi 1970, 127; 1976, 243). However, European member states did not wish to stir up Arab nationalism, neither were they keen on Israel becoming the first associate of the EEC (Weil 1970, 181). Negotiations were thus postponed until late 1962. The content of the first Israeli agreement, as well as the content of the agreement with Lebanon in 1965, focused on nonpreferential trade concessions which were hardly significant. While radically different from the Athens and Ankara agreements, these two agreements were able to boast compatibility with the GATT system sponsored by the United States. However even the GATT element showed a substantial difference in the two sets of accords: those with Greece and Turkey envisaged membership of the EEC, and put in place trading arrangements which would be GATT compatible over the long period planned before EEC membership was granted. Those with Israel and Lebanon on the other hand were much more restrictive and complied with GATT because of the limited concessions accorded.[5]

In the mid-1960s, the international environment, including in the Mediterranean, began an evolution that peaked in the détente of the early 1970s. Without a clear design or a single cause, superpower confrontation lost part of its urgency, giving way to a willingness to cooperate by the superpowers. At the same time, allies less subjugated by cold war imperatives became more open to new ideas and new priorities. There was still a long way to go before the cold war was to cross any threshold on its way down the securitization-politicization continuum that I sketched in chapter 1. But the Europeans' foreign policy agenda did acquire some leeway, which in turn promoted small-scale changes in Euro-Mediterranean relations

The gradual and relative downgrading of cold war tensions in the second half of the 1960s favored the economic aspirations that the Europeans nurtured vis-à-vis the Mediterranean nonmembers. Chased out of the political arena, the Europeans had developed a tendency to focus on economic relations. The foreign policy of de Gaulle aimed to maintain economic relations with the Maghreb after Algeria's independence, thus avoiding any attempt at being shut out of the region because of political reasons. Moreover, France also gradually developed profitable economic relations with Spain. In Germany too, the main drive was represented by the attempt to depoliticize most issues, in order to pursue economic and technological exchanges with both Israel and the Arab countries (Ismael 1986, 99). Moreover, Germany cultivated economic relations with Turkey, Spain, Portugal, Greece, Malta, and Cyprus, thus becoming, at the beginning of the 1970s, the major client and supplier of the Mediterranean countries as a whole (Papa and Petit-Laurent 1976, 272). Italy for its part concentrated its efforts on widening the share of its exports to the region, which increased steadily during the 1960s. The Benelux countries too, thanks to their traditional trading efficiency, acquired market shares in the Mediterranean countries (Papa and Petit-Laurent 1976, 275).

As the winds of détente started to blow, the Europeans begun to be more assertive about their economic position in the Mediterranean. This was reflected in the second group of agreements, which was signed between 1969 and 1972 with Morocco, Tunisia, Spain, Israel (second agreement), Malta, Cyprus, and Egypt. All these agreements, even when coated in the language of association, entailed a preferential element. Their intention was to protect European interests vis-à-vis the rest of the world, including the United States, whose erratic behavior in the Kennedy round had helped produce a wide interpretation of GATT rules (Tovias 1977, 34–35). However, the United States reacted immediately and negatively to the new wave of agreements and its complaints against the preference system of the EEC acquired an urgent tone (Lundestad 1998, 98). While the U.S. administration continued to adhere to the old logic of the Western bloc that had dominated the early post war years, the Europeans had begun to interpret international affairs in a slightly different light.

The importance of the early years of détente should not be overstated. I have magnified their effect for the sake of emphasizing a trend. In spite of the Europeans' decision to negotiate agreements, which the United States did not approve, during the period 1969–1972, the overall pattern of this period remained dominated by the cold war and by transatlantic solidarity. The fight against communism, which had such an importance in the strategic confines of the Mediterranean, did not relent during the period. European security perceptions, which I have hypothesized as contributing to the opening of a policy window, remained obsessed by the Soviet threat and, if we focus on the big picture, did not change. There was a partial influence of détente on member states' decision to adopt more preferential agreements in the second half of the 1960s. But this in no way amounts to changes in European political and security perceptions, nor to the opening of a policy window.

Actors' Dynamics Leading to the Agreements

Not only was there no policy window in this period: there was no policy entrepreneur either. The Commission hardly manifested an intention to play such a role, while the Council maintained a tight supervision of negotiations. The Council in turn was the place where several compromises were made, but no clear leadership emerged from it. On the contrary, domestic pressures at times led a southern European member state—Italy—to oppose negotiations. Therefore, agreements tended to emerge out of provisional constellations of positions or because of contingent plans concocted under the pressure of Mediterranean nonmembers. Every agreement had a story of its own, much of which was lost as time passed. As a consequence, I will limit myself to a few considerations of the patterns that characterize the lack of entrepreneurship between 1957 and 1972.

The legal basis of the agreements could have suggested a substantial role for the Commission, as the agreements were first and foremost trade accords. While three agreements were "mixed" (Greece, Turkey, and Lebanon I),[6] all the others involved just the EEC, thus potentially offering some leverage to the Commission. Moreover, the legal basis, which varied quite a bit (see table 2.1), was not tightly connected to the

Table 2.1 Legal Basis of Agreements between the EEC and Mediterranean Countries, 1957–1972

Country	Legal Basis	Type of Agreement
Greece	Art. 238 (Mixed Agreement)	Association Agreement
Turkey	Art. 238 (Mixed Agreement)	Association Agreement
Israel I	Art. 111	Nonpreferential Agreement
Lebanon I	Art. 111 (Mixed Agreement)	Nonpreferential Technical Cooperation Agreement
Tunisia	Art. 238	Association Agreement
Morocco	Art. 238	Association Agreement
Israel II	Art. 113	Preferential Agreement
Spain	Art. 113	Preferential Agreement
Malta	Art. 238	Association Agreement
Lebanon II	Art. 113	Preferential Agreement
Cyprus	Art. 238	Association Agreement
Egypt	Art. 113	Preferential Agreement

Source: *Journal Officiel des Communautés européennes*, various issues.

content of the agreements, which could at first be interpreted as the Commission overstretching its entrepreneurial capacities.

The Commission, however, seems not to have developed a position of its own.[7] Such a stance could be justified with the restrictive interpretation of EEC competence that prevailed before the European Court of Justice (ECJ) judgment in the 1971 AERT case. The Commission in fact enjoyed more freedom of initiative while carrying out the exploratory talks with the countries concerned than after the beginning of formal negotiations (Weil 1970, 50ff.) given the prevailing practice of following Art. 228 for all types of negotiations. This article granted member states a wide power of supervision of the Commission's role, through the constitution of committees. Moreover, the association agreements with Greece and Turkey broke with the tradition of association agreements that had until then prevailed in the European Coal and Steel Community, and all EEC member states were represented in the Association Council, instead of the Commission as the representative body of the EEC as a whole (Feld 1965, 238).

Does the ensuing bias in favor of the Council mean that the Council was the driving force, because of a strong entrepreneurial state or because it represented a powerful constellation of interests on the part of member states? The evidence shows that at the time no entrepreneurial state invested in the Mediterranean. France did obtain a better treatment for Morocco and Tunisia; it supported Spain's application for membership whenever the issue came up, but it managed to keep Algeria outside of any legal arrangement while blocking negotiations with Israel.[8] Germany on the contrary supported Israel for historical reasons. Belgium and the Netherlands opposed Spain on ideological grounds, whereas Italy opposed it on economic grounds. At first this created a double veto situation, with respect to Spain and Israel. The EEC thus rejected Spain's request for an agreement but signed a shallow one with Israel in 1964. The deadlock was broken in the late 1960s, when France adopted a more positive attitude, asking for equal treatment of requests coming from Israel and from Arab states. This attitude, which aimed at promoting Arab interests, opened the door to equal treatment being granted to Spain as well.[9] This development in turn paved the way for a more general settlement, on which the accords that followed with Israel, Spain, and other Arab countries were also founded (Henig 1976, 316–317; Minerbi 1976, 245; Tovias 1977, 81 fn).[10] In this mishmash of partially clashing, partially converging positions, no clear entrepreneur spoke up for the Mediterranean.

There was, on the contrary, an effective case of resistance on the part of a southern European country. Beginning from 1964, Italy, under pressure from its southern agricultural producers and particularly from the citrus lobby, demanded an accommodation to avoid competition from agricultural goods from Mediterranean nonmember countries. In fact, Italy was self sufficient in the most important market, oranges, while the other five member states were importing 80 percent of their internal consumption from the Mediterranean countries (especially from Spain, Morocco, Tunisia, and Israel). Negotiations under way with these countries, which had been put forward by the other five members, envisaged a cut in the Common External Tariff on all imports of oranges, but Italy rejected it, to protect its producers. After a lot of wrestling among the Six, prices valid for the Common Market were fixed at a high level and a variety of tariffs were imposed on non-EEC orange producing countries (Henig 1976, 318). In this case, therefore, a compromise between the member states was forced by the influence of a domestic minority actor on one country out of six, which forced the Italian government to take a harder stand than it would otherwise have adopted. The situation exemplified also the paradox of southern European countries. While they have a "natural" interest in their southern neighbors, they are by no means "natural" policy entrepreneurs in their favor. As we shall see in chapter 4, this paradox came to the fore again at the time of the southern enlargement of the EEC, as the accession of Greece, Spain and Portugal provoked at first a worsening of Mediterranean nonmembers' conditions in Euro-Mediterranean relations.

Finally member states managed to agree to address most of the Mediterranean nonmembers on a bilateral basis. This could be interpreted as an instance of European foreign policy, given that, at the end of the day, the EEC did conclude a web of agreements. The process by which it got there, however, reveals the absence of a conscious or coherent decision to do so. There was no moment in which member states' and EEC institutional representatives expressed any kind of vision for these countries. The outcome was instead guided by a constellation of provisional factors and contingent developments, thus running short of being a policy, never mind a "European" foreign policy.

Therefore, one conclusion which can be drawn about actorness from the analysis of this period of uncoordinated bilateral agreements, in accordance with what I have suggested in chapter 1, is that the absence of a European policy for the Mediterranean region correlates with the absence of a policy entrepreneur. Neither a member state nor the Commission acted in an entrepreneurial manner, investing resources in the formulation of a policy initiative directed toward Mediterranean nonmembers. Not only was the Commission limited in its independence of action, but also it appeared to be unable to conceive of the area as a region or to develop a position of its own. France hindered some agreements and supported some others, whereas Italy behaved entrepreneurially *against* most of the agreements.

This empirical evidence thus supports *a contrario* two of the key hypotheses of this research, that is, that a necessary condition for a Mediterranean initiative to take place is the existence of a policy window and a policy entrepreneur. As it was denounced at the beginning of the 1970s, the outcome was an "accidental" process (Hager 1974, 231), which was "apparently random" and incoherent (Shlaim 1976, 80), probably due to "a fit of absent-mindedness" (Tovias 1977, 1).

The EEC Agreements with Mediterranean Nonmember Countries (1957–1972)

So, what did this "patchwork" of agreements look like? Simplifying only slightly, the EEC agreements with the Mediterranean nonmember countries from the creation of the EEC to the formulation of the Global Mediterranean Policy in 1972 can be distinguished along two broad lines: (1) the country timing, that is, when an agreement is signed with a given country; (2) the content of the agreement, that is, what the agreement actually foresees for the relations between the non-member country and the EEC.

The first aspect (the country timing) spans more than a decade. While attempts by policy makers to rationalize EEC Mediterranean policy in the following decade will strive to deliver a comprehensive approach toward all the Mediterranean countries together at one point in time, during the period under examination, the signing of agreements was strung out over more than a decade, between 1961 and 1972, as shown by table 2.2. The agreements can be grouped in two sets. The first includes the agreements signed between 1961 and 1965, while the second covers those signed between 1969 and 1972 (Henig 1976, 316; Tovias 1977, 44). Some countries thus were the early-comers, belonging to the first temporal set, while others were de facto the late-comers. Some countries did not formalize economic relations at all, during this period.

Greece, Turkey, Israel, and Lebanon belong to the first group. The earliest mandate for the Commission to negotiate an agreement was prepared for the negotiations with Greece. The Athens agreement entered into force in November 1962.[11] It was soon followed by an agreement

Table 2.2 Agreements between the EEC and Mediterranean Countries, 1957–1972, Times of Negotiations

Country	Beginning of Negotiations*	Date of Signature	Journal Officiel	Date of Entry into Force
First Group				
Greece	9.VI.1959	9.VII.1961	L26 (18.II.1963)	1.XI.1962
Turkey	1961	12.IX.1963	L217 (29.XII.1964)	1.XII.1964
Israel I	1958, 1962, 1964	4.VI.1964	L95 (VII.1964)	1.VII.1964
Lebanon I		21.V.1965[a]	L278 (20.X.1975)[b]	1.VII.1968
Second Group				
Morocco	December 1963, 1965, 1967	31.III.1969	L197 (8.VIII.1969)	1.IX.1969
Tunisia	1959, 1965, 1967	23.III.1969	L198 (8.VIII.1969)	1.IX.1969
Israel II	October 1966	29.VI.1970	L183 (17.VIII.1970)	1.X.1970
Spain	1962, 1967	29.VI.1970	L182 (X.1970)	1.X.1970
Malta		5.XII.1970	L61 (14.III.1971)	1.IV.1971
Lebanon II		18.XII.1972	...	Never ratified by Lebanon
Cyprus	March 1971 January 1972	19.XII.1972	L133 (21.V.1973)	1.VI.1973
Egypt		18.XII.1972	L251 (7.IX.1973)	1.XI.1973
Algeria	1963	...	...	...
Jordan	...	...	...	...
Libya	...	...	...	...
Syria	...	...	...	...

* Not for all agreements was it possible to detect the precise date of the beginning of negotiations. For some of them, negotiations were undertaken more than once.
[a] Immediate entry into force of the part on technical cooperation, on the basis of a joint declaration adopted on the date of the signature.
[b] The agreement was renewed year after year. This was the last time that the agreement was renewed.

Source: *Journal Officiel des Communautés européennes*, various issues.

with Turkey, which formalized its application in 1961 and reached an agreement in 1963. The next applicants were Spain and Israel. Given its political features and the opposition it provoked in some member states, the Spanish request was acknowledged by the Commission "with a polite letter and no more" (Tovias 1977, 29). Toward Israel too, whose aspiration for an agreement with the EEC dated back to the early days of the EEC,[12] the Commission adopted a low-key approach, due to the opposition of some member states, notably France. The ensuing negotiations with Israel dragged on until a poorly substantiated agreement was rapidly put into force in 1964. Israel's example influenced Lebanon, which signed an agreement with the EEC in 1965. Thus the first phase of EEC activism toward the Mediterranean countries was marked by two strong candidates that managed to reach substantial agreements through complex negotiations, and by two minor applicants, with whom rather shallow, half-hearted agreements were quickly formalized, while Spain was excluded altogether from negotiations.

As the dates reveal, no substantial negotiations were undertaken between August 1965 and the late months of 1966, while the attention of member states was devoted to the attempt to solve and overcome the "empty chair" crisis, during which France boycotted the EEC. The event came to affect Euro-Mediterranean relations. The exploratory talks with Spain were "completely interrupted" (Tovias 1977, 30), while the possibility of an agreement with Algeria vanished. At the same time, in December 1965, Italy and the Benelux countries decided to stop the regime of intra-Community treatment from which Algeria had benefited up to then, thanks to its former status as a French department (Weil 1970, 176). Morocco and Tunisia, the most relevant applicants in the mid-1960s, were particularly unlucky, given that the first round of negotiations was due to take place in July 1965, right after the French "walk out." As a result, the talks did not lead anywhere (Guessous 1970, 45) and a second mandate was later required in order to relaunch the discussions (and to broaden the range of topics on the table).[13]

The halt in negotiations due to the "empty chair" crisis confirms the low ranking that Euro-Mediterranean relations commanded on the EEC agenda. EEC actors directed their attention to the most pressing issues, which were the future of the EEC and alternative interpretations of the organization's mission. Negotiations with Mediterranean nonmember countries not only did not bear any relevance to this debate, but also they were substantially controversial, with little chance to progress until a more general equilibrium was reestablished. As a consequence, even the fragmented progress in bilateral negotiations that characterized the early 1960s ground to a halt and talks resumed only after the EEC had fully regathered its sense of purpose.

The second group of negotiations, which begun in 1967, led to a set of agreements that were more homogeneous in terms of content. The group consisted of Morocco, Tunisia, Spain, Israel (second agreement), Malta, Cyprus, and Egypt. The new set of applicants was treated generally in pairs, though this did not always arise from the supposed commonalties shared by the countries in question. One such pair was Morocco and Tunisia. They had first been indicated as candidates for association in the Rome Treaty, but in spite of being relatively neutral from a political point of view, they were caught in the "empty chair" crisis and ended up in the second group (Grilli 1993, 183). The fate of the agreement with Spain and of the second agreement with Israel was linked to a package deal inside the EEC, which led to both agreements signed in June 1970, foreshadowing what would happen again in 1972. At the end of the 1960s, negotiations were undertaken by Malta, and later Cyprus and Egypt, while Lebanon did not ratify the second agreement it had negotiated, which was due to enter into force in December 1972.

It is important to note that agreements in this second group tended to be finite and come with an expiry date attached. The agreements with Morocco and Tunisia, in particular, had an early expiry date, fixed for August 31, 1974. The clause, inserted as a promise of future more intense cooperation, was to create an additional incentive to negotiate a comprehensive package at the time of the Global Mediterranean Policy.[14]

Libya showed no interest in formulating an agreement, as the only product exported to the EEC—oil—was duty free. Syria and Jordan too did not demonstrate any eagerness to formalize relations with the EEC. Relations with Algeria were completely unregulated in the early years after its independence, though in practical terms trade conditions were equaled to those written in for Morocco and Tunisia, thus adding one exception to another.[15] Discussions about a trade agreement with Algeria kept dragging on, but the agenda was ridden with points of contention.[16]

The end of 1972 can, therefore, be taken as the date by which the EEC accomplished the establishment of agreements defining its external relations with most of Mediterranean nonmember countries.[17] By then, the EEC had concluded agreements with almost all the countries bordering the Mediterranean, but there was no recognition of the Mediterranean as a region per se.

The variety to be found in the timing of the agreements is further accentuated in the content of the agreements, the second aspect of Euro-Mediterranean relations. Agreements not only covered different aspects of the relationship between the EEC and third countries, but even when addressing similar issues, they adopted different solutions. The final outcome shows a very differential treatment for the countries involved, which Ralf Dahrendorf, Commissioner for External Affairs from 1970 until 1973, justified by saying that each case had to be examined individually because of divergent traditions and systems.[18]

In spite of the evident disarray of the agreements, some general considerations can be made on the basis of recurring issues (Henig 1976, 319; Loeff 1973).[19] The agreements established a pyramid of privilege based on two aspects. The first was related to the number of issues included and the second to the degree of concessions granted on the issues, which in turn indicated the degree of closeness between the EEC and the partner country (Tovias 1977; Papa and Petit-Laurent 1976).

Future prospective developments, social provisions, financial and technical aid, trade concessions, all these were issues on which the EEC constructed the architecture of its relations with the Mediterranean nonmember countries. In such an architecture, Greece and Turkey achieved the most privileged position.

Future prospective developments toward membership were included in the Athens and Ankara agreements only. The Association Agreement with Greece foresaw the establishment of a customs union after a transitional period of 22 years. At the end of this period, if the main goals included in the Agreement had been successfully pursued, the Agreement envisaged the possibility of membership.[20] Similarly, the Association Agreement with Turkey established progressive convergence in three steps. After an initial preparatory stage of five to eleven years, Turkey would have entered into a transitional stage, to be accomplished by the creation of a customs union. The final stage was meant to lead to Turkey's official application for full membership, no later than 1995.[21] However, after 1970, relations between the EEC and Turkey entered a period of decline, which negatively affected the prospective deadline (Rosenthal 1982, 13). In the case of Malta, potential developments envisaged the creation of a customs union too, but that development was soon hampered by domestic Maltese politics.

Social provisions, again, were included in the Athens and Ankara agreements only. They regulated free mobility of workers from Greece and Turkey to the Common Market during a specific period of time. While in the Greek case the mobility of workers was implemented, together with other provisions related to services, the slowing down after 1967 of European economies, especially in Western Germany, hampered effective implementation in the Turkish case (Weil 1970, 88; Yannopoulos 1976).[22]

Aid provisions were of two types: financial and "technical." Greece and Turkey again received a preferential treatment, with soft loans granted through the European Investment Bank (on top of the vast aid program the two countries received from the United States).[23] The funds were intended to increase industrial productivity in the two countries, in order to enable them to compete with European goods. The other agreements did not include explicit provisions about financial aid. Technical assistance was granted to Lebanon, in the first agreement signed between the two parties. It focused on technical assistance and training programs, in exchange for information about investment possibilities for the EEC in Lebanon. This was the first case of common technical assistance to a state that had not previously been a dependency of one of the member states (Weil 1970, 192).

While social provisions and aid applied to relatively few agreements, trade was at the centre of all the agreements drawn up. It included provisions about industrial goods, agricultural goods and the degree of reciprocity in concessions. The basic elements of the EEC approach to these three issues was summarized by Joseph Loeff, at the time the Director of the Direction Générale Relations Extérieurs at the European Commission: "Ces accords, qui se fondent principalement sur la notion d'équilibre dans le secteur agricole et d'expansion dans le secteur industriel, s'articulent autour du principe d'une réciprocité dans les concessions"[24] (Loeff 1973, 104). These words, when not couched in such diplomatic language, indicated what was the core deal between the EEC and the Mediterranean nonmembers. For the case of industrial goods, the EEC offered substantial concessions to all Mediterranean nonmember countries while in the case of agricultural goods, the EEC increasingly avoided concessions to third parties. In terms of reciprocity, the EEC preferred reciprocal concessions to be made, but it showed a conciliatory behavior if third parties opposed them.

But let us examine the three aspects in detail, as they came to constitute key terms of references in the negotiations with the Mediterranean nonmembers in the decades that followed. Most importantly, these conditions reflected the economic doctrines that prevailed at the time, which favored economies of scale and import-substitution as the best strategy to promote development. The change in economic approach in the 1990s, as we will see in chapter 5, was substantial.

Trade in industrial goods from Mediterranean nonmember states to the EEC was favored to different degrees. The EEC granted a privileged access to the Single Market through tariff reduction on the Common External Tariff (CET), which had been the basis of the EEC customs union. Greece, Turkey, Morocco and Tunisia received the best treatment, as their industrial goods entered the European market duty free. Tariff concessions for the other partners varied: the rate of abatement of the CET was 70 percent for Cyprus, Malta and Spain, 55 percent for Lebanon (second agreement) and Egypt, and 50 percent for Israel (second agreement). In the first agreement, Lebanon and the EEC reciprocally granted each other Most Favored Nation status, as was envisaged in the GATT, in spite of Lebanon not being a member of the trade organization. The first agreement with Israel offered only a very small reduction of the CET (-20 percent) and on a very small set of goods.[25]

The rationale behind this approach was to offer a broader market to the new industries of the third countries in order to allow them to develop economies of scale and export their products to Europe. The small, unattractive local markets were to be complemented by the rich and wealthy European market, where the newcomers would have the opportunity to sell their products in exchange for much needed funds to spark development. This concession was not costly for member states as the industrial structure in the Mediterranean countries was nonexistent or in a stage of infancy and anyway did not represent a real threat for well established European industries. Moreover, the agreements did not exclude the possibility of exceptions, leaving the way open for further negotiations if needed. In some cases, safeguard clauses were already adopted to limit the dangers of competition. Most telling was the provision that all goods had to comply with the European rules of origin. This not only would imply an adjustment of industries of the nonmember states to European standards but it also biased trade in favor of goods produced from raw materials originating from Europe (Shlaim 1976, 90). In both cases, the mechanism of the market was unleashed in theory, but real competition was from the very start hardly possible.

Lack of competition was particularly evident in the agricultural sector, where southern European farmers received a substantial protection from southern Mediterranean goods. Greece was the sole country to receive intra-EEC treatment for agricultural goods. Having being associated soon after the creation of the EEC, Greece was involved in the process of definition of the Common Agricultural Policy (CAP) and this early participation, together with the prospect of membership, contributed to an agreement favorable to Greek farmers. Morocco and Tunisia did not fare too badly either. They obtained a relatively profitable treatment, with concessions similar to those they had enjoyed in their relations with France. However, clear precautions were taken in case the prices of exported goods fell below the European average level and thus might endanger the foundations of the CAP. Turkey struck a surprisingly bad deal, as in the first preparatory phase 40 percent of its exports were restricted by quotas and in the transitional stage too the concessions did not go beyond 40–50 percent of the CET for olives, grapes, and some fresh and dried fruits, which constitute a crucial Turkish export (Bridge 1976, 167). The remaining countries saw the vast majority of their requests about agricultural goods turned down by the EEC, in the name of preference for Community production.

The degree to which Mediterranean nonmembers decided to grant reciprocal concessions and stick to them introduces a dynamic element in the discussion about trade concessions. Although the principle was supposed to be equally valid for all the partners, the degree of reciprocity varied even more than in the case of other aspects. Moreover, even when accepted in theory, Mediterranean countries profited from an international discussion about reciprocity in trade to renounce it after the entry into force of the agreements.

At one end of the spectrum, the treatment of candidates for EEC membership tended toward free trade, customs union and thus full reciprocity. In the case of Greece, a customs union with full acceptance of the CET was scheduled after a period of 12–22 years, while for Turkey, the customs union and the adoption of the CET were supposed to come into force during the second stage toward the final membership. In both cases, the last sectors to be liberalized included machinery and chemicals, as well as other goods for which Greece and Turkey were dependent on protection from European industries, so as to leave time for local industries to develop before facing strong competition. States on the contrary that basically did not reciprocate trade concessions were Israel, Morocco and Tunisia. Their concessions accorded to EEC goods were as minimal as a reduction of 10 percent in duty levies in the case of Morocco. In the remaining cases, some kind of balance was sought, the degree of reciprocity ranging from a concession of 30 percent up to 50 percent on the existing levy, vis-à-vis larger EEC concessions in the industrial field and smaller concessions in the agricultural sector.

The EEC initial request for reciprocity raised several issues. It was justified in two ways: first, the creation of a free trade area was the necessary condition for approval within the GATT framework, the main aims of which were to promote multilateral trade and to phase out privileged trade relations. Second, it was said to be a way to place on an equal footing both parties to the agreement, through their reciprocal commitments (Loeff 1973, 105). Both points were, however, soon to come under attack from different perspectives, as we shall see in chapter 3. As a consequence, several Mediterranean countries jumped at the first opportunity to renounce reciprocity in trade concessions. Turkey defaulted on the principle shortly after the entry into force of the agreement, in line with the decline of the relationship experienced in the following decade. Morocco and Tunisia also retreated from the privileges accorded, as did Malta and Cyprus (Pomfret 1986, 40).

The overall picture that thus emerges from the analysis of the timing and content of EEC agreements with Mediterranean nonmembers is one of little coherence, depicting a "pyramid of privilege." At the top, Greece and Turkey benefited from the cold war environment of the early days of the EEC and obtained two early and substantial agreements, envisaging eventual membership. At the bottom of the pyramid a few countries, including Jordan, Syria, and Libya, did not conclude any agreement with the EEC, for a variety of reasons. In between, several Mediterranean nonmembers managed to extract a few concessions, the value of which was more rhetorical than real. The timing of the agreements shows the relatively little importance that the area in its own, as a single region, had in the eyes of the Europeans. The content of the agreements confirms this. There were some common principles, but the range of variation in their application was huge. The Global Mediterranean Policy in 1972 would go in the direction of redressing this situation.

Conclusions

This chapter has been devoted to the analysis of a case of nonpolicy, according to the definition of EFP adopted in this research. The bilateral agreements negotiated between the EEC and the Mediterranean nonmember countries during the period 1957–1972 neither amounted to an EFP initiative, nor did they address the Mediterranean as a region. They bore little substantial uniformity in terms of timing, content and legal basis. As we have seen, they were a diverse assortment of conditions and concessions which require a magnifying glass to spot the common threads running through them. The main findings confirm the hypotheses I described in chapter 1 *a contrario*. The lack of an EFP initiative for the Mediterranean correlates with the absence of a policy window as well as of a policy entrepreneur.

The overwhelming importance of the cold war during this period prevented any substantial innovation in international relations. When the EEC came into being, the pattern of the cold war was well established, and the Mediterranean played a central role in it. Accordingly, the seemingly permanent international scheme of superpower confrontation excluded any real innovation, as well as any need for it. Divergences among agreements are partially explained by their relation to the cold war. In the first wave of agreements, in particular, Greece and Turkey managed to conclude very good agreements with the EEC because of their positions in the international arena.

The internal dynamics of the EEC also affected the agreements. The dynamics between the Council and member states, on the one hand, and the Commission, on the other, saw the latter in a relatively passive position. At the same time, no member state undertook an entrepreneurial role. None of the member states displayed any activism in favor of a common regional approach to the Mediterranean. The notable but negative exception was Italy, which invested to *block* the agreements in order to defend the interests of its domestic citrus lobby. The idea of an EFP for the Mediterranean, conceived as a single region, was never taken into serious account at this stage.

Therefore, the analysis of this "time zero" of European foreign policy toward Mediterranean nonmembers has led to two conclusions. First, in the early years of its existence, the EEC was aware of the issue of its relationship with Mediterranean nonmember countries, but the outcome was a set of different agreements which covered only some Mediterranean nonmembers. Thus we are now in a better position to understand the qualitative change that takes place in the following period, when the Europeans did succeed in formulating a common policy initiative. Second, the set of hypotheses put forward for the explanation of European foreign policy making in the case of the Mediterranean have also contributed to the understanding of the *lack* of European foreign policy in this period, and to the analysis of the timing and content of the bilateral agreements. This case of "dogs that did not bark" thus supports the approach adopted insofar as the absence of an EFP toward the Mediterranean coincided with the absence of a policy window and of a policy entrepreneur.

CHAPTER 3

Inventing the Mediterranean: From the Global Mediterranean Policy to the Euro-Arab Dialogue

Introduction

Between 1972 and 1974, European member states "invented" the Mediterranean. Such an endeavor was accomplished by putting forward a foreign policy initiative aimed at Mediterranean nonmember countries, under the name of "Global Mediterranean Policy" (GMP). It consisted of a legal framework to regulate relations between the EEC and all the Mediterranean nonmember countries on matters of mainly trade and aid. With the GMP, the EEC for the first time addressed the Mediterranean nonmember countries as a region, within a single policy framework. The policy, which was formulated in the EEC framework, was soon complemented by an initiative directed to the Arab countries, namely the Euro-Arab Dialogue (EAD). This time the initiative was formulated within the newly created European Political Cooperation (EPC) framework, inaugurated in 1970. Therefore, within two years, the European member states developed two specific initiatives, which were largely seen as complementary and relied on the same basic principles. They represented the two facets of the first instance of European foreign policy toward the Mediterranean.

What explains this burst of activism on the part of member states? What factors pushed the Mediterranean up the agenda and triggered the formulation of this first instance of EFP toward the Mediterranean? Between 1970 and 1974, a policy window was open, while between 1972 and 1974 France behaved as the main policy entrepreneur.

The simultaneous existence of these two factors sparked a debate at the European level about Euro-Mediterranean relations, which laid the basis for a decision on the two initiatives. The existence of two policy initiatives toward the Mediterranean thus correlates with the existence of the conditions I have put forward in chapter 1.

The window of opportunity that opened between 1970 and 1974 was founded on shifting perceptions among member states. During this period, cold war tensions abated, as détente pervaded international politics. However with this, two fresh challenges emerged on the European horizon. The first was terrorism, due to a shift of strategy by Arab-Palestinians determined to bring their fight closer to the Europeans. The second issue focused on economic relations, which after a decade of turbulence culminated with the oil shock in 1973. Both security challenges revolved around the Arab-Israeli conflict and the need of the Europeans to contribute a solution to this, something that was made more difficult by disagreements among Western countries. These divergences acted as an intervening variable to widen the policy window. All these elements contributed to strengthen the urgency for European policy makers to "do something" for the Mediterranean, while at the same time they magnified the cognitive uncertainty about exactly what it was that Europe should do.

The debate about this dilemma was raised at the European level by several actors, among which the most successful was France. In the case of the Global Mediterranean Policy, Italy and the Commission provided early and important inputs, though their efforts did not bring about a lasting change to the EEC/EPC agenda. France's action, motivated by the desire to strengthen its international status, managed to spark the debate that led to the GMP and to the EAD. It did so by feeding proposals into the discussion, but then in broker-style it was open to change them to incorporate other actors' suggestions.

In the course of the process leading to the GMP and the EAD, the cognitive basis of the two initiatives came to be defined through interaction among fellow partners. In the case of the GMP, Italy and the European Parliament stressed the political relevance of the Mediterranean. The Commission led a debate about the need to contribute to the development of Mediterranean economies. This fed into a more general debate on the geographical scope of the Mediterranean. By establishing a series of parallels, the EEC framed the area as a homogenous region, toward which it had political and developmental responsibilities. But when the issue reached the stage of defining substantive details, the framing process met its limit. A similar story applies to the EAD in the EPC framework.

There are two underlying and crucial issues that are central to this period, and thus to this chapter. The first is the myth that the Europeans mobilized only after the oil shock. While the oil shock was crucial to gather support for the Euro-Arab Dialogue, much of the debate took place—and the Global Mediterranean Policy was agreed—before that. The oil shock itself was the culmination of years of tensions over economic relations. Although no one foresaw the drastic reaction of Arab countries after the Yom Kippur war, the issue of oil and economic relations had been on the political agenda for quite a while. It was the growing awareness among the Europeans about economic relations that led to the politicization of Arab-European relations, while the oil shock brought the issue into the security domain.

The second issue that is central to this period is more analytical. The whole period could be read as a powerful realist story. As will be seen, several realist or liberal intergovernmentalist elements characterize Euro-Mediterranean relations at this time, ranging from power-seeking France to oil-scared member countries. Although these elements do wield explanatory power, focusing exclusively on them would, however, miss a very important point, namely the cognitive shift that underpinned the adoption of the two initiatives and the type of motives and processes connected to French entrepreneurship. If realist factors and realist-motivated actors were so strong, then the entrepreneurial behavior would approximate the "believer" type of entrepreneurship, and the outcome would reflect the preferred option of the entrepreneurial actor. This, as we shall see, was not the case. Therefore, the challenge of this chapter is to grasp the elusive nature of the context conditions and of the key actors, and look beyond their realist appearances, in order to highlight how realist rationales in fact sparked ideational processes, the consequences of which went beyond what liberal intergovernmentalists would expect.

I have divided this chapter as follows. First, I will analyze the conditions that existed for the opening of a window of opportunity. I will thus analyze the nature of Mediterranean détente, the challenge of terrorism, and the troublesome economic relations. I will also focus on the intervening variable, in the form of divergences among Western countries about the Mediterranean. Second, I will analyze France in this context, with a particular emphasis on what motivated its entrepreneurial action. Third, I will focus on how France conducted its entrepreneurial activity and how negotiations developed, leading to the idea of a "Mediterranean" and to the adoption of the GMP and the EAD. I will then conclude the chapter by describing the main tenets of the two resulting initiatives.

The European Definition of Challenges Originating from the Mediterranean

European perceptions of Mediterranean nonmember countries worsened at the beginning of the 1970s. At the time, the cold war entered a less dramatic stage. While it lingered over the Mediterranean, EEC member states did not dedicate to it the same amount of attention they had in the previous decade. The area remained heavily militarized and the links with the USSR were still in place, but the Europeans believed that there was a decline in the military threat posed by communism in the area. As the military dimension of security receded on the agenda, two "new" issues became more salient, namely terrorism and economic relations, which included oil. In both cases, the Europeans were slow to react, but then responded with strong emergency measures. The first part of this chapter is thus the story of how terrorism and economic relations moved up the political agenda in the early 1970s from purely private matters to security issues, demanding an urgent policy answer. In other words, how a window of opportunities opened to redefine national priorities and to generate a debate about the Mediterranean at the European level.

The Mediterranean Détente

At the beginning of the 1970s, the well-established cold war pattern of relationships in the Mediterranean began to slowly loosen its grip on the area, unleashing a whole set of new possibilities. The perception of European policy makers, and of diplomats in foreign ministries in particular, was that the threat represented by the superpower confrontation was more a part of the "ordinary politics" of foreign affairs, than a "high security" issue justifying emergency measures. The Soviet threat remained in place, but it lost the urgency it had in the late 1950s and remained that way until the late 1960s. Détente, attempts by Mediterranean nonmembers to create a nonaligned pole, and revised estimates of Soviet challenges, all these factors contributed to a shift in European perceptions.

At first glance, however, the situation seemed to be as threatening as ever, judging from the presence of armed forces and the number of military alliances.[1] Since 1969, the USSR had been providing military, technical, and commercial cooperation to Algeria.[2] In May 1971, Egypt signed a 15 year treaty of friendship and cooperation with the USSR. Military bases, whether for naval or air forces or both, were granted by Algeria, Tunisia, Libya, Egypt, and Syria, as well as by Yugoslavia and, to a lesser extent, Morocco. More generally, the Arab radical movements were linked to the USSR.[3] The United States also had varying types of military arrangements, with Greece, Turkey, Spain, Israel, Tunisia, Jordan, and Lebanon. The United Kingdom supported Jordan, Cyprus, and Malta, while keeping a presence in Gibraltar. France provided arms to Greece and Libya. The Mediterranean thus saw an impressive military presence of cold war opponents. Tensions seemed to reach a tipping point at the time of the Yom Kippur war in 1973, when Nixon put U.S. forces (including nuclear arms) on Defcon 3 alert after the USSR launched an ultimatum linked to the ceasefire. Until the mid-1970s, the Middle East and more generally the Mediterranean appeared to be the place of continuous frictions between the two superpowers where the limits of détente were tested.[4]

On the other hand, as Yapp points out, "[i]t was not so much the cold war as the myth of the cold war which was imported into the Near East in this period" (Yapp 1996, 421). In the early 1970s the superpowers embarked on a period of détente.[5] Moreover, the Soviet expansion in the Mediterranean was quickly losing the momentum it had gathered at the end of the 1950s. July 1972 marked a turning point in the USSR's role in the Middle East when Sadat expelled around 20,000 Soviet "advisors" from Egypt and withdrew Soviet privileges to use the country's bases (Golan 1977, 21; Freedman 1991, 47–48).

Most importantly for the point of view of this book, European policy makers increasingly sensed the fading risks of superpower confrontation in the area. The main indication in this direction came from the attempts of several Mediterranean countries to create a "third" nonaligned group in the area. Documents in the French archives show that since the end of the 1960s several proposals existed to "demilitarize" the Mediterranean. Yugoslavia was the most outspoken supporter of the idea. Most Arab countries supported it too, with traditionally nonaligned countries (Algeria, Tunisia, Libya) particularly enthusiastic about it. They saw the creation of a "demilitarized" Mediterranean as an avenue for redirecting attention to the Arab-Israeli conflict, while loosening their ties with the Soviets. Like most external actors who were only lukewarm about the idea, Western European countries encouraged it, if only to cultivate any distance between the USSR and the Mediterranean. The idea was met with skepticism on the part of the United States and of the other Western European countries.[6] It did not encounter a favorable reception from the USSR or from Greece and Turkey.[7] French diplomats, while striving to remain abreast of diplomatic developments among contributors to the initiative, soon came to believe that, apart from a widespread desire to get rid of both superpowers, too many differences existed among the participants for any momentum to develop. Their Italian colleagues agreed.[8] Negotiations, which dragged on for years,[9] demonstrated to European policy makers that the Soviet penetration was not as thorough or as menacing as the military situation would have suggested.

The Soviet threat was rather perceived in ideological terms, in relation to development and to a New International Economic Order.[10] While Mediterranean nonmembers suggested "demilitarizing" the area, what happened instead was that EEC member states "demilitarized" their conception of the Mediterranean and of the challenges it posed.

The Europeans' perception of a relative Western European security in the Mediterranean translated into a low-key military engagement in the area. While their contribution in terms of ideas, finances and troops was concentrated on the Central European "front line," their strategic contribution to counter Soviet expansionism in the Mediterranean in this period became almost nonexistent. France completed the withdrawal of its forces from the Eastern and Western Mediterranean in 1968. The United Kingdom achieved the withdrawal of its military forces from East of Suez in 1971, while maintaining a reduced military presence in Cyprus and Gibraltar.[11] As a consequence, the U.S. Sixth Fleet became the main force responsible for countering the Soviet fleet, which was equal in numbers but not as efficient as the U.S. fleet. As the French already put it in 1968, in an internal note of the Quai d'Orsay: "les moyens militaires dont l'U.R.S.S. dispose en Méditerranée ne constituent pas aujourd'hui encore une menace préoccupante."[12] And again: "la disproportion entre l'U.R.S.S. et les États Unis reste grande sous le rapport de la puissance de feu, des moyens d'intervention et de l'autonomie d'action."[13] Even though the domestic debates about the cold war, especially in Italy and France, continued, they rarely addressed the Mediterranean as such.

Therefore, the conclusion that can be drawn from this overview is that the European policy makers' perception of military challenges originating from the Mediterranean in this period decreased. The cold war did not command any longer the sense of urgency that characterized the 1950s and most of the 1960s. The new decade thus opened with a downgrading of military issues in the Mediterranean in the ranking of foreign policy priorities among European policy makers. Room thus existed for new priorities to reach the top of the agenda.

Terrorism Spilling Over from the Middle East

A different type of threat was on the rise during this period: terrorism. The early 1970s marked the beginning of modern terrorism (Engene

2004). In Europe, this trend was led by a dramatic increase in activism by Arab-Palestinian terrorists. Terrorism came to have a profound impact on the perceptions of European policy makers, to whom it presented a multifaceted political challenge that needed to be addressed. Terrorism by Arab-Palestinian groups created a connection between the domestic arena of Western European countries, and the Middle East, the Mediterranean and the Arab world more generally. Over the period 1968–1972, the phenomenon quickly escalated from the private sphere, involving criminal means and policing measures, to the security arena, demanding emergency measures, passing through an intermediate stage of politicization. The emergence of terrorism is thus a clear example of preference deconstruction and cognitive uncertainty, as I described in chapter 1. I will illustrate this *destruens* process through the use of three indicators: (1) the number of violent incidents in Western Europe, displaying a sharp increase during this period; (2) the shifting emphasis in the public debate[14] about whose responsibility terrorism was; (3) the changing legislative context. I will conclude this section with a short description of consultations about terrorism at the European and international level, which indicate the type of cooperative environment within which the EFP making efforts developed.

Over the period 1968–1972, the number of violent incidents in Western Europe increased sharply, with a substantial percentage of the international attacks being linked to the Arab-Israeli conflict. This was not an isolated phenomenon. Terrorism was on the rise everywhere in the world. Terror attacks (of all kinds) as a percentage of the total number of violent episodes worldwide rose from 18 percent in 1968 to 30 percent in 1970 to 49 percent in 1972 (Carrère and Valat-Morio 1973, 48). Europe in particular became, from the end of the 1960s onwards, "the most active terrorist environment in the world" (Pluchinsky 1982, 40). The novelty of the phenomenon lay in the scale and type of terrorism fuelling violence during this period. As shown by Engene (2004), in the early 1970s, the appearance of "international" terrorism was accompanied by an increase in magnitude of "home grown" terrorism. International terrorists struck West European countries not only to punish the involvement of Western European countries in international politics, but also and especially to attract the attention that spectacular and televised attacks could bring to their cause. Terrorism perpetrated by Arab-Palestinian groups was particularly active, as well as effective. As shown in figure 3.1, the number of terror attacks carried out by terrorists claiming some connection with the Palestinian cause on the territory of EEC members took off in the period under examination.[15] The way forward for the Palestinians after the 1967

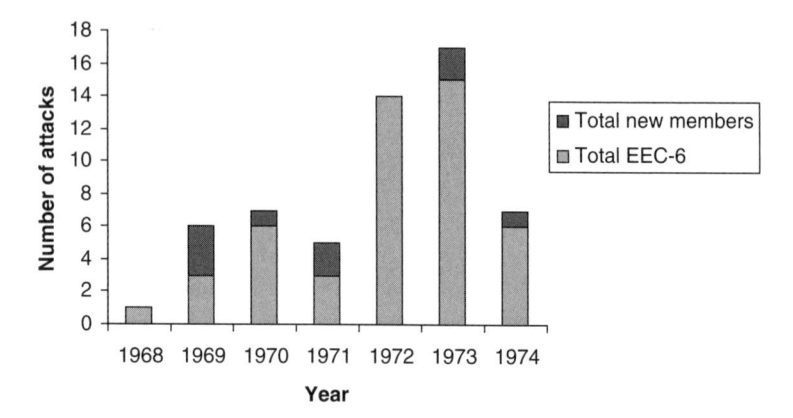

Figure 3.1 Number of Terror Attacks Attributed to Arab-Palestinian Terrorists on EEC Territory, 1968–1974
Source: Author's calculation, based on Mickolus 1980.

defeat was to organize their fight by all possible means (Cooley 1997, 298). Terrorism was an arena where they could wield an advantage.

It is interesting to see the link between the increase in terrorist attacks connected to the Arab-Israeli conflict and the shift in the way in which terrorism was defined and whose responsibility it was to address it. The definition of terrorism changed during this period from a predominantly private matter to a security issue, driven by a discussion about the responsibilities to combat it.

At first, terrorism clearly belonged to the private sphere. The first period of Palestinian-Arab international terrorism began with the hijacking of an El Al plane from Rome on July 22, 1968. Members of the Popular Front for the Liberation of Palestine (PFLP) forced the plane to land in Algiers and demanded the release of prisoners detained in Israel (Sobel 1975, 19; Mickolus 1980, 94). After this first skyjacking, several other attacks against Israeli targets followed. The reaction to this first wave of attacks, which were targeted more at the Israelis than Europeans, involved European governments only at the margins. Actors who mobilized were mainly private. The most active was the International Federation of Airlines Pilots' Associations (IFALPA), which organized a boycott of Algerian airports and threatened to boycott El Al. Despite a call by the IFALPA upon the UN, governments in Western Europe limited their action to briefly tightening visa conditions for Arab citizens, while pressing airport authorities to improve airport security conditions.

In 1970 Arab-Palestinian terrorists began to explicitly attack European interests, and Western governments could not avoid responsibility for addressing the issue, but they did so at first by taking relatively small-scale actions. Terrorism at this stage could thus be said to enter the political arena, but not the security one. This second stage was marked by the spectacular hijacking of four planes during September 6–9, 1970 (Mickolus 1980, 212–213). Three of the planes were diverted to Jordan where hundreds of passengers of American, Israeli, British and West German nationality were kept as hostages. The crisis soon escalated in Jordan, leading to the "Black September" campaign (Yapp 1996, 298; Sobel 1975, 29–38). Western European governments too were directly called into question. When the negotiations to liberate the hostages of September 1970 were organized, the United Kingdom, West Germany, Switzerland, Israel and the United States,[16] formed a common crisis committee. Interestingly, the tasks of the committee included also drawing up additional security measures, especially for German airports, which were seen as the most vulnerable to terrorist attacks.[17] The terrorist attacks perpetrated by the PFLP were defined as an act of war and a security threat to all travelers (though not to states or people in general).[18] Moreover, the United Kingdom and the United States decided to entrust the issues to the UN Security Council, which examined the issue for the first time on September 10, 1970. No initiatives were taken at the EEC level. At this point in time, a whole set of public actors were thus involved in the protection of passengers (only).

The third stage of Arab-Palestinian terrorism, focusing on attacks inside Europe, began in 1972 and it marked the full assumption of responsibilities on the part of governments. Terrorists conducted a large-scale campaign of letter bombs, sabotaged oil industries in Italy, Germany, and the Netherlands and detonated several bombs against Israeli-connected targets. Pro-Israeli guerrilla groups begun to strike back, within Europe, in revenge for these attacks. The highpoint was when a commando of Palestinians broke into the Israeli quarters at the Olympic Games in Munich, on September 5, 1972, killing two Israelis and taking nine athletes hostages. For the first time, a European government decided to counter the attack, but with dreadful result. All hostages were killed, so were some of the terrorists and a policeman (Mickolus 1980, 338–343). A wide polemic followed, dominating the media for days. One year later, a rumor spread in Germany that Arab terrorists were blackmailing the government with threat of germ warfare through mail (Mickolus 1980, 418).

The reaction to these developments shows that terrorism at this stage became a security issue. It is in the period 1972–1974 that the legislative context in relation to the use of force—my third indicator of securitization—underwent a significant change across Western Europe. Counterterrorism forces were created in all member states, though reforms were not achieved with a single legislative act.

As a consequence of the Munich attacks, the federal and national authorities in West Germany launched a thorough plan of modernization and increase in the number of police forces, aimed at increasing their efficacy (Funk and Reinke 1992, 42). The implementation of the plan was, however, to take a decade. In France, the Palestinian issue and more specifically the Munich massacre led to the creation of the *Group d'intervention de la gendarmerie national* (GIGN) in 1974 (Hermant and Bigo 2000, 86). Also the number of French forces devoted to public order kept increasing between 1972 and 1978 (Roach 1985, 121). In Italy, the Olympic Games attack resounded in a national parliamentary debate.[19] The changes that ensued, while they increased the individual responsibilities under criminal law between 1969 and 1974, in 1974–1975 also added new and more intrusive police powers (Stortoni-Wortmann 2000, 152).[20] In Belgium, the *Escadron Spécial d'Intervention* (ESI) was created in November 1972 with the explicit aim of fighting international terrorism and in particular skyjacking (Ponsaers et al. 1992, 78). Measures were taken to prevent immigrant networks from becoming a seedbed for terrorism. In Germany, measures against Arab residents were progressively tightened and several people were expelled from Germany. In France, the rumor spread of an Israeli infiltration of German police identifying Arabs with terrorist connections.[21]

While it can be debated whether terrorism had become a low or a high security issue, and how much of the change was exclusively linked to Arab-Palestinian terrorism, international terrorism at the hands of Arab-Palestinians definitely contributed to these changes and fuelled the uncertainty that surrounded them. The rapid shift from a private matter to a security issue thrust on public authorities as a responsibility was dramatically evident in the Munich episode. It was also clear that public authorities where not ready for such a responsibility. Policy makers struggled to frame the new phenomenon in a policy relevant discourse, and the successive waves of legislative actions taken pointed to perceived causes of the problem and policy options. Governments thus experienced cognitive uncertainty, as I have defined it in chapter 1. As a consequence, they were available and also willing to discuss terrorism with friendly partners.

A first instance of this tendency to "rally around the table" and debate policy problems occurred at the European level. Following a

German proposal, the Six plus the applicant countries (Denmark, Ireland, Norway, and Great Britain) decided to organize their discussions within the EPC framework. A first meeting was held in Frascati on September 12, 1972, in which it was decided to try and establish a form of coordination between intelligence services in member states.[22] The issue of secrecy was immediately problematic, as shown by the leaks that took place right after the second meeting of the Political Committee (POCO) in which the idea of a European "Interpol" was raised, on September 21, 1972.[23] At these meetings, the POCO discussed the possibility of exchanging information on terrorist activities, sharing analyses of technical methods through which attacks were perpetrated, harmonizing visa regimes and strengthening surveillance of foreigners. Members of working groups set up to look at these measures would report to ministers of Interior and of Foreign Affairs. No coordination committee was established, but a declaration was eventually issued.[24]

The European effort at coordination also took account of the initiative of the UN Secretary General Waldheim in the autumn of 1972.[25] Here however, efforts were blocked by internal divisions within the UN, most notably between the United States and the nonaligned countries.[26]

Terrorism thus highlighted the need for the Europeans to "do something" about their southern neighbors, at a time when economic relations were turbulent and the Europeans' capacity to act in the area continued to shrink.

Turbulent Economic Relations

Economics was the second aspect of European security to become progressively sensitive during the 1960s, culminating in the oil shock of 1973. Arab states in the Mediterranean showed themselves as increasingly assertive in economic relations with the European countries, as their quest for economic independence tackled the remnants of colonial legacies. In a long wave of nationalizations lasting from 1956 to the early 1970s, they addressed issues including ownership in all the productive sectors. During this period, member states came to understand the importance of Mediterranean countries and the Middle East for their welfare (de la Serre 1979, 81). Economic relations became thus progressively politicized, while oil was securitized in November 1973. It is interesting to note that what changed was mainly the terms of economic negotiations, rather than economic relations themselves.

Trade remained largely constant. European perceptions of the Arab countries did however change, as negotiations became more aggressive. This section thus shows a second element that contributed to the cognitive uncertainty of European policy makers in the early 1970s, namely the growing tension in economic relations between EEC member states and Arab countries. I will describe the politicization of economic relations, the securitization of oil and the cognitive uncertainty related to the two processes by making use of three indicators, namely (1) the extent and style of nationalizations; (2) changes in how the Europeans approached the terms of negotiation with the Arab countries; and (3) number of books published on the subject of oil and energy.[27] Apart from these indicators, I will also consider flows of trade and oil imports. While I will show that flows of trade remained basically stable, the other three indicators point to a clear shift in the relationship.

Let us start with the issue of nationalization. As a legacy of colonialism, Arab countries had not only a strong foreign presence in all sectors, but also a legal system biased in favor of foreign capital. In Morocco, for instance, the percentage of foreign ownership in the industrial sector in 1970 (and thus years after the country's independence) was of the order of 60–70 percent in sectors such as mechanical industries and pharmaceuticals (El Oufi 1990, 26). Processes of nationalization in the Arab countries, though proceeding in different ways and with a varying degree of aggressiveness, were designed to achieve economic independence through unilateral decisions. Egypt was the first to embark on peremptory nationalizations, the first example of which came with the seized nationalization of the Suez canal in 1956 (Magdi Wahba 1994), an operation fraught with military consequences. The Development Plan of Tunisia for 1962–1971 specifically indicated as an objective the decolonization of economic activities. The bulk of Tunisian nationalizations, which were carried out in the mid-1960s, included the nationalization of services (such as railways), of rural lands, and partially of industrial activities (Duwaji 1967). Morocco, a late comer to nationalization, introduced between 1971 and 1973 a law on "Moroccanization," as well as laws on investment, rural lands, and activities linked to the distribution of oil, and imposed a national sea area for fishing (World Bank 1981, 13). Algeria, also a late comer, was particularly radical and aggressive in the solutions it adopted. Rural land was nationalized without compensation for the (largely French) ownership. The Development Plan for the period 1967–1969 managed to take over most of foreign industrial assets to the point that, by the end of 1969, only around 20 French industrial enterprises remained under French control, out of the 700–800 which existed in 1962 (Bennoune 1988, 125–126). Moreover, Algeria nationalized oil. After having nationalized most non-French companies' assets in the sector, in February 1971, Algeria announced the nationalization of 51 percent of all French interests in Algerian oil (Diallo 1992, 206).[28] The Libyan revolutionary government, for its part, first nationalized the oil distribution companies and then, after having exacted higher royalties from all companies, nationalized all holdings of British Petroleum, in December 1971 (Sobel 1974, 82).

The nationalization process put the Arab states and European member states with possessions in the Arab countries on a collision course concerning their economic interests, as the Europeans were forcibly made aware of the change in the relationship. The tendency of the Tunisian government to act unilaterally led to a clear strain in relations with European countries between 1964 and 1966–1967 and in particular with France (Couve de Murville 1971, 438–439). The issue of compensation by the Algerian government for French citizens' properties was to drag on for years,[29] while the two countries reached the nadir in their relations between June 1970 and April 1971, coinciding with the nationalization of the oil industry (Ecrement 1986). Even in the case of Morocco, which carried out the least aggressive nationalization process, the attempt to "Moroccanize" enterprises with 51 percent Moroccan and 49 percent foreign capital did not lead to partnership, as expected, instead by 1975 more than half of Western entrepreneurs had shut down their businesses or sold up, rather than enter into coparticipation deals (El Oufi 1990). Governments were dragged into negotiations about the future of commercial assets, and, as actors they tried to consolidate and stabilize economic relations, but no one suggested resorting to emergency measures. In other words, economic relations with the Arab countries became politicized at the turn of the decade, although they did not cross the threshold of security. This further step was only achieved with the oil shock.

There was, however, an inescapable ambiguity in the process of nationalizations, in that Arab countries wanted control over their economies but at the same time they relied on foreign capital and trade with Europe to foster development. As a consequence, while former European colonial powers and the new regimes struggled over terms and conditions, trade relations tended to remain on the same level or even improve (see table 3.1). The country in the most awkward position was France, which saw both imports and exports with Mediterranean

Table 3.1 Trade of EEC Countries with Mediterranean Countries. Percentage on the Total of Imports and Exports of EEC Countries[a]

EEC Countries	Imports from Mediterranean Countries			Exports to Mediterranean Countries		
	1970	1971	1972	1970	1971	1972
France	6.6	4.6	4.8	8.8	8.1	7.4
Italy	2.6	3	3.3	5	5	5.8
Germany	2.5	2.7	2.7	3.4	3.3	3.6
Belgium-Luxembourg	1.5	1.7	1.8	2.4	2.5	2.8
Netherlands	1.8	2.2	1.7	2.3	2.2	2.5
United Kingdom	2.6	2.7	2.7	4.7	4.7	5.2
Ireland	1.7	1.7	1.6	1.1	1.8	1.5
Denmark	1.3	1	1.4	1.9	2.2	2.7

[a] By Mediterranean countries, in this case I mean Spain, Morocco, Algeria, Tunisia, Egypt, Israel, Jordan, Lebanon, Syria, Malta, and Cyprus. I did not include Portugal because it was part of EFTA; Turkey and Greece because they had a free trade agreement (as analyzed in chapter 3). I also excluded Libya, Albania, and Yugoslavia as they were never involved in any discussion about a European foreign policy towards the Mediterranean. Oil is included in the percentage.

Source: UN Yearbook of Trade Statistics, 1974.

nonmembers drop in 1971 and 1972.[30] But this case should not be overstated, as the diminishing share of trade, with imports falling more sharply than exports, was predominantly due to trade with Algeria, and most notably in connection with (and in retaliation to) the nationalization of oil.

Among all the commodities which crossed the Mediterranean sea, oil was—and still is—by far the most important. The heavy European dependence on oil in 1970 grew out of a long history of European mismanagement of alternative resources (Lieber 1976, 3–4). Oil quickly substituted coal in fueling economic development in Europe. In 1950, approximately 75 percent of Europe's energy requirements were met by European coal, and only 10 percent by oil. By contrast, in 1970, the relative positions had dramatically reversed to 30 percent and 60 percent respectively.[31] Whereas coal was available within Europe, oil needed to be imported. As shown in table 3.2, almost the entire supply came from abroad. Moreover, oil imports increasingly came from the Arab oil-producing countries. In a nutshell, not only was EEC economic development largely dependent on *oil* and on *imported oil*, but more precisely it was dependent on *oil imported from the Arab countries*.

The percentages presented are aggregated data, which means that within the general European dependency, some countries were even more reliant on Arab oil than the average. Italy and France were the extreme cases. In 1973, Italian imports of Arab oil reached 86.6 percent of its total

Table 3.2 Supply of Oil for OECD Europe, by Region of Origin, 1960, 1965, 1970, in Million Tons

Origin	1960	1965	1970
Western Hemisphere[a]	17.8	24.9	24.2
Middle East	133.7	199.3	309.0
North Africa	8.1	76.2	193.7
West Africa	1.0	14.6	42.7
Other	8.4	13.2	24.2
Total crude imports	169.0	328.2	593.8
Total supplies for OECD Europe	*183.5*	*348.9*	*616.3*
Imports as per cent of supply	*92.1*	*94.1*	*96.3*

[a] Excluding movements in the European area.

Source: OECD 1973, 68.

energy consumption while in France they amounted to 65 percent (Maull 1980, 116). Germany, while producing and consuming coal, had left the control of oil supplies to the international market and therefore had no control on oil negotiations. The United Kingdom, rich in coal and oil, should have been in a better position to avoid dependency. Nevertheless, the rigidity of its labor market further complicated the issue. The member state in the best position was the Netherlands, which was a key trading and refining area for oil and oil products (Hager 1974, 36–37).

Threats to oil supplies were however gathering on the horizon. As mentioned earlier, the oil-producing countries went for unilateral nationalizations and expropriation which left Western oil companies or the oil consuming countries little chance of comeback. Every successive meeting of the OPEC producers hiked the price of oil higher. Power relations between consumers, oil companies, and oil-producing countries were shifting decisively in favor of the latter.[32] Moreover, in 1969–1970, world demand appeared to be "ahead of all predictions" (Sampson 1975, 240), while the United States began to import large amounts of oil—from the Arab countries.

Even more worrying, there were early signs that the Arab-Israeli conflict was beginning to impinge on the oil trade. On May 15, 1973, Algeria, Libya, Iraq, and Kuwait temporarily halted the flow of oil as a protest at the Western stance on the Arab-Israeli conflict (Sobel 1974, 178). At the end of August 1973, Saudi Arabia, lobbied by Egypt, threatened the United States that it would be "extremely difficult" to continue supplying oil if the United States did not change its policy toward Israel (Sobel 1974, 180; Sampson 1975, 248). Oil had suddenly become a potent weapon.

What was the European perception of the oil issue before the 1973 shock? Within the EEC, at the beginning of the 1970s, oil had become a political issue because of the loss of European countries' leverage on oil sellers. Still, at that stage it was not a security issue. The political flavor of the time can be gauged from a report published by the OECD on the eve of the oil shock.[33] It started by defining changes in the oil industry as "massive, rather than catastrophic" (OECD 1973, 11). Moreover, it suggested that the direction of change showed a clear increase in the power of the Arab countries in relation to Western countries (OECD 1973, 74). The report devoted only four scant paragraphs to the issue of reliability of sources, and indicated as potential causes the possible domestic instability of Arab countries and commercial problems (OECD 1973, 77). Similarly, a report prepared by the Netherlands about Libya and presented within the EPC framework, in the Working Group "Problems of the Mediterranean," alerted member states to the fact that, thanks to its huge financial reserves, Libya could afford to halt oil production if that was deemed to be in the interest of the Arab countries.

The politicization of oil had consequences in terms of cognitive uncertainty, as was evident from the contradictions contained in the analyses of the European Commission.[34] The Commission defined the core European interest as the need to "secure cheap oil" (Lieber 1976, 6–7), yet the EC did not feel any urgency to pursue such a strategy, and even dropped an offer from Algeria to deliver long term oil supplies at the beginning of the summer of 1973 (de la Serre 1979, 81). The Commission also raised the possibility of alternative ways to secure cheap oil, but it left the debate wide open. As discussions within the EEC and within EPC showed, cooperation with the United States was barred by France, while cooperation with the Arab countries created difficulties for Germany and especially the Netherlands.

Therefore, on the verge of the oil shock, the Europeans were conscious of the stakes of a future oil crisis but perceived oil as just another bone of contention in the turbulent economic relations of the time and yet another hint that the Middle East conflict required a solution. Negotiations about oil supplies were not considered to pose a threat to national security.

The oil shock started with a painful recognition by developed countries that, in fact, they did not possess any leverage on one of the most important commodities for their economies. OPEC was strong enough to unilaterally increase the price per barrel from $3 to $5.12, on October 16, 1973. It also announced a 5 percent cut in monthly production until Israel withdrew from the territories it had occupied in

1967. Saudi Arabia, the world's biggest oil producer, further shook the markets by cutting its own production by 10 percent and imposing an embargo (immediately imitated by the other Arab producers) on the United States and the Netherlands, to punish them for their support of Israel.[35]

There is little need here to recall the panic reaction of Western European governments and societies to the oil shock. Newspapers reported the developments in dramatic terms. Long queues formed at petrol stations to the point where the consumer panic forced some countries, such as Italy, to send out the army to patrol supplies and supervise rationing.

Instead of analyzing this complex dramatization, I will focus on a different indicator of the "collective puzzlement" and confusion of Western societies on the subject of energy and oil, namely the number of books and articles on this subject published between 1971 and 1975.[36] As shown in figure 3.2, 39 publications were recorded in 1971, and 56 in both 1972 and 1973, climbing to 148 and 198 publications about oil and energy in 1974 and 1975 respectively. The dramatic increase in the number of analyses on the "guerre pétrolière" (Madelin 1974) is a useful indication of the extent to which Western societies struggled to provide an answer to the new challenge.

What is interesting, from the point of view of the European definition of security, is that all of a sudden "oil had become a matter of

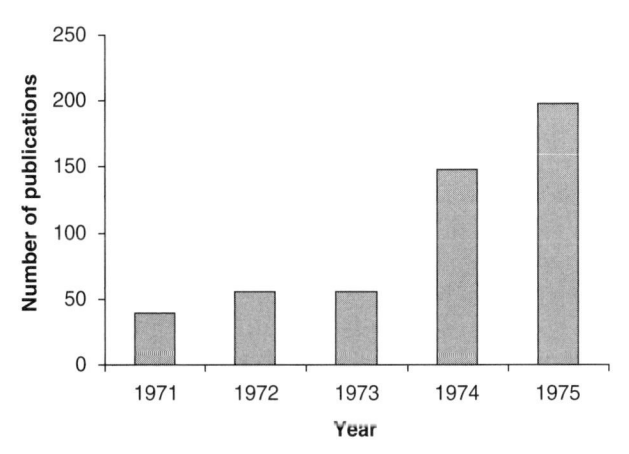

Figure 3.2 Number of Publications on the Subject of Energy and Oil, with Particular Reference to Western Germany, Western Europe, and the Middle East, 1971–1975

Source: Bibliographie der Wirtschaftswissenschaften, 1971–1976.

national security" (Lieber 1976, 15). In the face of the loss of reliable supplies there were no doubts that oil was a strategic asset upon which depended the economies and welfare of European citizens. If before the oil shock European security had been equated with stability and status quo, afterward neither of those things was enough. Security meant *re*establishing secure oil supplies, which in turn implied a drastic change in the fundamental terms of European Arab relations (Waterbury 1979, 25). The Arab world was not only a potentially interesting economic partner and at times an aggressive negotiator; it was also a source of economic threats attacking Western welfare states at their core. But how could equilibrium be reconstructed? This was the question which opened up the possibility of constructing a European debate on the issue.

To summarize what has been discussed so far, new challenges emerged in the Europeans' perceptions at the beginning of the 1970s, as cold war tension receded. The two new issues moving rapidly up the political agenda were terrorism and economic relations, and both were connected to the Arab-Israeli conflict. Beginning in the late 1960s, economic relations with the Arab countries emerged as a political problem for Europe, which turned into a security issue about secure and stable oil supplies after October 1973. These simultaneous changes shook previously established foreign policy priorities of European governments and created uncertainty about the appropriate response. European policy makers were cognitively motivated to explore new information about their southern neighbors and new policy solutions, in order to come up with ways of tackling the new international situation. This context constituted a window of opportunity to rethink relations with the Mediterranean and with the Arab world. It could be argued that it was not a particularly wide policy window, as it was initially formed mainly by the securitization of terrorism and oil. However, the cognitive uncertainty was helped by a strong intervening variable, in the form of divergences among Western allies about how to read the situation on the ground and how to address it.

Divergent Priorities: Increasing Divergences with the United States over the Middle East

The reading of the Middle East situation differed significantly across the Atlantic, between the United States and the Europeans at the beginning of the 1970s. In the eyes of the Europeans, the U.S. attitude toward the Middle East under the influence of Kissinger added to Middle East tensions instead of toning them down. U.S. foreign policy tended increasingly toward privileged relations with Israel and high level contacts with the Soviets about the Middle East. This antagonized Arab countries with which the Europeans struggled to find an agreement, and precluded alternative approaches to the area. Therefore, the cognitive uncertainty created in Europe by new foreign and domestic policy priorities was magnified by the Europeans' need to define a European explanation and a European solution to European concerns.

U.S. foreign policy toward the Middle East under Nixon underwent a profound transformation, marked by the arrival of Henry Kissinger at the State Department (Quandt 1977, 103). Taking advantage of the presidential election in 1972, which distracted candidates and the political establishment, Kissinger managed to gain a firm grip on Middle East affairs. Kissinger's approach was based on three main tenets: (1) privileged relations with Israel, after the low point experienced in 1969–1970; (2) dismissal of the aspirations of radical and moderate Arabs alike until U.S. leadership in the region was fully recognized (Rubin 1985, 164); (3) containment of the Soviets in the Middle East, but through bilateral dialogue within the broader framework of détente (Spiegel 1985, 175). To achieve these aims the best strategy was, according to Kissinger, the maintenance of the status quo (Kissinger 1979, 1290ff.), which was later critically described as "standstill diplomacy."

The limitations of the U.S. approach were dramatically evident to European diplomats and politicians of the time, who disagreed with every single element of it. First, the pro-Israel drift of the United States came at a moment in which the Europeans were slowly turning toward a pro-Arab position.[37] All European countries, including Germany and the Netherlands, criticized Israel's territorial conquests after 1967 (Soetendorp 1999, 98ff.). European leaders wanted the United States to put Israel under pressure.[38] The failure of the United States to do so was perceived as one of the main causes of regional instability[39] and presented a permanent source of disagreement between the Europeans and the U.S. administration.

Second, the European countries estimated that the "standstill diplomacy" conducted by Kissinger was antagonizing the Arabs unnecessarily, with direct risks for Europe. According to the Europeans, the moderate Arab states deserved a better treatment, if only because they possessed the largest oil resources in the world. While there was a widespread feeling in the United States that the government could confidently keep diplomacy separated from oil industry matters (Spiegel 1985, 171), the Europeans were not so sure about that and deemed that the United States had underestimated the risks of such a strategy for their European allies (Campbell 1993, 349). Moreover, terrorist attacks in Europe brought the Palestinians to the center stage and prodded the Europeans toward some form of recognition of Palestinian rights. The United States on the contrary seemed to ignore the existence of the Palestinians (Mansfield 1970, 182), thus leaving the Europeans dangerously exposed to the consequences of the problem in terms of European security.

Third, the Europeans resented their exclusion from the dialogue on the Middle East which involved only the United States and the USSR. In 1969 De Gaulle relaunched his proposal for Big Four Talks (United States, USSR, United Kingdom, and France) on a settlement in the Middle East, with the backing of the United Kingdom (Kissinger 1979, 933). The United States was unenthusiastic about the proposal, which could have been perceived as a nuisance by Israel, as both France and the USSR were expected to act as advocates for the Arabs (Spiegel 1985, 183). The United States chose however to support it, along with bilateral consultations between the United States and the USSR, the Jarring initiative,[40] and a series of direct contacts with regional actors. In Kissinger's view, this was the best strategy to water down any European interference, maintain constructive relations with the USSR, and gain time (Kissinger 1979, 351–352).

Yet the U.S. attempt to dispel European grievances did not manage to close the transatlantic gap. In 1973, the United States launched the "Year of Europe," with the aim of strengthening and formalizing transatlantic cooperation. The initiative however was not welcome in Europe. Western European countries disliked its unilateral management, as well as its timing, as they "were trying to build Europe in 1973, not rebuild the Atlantic alliance" (Campbell 1993, 346).

Therefore, when Middle East crises erupted, the transatlantic allies were deeply split. The Europeans strongly disagreed with the U.S. approach during the Yom Kippur war, which epitomized the principles adopted by Kissinger in the preceding years. Western European countries were determined to avoid clashes with the Arab states and looked upon Arab aggression with mixed emotions. Not only did they fail to provide arms to Israel but publicly refused the use of NATO facilities to U.S. supply flights on their way to the war area.[41] The unilateral U.S. alert called on October 25, 1973, which included U.S. strategic nuclear forces in Europe, came to them as a shock.[42] The real threat to the Europeans seemed to come "from unwise actions by the United States, taken unilaterally and without consultation" (Garthoff 1985, 404).

The management of the oil shock led again to opposite approaches. The United States chose a tough stance, advocating a cartel of consumers based on horizontal cooperation between oil-importing states along OPEC lines (Nuttall 1992, 97). However, given the hegemonic leadership of Kissinger on Middle East affairs, the risks of such a horizontal cooperation being transformed into a U.S. crusade against the Arabs with reluctant European backing were very high. The Europeans were thus more inclined to promote vertical cooperation between consumers and producers. Instead of antagonizing the Arab countries through stark confrontation, they preferred dialogue with the Arabs, which was the rationale for launching the Euro-Arab Dialogue in 1974.

This period thus shows a profound rift between European and U.S. approaches over the Middle East. This divergence spanned the period 1970–1972, and covered the formulation of the Global Mediterranean Policy. It was brought to a head by events in 1973 and 1974, thus also affecting the policy window for the second European initiative toward the Mediterranean countries, that is, the Euro-Arab Dialogue. Disagreement with the United States about how to interpret new phenomena and political developments in the Middle East galvanized the Europeans to combine their efforts to define a path toward Euro-Mediterranean relations other than the one suggested by the United States. But transatlantic disagreements were also among the reasons for the shallow implementation of the two EFP initiatives directed to the Mediterranean.

The Changing External and Internal Balance of the EEC: UK Accession and Western Germany's Ostpolitik

One last intervening factor should be mentioned in relation to the policy window, namely the divergent priorities among member states in the period 1969–1973. Two changes were simultaneously taking place, both affecting the pattern of external commitments of the EEC. First, the United Kingdom, along with Ireland and Denmark, was eventually accepted as a member of the EEC. Negotiations formally opened on June 30, 1970 and the three applicants became full members on January 1, 1973. This was the first EEC enlargement and entailed a readjustment in external relations given the wide range of international commitments the United Kingdom had at the time of its entry. Second, in 1969, Brandt, the newly elected Chancellor of West Germany, launched a new foreign policy toward East Germany aimed at normalizing relations with the DDR (Deutsche Demokratische Republik) and the Soviet bloc. By changing the terms of relations with the East he developed a strong Ostpolitik by which West Germany created privileged relationships with Eastern Europe and the USSR. This development upset the well established equilibrium within the EEC and contributed to a lively discussion within the EEC and among member states about Western Europe's international relations. This new turn to the east forced the foreign policy priorities of northern European members on a collision course with southern European members whose own foreign policy priorities were different and who had also developed a different understanding of EEC interests as a whole. Therefore, a second rift among the Western allies increased the urgency of resolving uncertainty toward the Mediterranean. Let us examine the two internal European developments in turn.

The first enlargement of the EEC led to a debate about the EEC external relations for two main reasons. The first one had a legal basis. Enlargement raised the technical issue of "adjusting" existing agreements with the Mediterranean nonmembers so as to incorporate the new members into old agreements (Tsoukalis 1977, 429). The United Kingdom, Ireland, and Denmark were to be included in the Common External Tariff, mainly to the disadvantage of the Mediterranean nonmembers, and this required amendments to the various agreements in force (Pierros et al. 1999, 83). As a result, the Mediterranean agreements were automatically put on the EEC agenda in 1970, alongside accession negotiations, and the discussion leading to the adoption of the GMP was later to develop from such an agenda.

The second reason why EEC enlargement contributed to a debate about the Mediterranean lay with the international position of the United Kingdom.[43] The United Kingdom at the time of its third application to the EEC had downsized its involvement in the Commonwealth, but still had a substantial role.[44] While the military and the financial components of this relationship faded during the 1960s,[45] trade flows with the Commonwealth remained strong and directly contradicted the principle of EEC preference on which the Common Market was founded (Ward 1997). The problem had an ideological aspect, namely how best to frame relations between the North and the South, and between developed and developing countries.[46] The answers provided by the United Kingdom and France were traditionally very different. Broadly put, France was in favor of regionalism, while Great Britain preferred broad multilateralism (Grilli 1993, 21). From the point of view of some British commentators, the EEC should have stopped being prey to out-of-date French notions such as "EurAfrica" and association agreements that disguised a clientelistic approach. An influential commentator, for instance, openly attacked "the Community's geographical obsession with the area to the south of it" and the notion of "the Mediterranean as a European lake, in which neither the United States nor Russia have any business to be in the long run" (Shonfield 1973, 58). Other countries, such as the Netherlands and Germany, would also have preferred to abandon the geographically restricted nature of the association with Mediterranean countries (Faber 1982, 38). France, on the contrary, with the lukewarm support of Italy and Belgium, maintained the opposite view. Therefore, although relations with the Mediterranean countries during the 1960s could not be said to bear the hallmark of regionalism or regional favoritism as their detractors accused,[47] the ideological tone of the discussion magnified the contrast between visions of EEC external relations.

In parallel with the first northern enlargement, the EEC experienced another rift in foreign policy priorities of its member states, prompted by Western Germany's Ostpolitik. The philosophy was simple, although revolutionary for West Germany at the time: the overturning of the cold war status quo was to be reached in the medium-long run through rapprochement (*Wander durch Annäherung*) with Eastern Germany rather than by denial of any form of contact. The main consequences of this new approach were that the DDR was to be recognized, not banned, and recognition could only be done by first addressing the USSR, which in exchange for economic concessions could put pressure on the reluctant DDR leadership. The newly elected German government took upon itself to this task in 1969 with the final goal of achieving a broad framework of agreement with the USSR, the DDR and the Eastern European countries and settling all the issues still pending after the end of the World War II.[48] The whole idea represented a "dramatic turnabout" in German foreign policy (Pfetsch 1988, 218). For the first time since 1949, Germany played with Ostpolitik "un rôle international propre"[49] (Soutou 1996, 315).

West Germany's overture to the DDR, Eastern Europe and the USSR had repercussions for the established balance within the EEC. Ostpolitik represented a challenge to France and especially to France's role in the EEC and in the world (Fritsch-Bournazel 1987, 73). Ostpolitik would have permitted West Germany "to redress the political imbalance that had developed in the Franco-German relationship of the 1960s" (Hanrieder 1989, 202). From this perspective, the years 1971–1972 were a period of disorder in the relations between the two countries, which often led to discord in European affairs (Simonian 1985, 101ff.). Such a situation increased the pressure on France to define a new way forward for the European foreign policy agenda, while for all member states Ostpolitik meant venturing into uncharted territories. It was the sign of a new and uncertain era of international relations.

These two parallel developments (UK accession and Western Germany's Ostpolitik) contributed to increase the relevance of defining new Euro-Mediterranean relations. They did so not because they had any direct bearing on the issue. Paradoxically, they did so *a contrario*, because France was faced with the need to redefine its position, while questioning the other member states about their preferred course of action. Together with the rift within the transatlantic alliance, clashing foreign policy agendas within the EEC contributed to bring home to member states the urgent need for a systematic and shared approach to EEC external relations. Whereas changing European security perceptions created cognitive uncertainty, different understandings about how to address new issues offered an important (if secondary) contribution to policy making by highlighting the pressing nature of the endeavor.

The Policy Entrepreneurship of France

On France fell the role of the policy entrepreneur who made use of the policy window which emerged. In a variety of ways, France was crucial in turning the passive concern of the other member states for the Mediterranean into an active process of EFP formulation, leading to a new initiative toward the Mediterranean (the Global Mediterranean Policy—GMP) and another one aimed at the Arab states (the Euro-Arab Dialogue—EAD). The Commission played a role, but as we shall see, it was not a main player, and was also placed in a position of disadvantage in the EPC intergovernmental framework which developed the EAD.

However, France was not the typical entrepreneur that much of the literature would expect. In fact, France acted very much as a "broker," rather than as a "believer," the main difference being the degree of flexibility it showed in relation to the initial policy proposal and its eventual outcome. While a "believer" sticks to their stated vision, a "broker" has a more general interest in change and is prepared to put up with substantial alterations to the original proposal as long as the final result is policy change (see chapter 1). In the case of France's goals, the reasons for its action were broadly defined in ideational terms, to do with winning international recognition of its "big power" status. The main avenue for this was by championing the cause of the Mediterranean, although first France had to strengthen its own relations with the area, which had been neglected under de Gaulle in favor of a much grander world-scale policy. Setting Franco-Mediterranean relations on a firmer footing was to be the springboard for France's quest for international recognition.

French Mediterranean Policy and Its Uses

The main challenge faced by France in the period 1969–1971 was how to respond to a much more complicated international scene while keeping faith to its Gaullist tradition and maintaining a "big power" profile. The challenges outlined earlier, ranging from terrorism to Ostpolitik, affected French foreign and domestic politics, and prompted Pompidou to consolidate France's self-image after de Gaulle's departure. By reinforcing relations with the Mediterranean countries and with Western Mediterranean countries in particular, Pompidou hoped to project a familiar if more realistic, image of France as the international, independent power, which was the project of the Fifth Republic. The entrepreneurial attempts within the EEC and EPC were to represent the last stage in this strategy.

Pompidou's policy continued on the line adopted by his predecessor (Berstein and Rioux 1995, 35; Roussel 1994, 342).[50] De Gaulle's policy toward the Mediterranean since 1962 had been based on three, interrelated principles: (1) independence from the superpowers; (2) embargo on arms' sales to "states on the battlefield" (meaning Israel, Egypt and Jordan);[51] (3) a de facto pro-Arab policy supporting neutralist claims. Once elected, Pompidou largely adhered to these principles, but he looked for a more solid basis from which to bring them to life. According to de Gaulle, Algeria was the privileged "narrow door" to the Mediterranean, through which France was penetrating the Third World and could present itself as the champion of Third World interests. From there, it was to rise to "big power" status and it could sit at the negotiating table of the Big Four talks about the Arab-Israeli conflict (Kolodziej 1974b, 84–87). Pompidou's aim was to widen this fragile Algerian base to include the whole Mediterranean area, starting from North Africa and Spain.

Therefore, shortly after coming to power in June 1969, Pompidou directed his staff to reinforce relations with the Western Mediterranean countries. The diplomatic activity was spectacular. Maurice Schumann, minister of Foreign Affairs, visited Algeria in the beginning of October 1969. In the following month, he went to Tunisia, where he also discussed the subject of relations between Tunisia and the EEC. Financial aid to Tunisia was restored, joint military exercises were held, and the (re)establishment of French firms was initiated by the French government (Kolodziej 1974a).[52] After four years of suspension, relations with Morocco were reestablished in December 1969, leading to a flurry of cooperation agreements (including military cooperation), and King Hussein of Morocco visited Paris in February 1970.[53] Furthermore, the government announced in January 1970 its intention to sell 100 Mirage planes to the new Libyan regime of Qadaffi and to train Libyan pilots to use them.[54] Continuing the trend, at the beginning of February 1970 the Spanish minister of Foreign Affairs Lopez arrived in Paris, for the first official visit to France since the beginning of Franco's authoritarian regime, reciprocating a visit by Debré.[55] In a presidential speech in December 1969, Pompidou described the "renforcement de la présence française en Méditerranée, notamment en Méditerranée occidentale, marqueé par la visite de M.Maurice Schumann à Alger et à Tunis, par le rétablissement prochain de toutes nos relations traditionnelles en Afrique du Nord, par l'aménagement de rapports cordiaux avec le gouvernment libyen."[56]

Therefore, between June 1969 and February 1970, France radically improved its relations with North African countries and Spain, institutionalizing a set of bilateral ties with all the countries of the region. Cooperation crossed all fields: cultural,[57] financial, economic, political, and military. The military component was often a particularly important part of the agreements signed or on the agenda for discussions, Libya being the most typical example of a general trend. In fact, the final seal on the new priority France attached to relations in the Western Mediterranean was set by a grand military exercise lasting 10 days in Toulon in June 1971, which marked the permanent return to Toulon of part of the military command. "A tous les égards, la France a un rôle à jouer en Méditerranée"[58] declared a satisfied Pompidou at the end of the maneuvers.[59]

It is interesting to notice how France's new attention toward the Western Mediterranean was portrayed as part of a "normal" French vocation, meriting descriptions such as "natural,"[60] or "necessary."[61] France was "essentially a Mediterranean power"[62] and its border with the Mediterranean sea meant, according to Pompidou, that "it is not a matter of politics, it is a matter of realities, of geography."[63] French foreign policy toward the Mediterranean, and particularly toward Western Mediterranean, was thus portrayed as the logical consequence of France's existence and of its mission in the world. However, as has been shown, the relaunching of Mediterranean relations was an explicit political choice.[64]

The real continuity between de Gaulle and Pompidou in France's foreign policy was ideological, and aimed at creating an international role for France. What Pompidou did was to set out a means of achieving this against the backdrop of, first, the cold war, and then later, détente, by making use of the Mediterranean. France intended to transform the Mediterranean into a "lac de paix," outside of superpower confrontation.[65] The justifications put forward for the supply of Mirages to Libya centered on an argument that, if France had not supplied Libya, the USSR would have done so and Libya would have thus entered the Soviet bloc (Fontaine 1970, 11–14). France tried to combine the "politics of grandeur" with the "politics of weakness," justifying its international status by opposing the international order of the time (Kolodziej 1974a). By using its ideational and diplomatic resources, France managed to set in train a domino effect that from its colonial heritage led to its demand to be treated as a major international power and the champion of newly independent countries (cf. Chérigui 1997, 19).

However, to achieve this goal, France needed international recognition of this image. In fact, its bid for grandeur could only be successful if the other Western countries "bought" this discourse in some form and thus acknowledged (and validated) France's role in world politics. Direct recognition was sought through the attempt to revive the Big Four Talks on the Arab-Israeli conflict. However, by 1970 Pompidou realized that this was not going to work.[66] He then sought indirect recognition through the EEC. Here though, the importance of France and of the Mediterranean faced a competing challenge from Brandt's Ostpolitik and by the membership of the United Kingdom. It was here that France played the Mediterranean card, in order to be considered as "a kind of EEC [. . .] vanguard in the Mediterranean" (Gasteyger 1974, 6).[67] In Pompidou's words, as he commented on the military agreement with Spain signed in June 1970, the heart of the matter was to "équilibrer cette Europe, en rendant plus évidente l'influence méditerranéenne et latine."[68]

It is important to note that the attempt to "go multilateral" on the Mediterranean together with the other member states did not spring from a unanimous consensus within the French policy making community. It was an executive choice, crafted from above by Pompidou and Schumann, and resistance to it came from two sides.

First, some diplomats at the Quai d'Orsay believed that France should continue to focus on bilateral relations, instead of watering down its privileged position with multilateral discussions. Burin de Roziers, who was first ambassador of France in Italy and then from March 1972 the head of the Permanent Representation in Brussels, was for instance openly skeptical about the benefits of a multilateral approach within the EPC framework. Raising the Mediterranean in such a context would lead in his opinion to "vaines et fâcheuses entreprises communautaires,"[69] because of the NATO (i.e., pro–United States) allegiances of the other member states.[70] Jacques de Beaumarchais, at the time Director of the Directorate of Political Affairs of the Quai d'Orsay, was also reported to think along similar lines.[71] The reply by Maurice Schumann was however equally clear: there was room for both bilateral and multilateral relations on the subject of the Mediterranean.[72]

Second, the Ministry for Industry and Scientific Development and for Agriculture and Rural development stressed the potential risks of uncoordinated parallel negotiations between the EEC and the North African countries, which could have led to generous offers.[73] They thus resisted in principle all concessions that would have had an impact on producing sectors. This resistance was overcome by Schumann once the GMP was beginning to take place, by stressing the simultaneity of negotiations[74] and by ruling out substantial agricultural concessions.

These considerations show that the period 1969–1971 marked a change in French foreign policy, cloaked in a language of apparent continuity. Within two years, France had managed to reconstruct its relations with Western Mediterranean countries and establish a network of strong cooperation agreements in all fields.

The analysis of France's motives is important also in analytical terms. It contributes to clarify what kind of reasons pushed France into actively promoting an initiative for the Mediterranean *at the European level*. The typical rationalist account would suggest that France provided entrepreneurial leadership principally in order to reap material benefits, very much like an investment bringing material gains.[75] The story just told shows, however, that an improvement of relations with Mediterranean countries, and the material gains that would follow from it were largely obtained before France started its entrepreneurial action. The strengthening of France's *national* Mediterranean policy in the early years of Pompidou's Presidency created the conditions for a clear improvement in terms of trade and also in terms of security. European initiatives brokered by France, while prestigious and important, were not to add much to that effect. Clear enough, influence could be seen as delivering material benefits too, but my point here is that interpreting influence and the quest for international recognition only in terms of material benefits would be grossly reductive. If material benefits were France's main goal, it could have largely achieved its foreign policy objective toward the Mediterranean by improving bilateral relations.

Imagining the Mediterranean: Entrepreneurial Actions and Cognitive Interaction

Between 1970 and 1972, there were several strands of thought about Euro-Mediterranean relations, expressing a variety of economic, political, and social nuances. Italy, with the backing of Germany and in parallel with the European Parliament, promoted a political initiative to anchor southern neighbors to Europe at a time of detente. The Commission suggested injecting developmental concerns into economic relations. But it was the debate in the EEC that resulted in a solid foundation on which these floating ideas could be realized. Thanks to the entrepreneurial efforts of France, member states came to look at the area as a single region, with which to establish free trade with a developmental character.[76] On that basis, the EEC launched in October 1972 the Global Mediterranean Policy, addressing its southern neighbors from Spain to Turkey. The story of these years thus chronicles how, from these separate and at times conflicting strands, a single vision of the Mediterranean emerged.

What we are going to examine in this section is how the debate unfolded, how France offered crucial inputs and how a common policy framework emerged out of actors' contributions. Therefore, it will be a story on two levels. On the one hand, it will describe the entrepreneurial attempts of some actors and the success of entrepreneurial France. On the other hand, it will show how the collective puzzlement about the Mediterranean turned into a cognitive process by which relevant concepts, interpretative frames and specific policy options were evaluated and codified. In the following section, I will continue on these parallel tracks, but the focus will be on the definition of the Euro-Arab Dialogue.

Early Starts, Different Frames, Same Direction

The first mention of a "global" Mediterranean policy came by the European Parliament, in the context of a report prepared by the French Member of the European Parliament (MEP) André Rossi. He presented it in February 1971 to the Commission and to member states, suggesting the formulation of an overall scheme of principles governing relations with Mediterranean nonmember countries.[77] The debate that followed in the European Parliament (EP) demonstrated however a lack of agreement about the utility of a global approach to the Mediterranean not only among MEPs, but also within the Commission. The German Commissioner for External Relations, Ralf Dahrendorf, defended the "mosaics" approach which prevailed in the 1960s as the best way to address different partners.[78] In contrast, the Commissioner for Developing Countries, Deniau (French) was more favorable to a holistic solution.[79] The case for a common approach to the Mediterranean was thus not taken as a concrete option. When Rossi presented a second report, in June 1972, which basically endorsed the French proposal and the work done in the Council, the tone turned out to be very different (see below).

The second, more consistent, attempt to promote the Mediterranean came from Italy, with the support of Germany and the resistance of France. The setting in this case was EPC. The aim was a political initiative for the whole Mediterranean area. The Mediterranean apparently received a first mention at a meeting between Colombo, the Italian President of the Council, Moro, the Italian minister of Foreign Affairs, and Brandt. It is likely that as a consequence of that meeting, in April 1971, Moro suggested at the Council of General Affairs that the POCO examine the issue of the Mediterranean.[80] Italy also circulated a document on the Mediterranean, in which it stressed Soviet penetration in the area through nonmilitary means. The document emphasized the way in which not only the Arab-Israeli crisis, but also economic underdevelopment represented an avenue for the USSR to exploit regional tensions. It was thus important, according to Italy, to try and ease social and economic problems in the area.[81] Germany openly supported the document, while Belgium saw in it a way to improve its relations with Spain without compromising its national position.[82] The debate continued. In November 1971, Italy, which was holding the Presidency, proposed the creation of a Working Group, within the EPC framework, devoted to the "Problems of the Mediterranean"[83] (in the plural). Meetings of the Working Group started on November 30, 1971.[84]

This Working Group became the forum where information was exchanged and common assessments of the situation on the ground were crafted, but it never generated a debate in which the Mediterranean was taken as a single region. Member states undertook to write reports about specific areas of the Mediterranean. It is in this context that the Netherlands examined the potential political uses of oil on the part of Libya, which I mentioned earlier.[85] Germany produced a report on Spain and Portugal, in which it stressed their European character and the fact that they should be allowed to develop tighter links with the EEC.[86]

The Working Group on the Middle East, created in 1970, for its part became a forum for convergence on a joint understanding of the Arab-Israeli conflict. Although member states started from very polarized positions, in May 1971 they produced a document that called for the withdrawal of Israel to 1967 borders, options for Palestinian refugees, the internationalization of Jerusalem, and international interposition forces in demilitarized zones. The document, however, was not published, due to the opposition from the Netherlands and Germany, and Italian reservations (Ifestos 1987, 420).[87] The Working Group continued its duties and a couple of years later it was given the task of sketching out the Euro-Arab Dialogue, before member states decided to create an ad hoc Working Group on the topic (Allen 1982, 73). But it was only in 1980, with the Venice Declaration, that member states achieved *and* publicly supported a common position on the Middle East.

It is important to stress that France represented the main obstacle to any more substantial development in the Working Group on the Mediterranean. Italy, in an attempt to generate more political momentum into the discussion, prepared a framework document that mentioned the need to develop a global policy so as to contribute to development in the Mediterranean. But next to this France put a big question mark.[88] From the beginning of the discussion, the French representative in fact expressed a subtle but consistent resistance to common initiatives being taken within the EPC framework and stressed that he preferred initiatives on the part of the EEC *member states*, rather than in the EPC framework.[89]

The issue was not solely linked to prestige. Italy was ready to forgo the glory of leadership in recognition of the fact that French leadership was a necessary condition for any initiative on the Mediterranean.[90] The point for France at this stage was to keep the EPC framework separated from the EEC and from any attempt of fellow partners to push France toward transatlantic solidarity. Mentions of the EEC or British attempts[91] to discuss transatlantic relations in the (EPC) Working Group on the Mediterranean met repeatedly with French ripostes that the mandate was more limited than other representatives seemed to assume.[92] While Italy and in part also Belgium and Germany strove for convergence of opinions in the framework of the Working Group, France's participation strictly adhered to its Gaullist tradition.

Despite French resistance and internal contradictions, this strand of activism in favor of the Mediterranean is noteworthy as it signals not only the broad ferment surrounding the issue, but also the role of the recently created EPC framework as a forum for cognitive interaction among member states. The Working Group was probably too low in the hierarchy to have an impact on the established French tradition of foreign policy, but it indirectly contributed to the political relevance of initiatives taken at EEC level.[93]

There was a third substantial discourse about Euro-Mediterranean relations that punctuated member states' agenda in 1970–1972, and it came at the hands of the Commission in connection with the issue of "adjustments." The Commission had to present proposals to the Council not only because of the EEC accession of three new countries, but also because there still was no agreement with Algeria and agreements with Tunisia and Morocco were to expire in August 1974 (and the understanding at the time of signing had been that the deadline would have constituted an opportunity to revise the agreements). Instead of limiting its action to the technical aspects of adjustments, the Commission used the opportunity to analyze the content of the agreements. Its vision was that the EEC should shoulder part of the burden of economic development in countries such as those in the Mediterranean, and therefore member states had to infuse their external economic relations with some form of development policy. The Commission first expressed these ideas in a memorandum devoted to development (Faber 1982, 40; Mureau 1984, 82–84).[94] The part on the Mediterranean expressed the view that the EEC should pay special attention to the region and include cooperation into existing agreements. Similarly, when reporting on adjustments,[95] the Commission suggested expanding the range of products addressed by the agreements and it stressed the importance of financial cooperation, to spark economic development.

Member states were at first strongly against such a drive, with France and Italy at the forefront of opposition, but the mood then changed.[96] The mainstream consensus among member states in the early months of 1972 pointed in the direction of simply adjusting existing relations and, where appropriate, negotiating new agreements, but with a limited scope. Belgium, supported by France and Italy, drafted a document in which it stressed that "la substance et la structure des accords existants"[97] should not be questioned and changes were to be limited to "difficultés spécifiques et réelles."[98] The opposition front began however to soften once discussions got going in the Council. The debate confirmed that the substance and the structure of existing agreements was not to be changed, but it also acknowledged that it was probably impossible to keep the technical aspects separated from the "economic" (i.e., substantial) ones. Therefore, the Council entrusted the COREPER to continue the discussion with an eye to the propositions of the Commission.[99] Moreover, at the meeting on May 10, 1972, the Council gave a mandate to the Commission to negotiate with Algeria, Morocco and Tunisia what were referred to as "global agreements."[100] This was a significant development. It was the first time that the word "global" appears in the workings of the Council and it is most likely that it came at the initiative of France.[101] The term at this stage referred to the substance of the agreements. While the first generation of agreements centered principally on limited concessions about trade, the understanding within the Council marked a substantial shift in favor of agreements including also developmental elements, namely financial and technical cooperation, as well as a broadening of the type of goods the agreements covered. The Council envisaged such a change only for Algeria, Morocco and Tunisia, though, which were the most pressing cases. No reference to the Mediterranean was made at this point. Still, the grouping of the three North African countries in the mandate to the Commission created the idea of a geographical bloc and attached a developmental agenda to external economic relations. It was a clear example in which the debate among participants had led to an innovation in thinking about the Mediterranean.

The entrepreneurship of the Commission had thus sparked a debate leading to a new understanding of the substance of the agreements. While formally member states stuck to their position of "technical" adjustments, their acknowledgement of the intrinsic links with the broader environment in which the agreements existed opened the door to changes in the substance of the agreements, and to a broader approach to Mediterranean relations.

Framing the Global Mediterranean Policy

This was the situation shortly before France's entrepreneurship. Mediterranean nonmembers were on the agenda, member states acknowledged some responsibility for development in North Africa and the need for some form of political initiative, but the debate was fragmented and limited. The time was ripe for systematizing these "floating ideas" into a more coherent ideational framework and then into a European initiative. The spark igniting such a broader debate was provided by France, within the EEC framework.

France began its entrepreneurial action within the EEC framework at the same Council meeting on May 10, 1972 in which the Council gave the mandate to the Commission for negotiations on "global agreements" with Maghreb countries.[102] In that venue, France put forward two conceptual leads, one based on geography, the other one on the substance of the agreements. The geographic concept consisted of a parallel between Spain and Israel. France argued in favor of addressing both countries in the same way, as they were the two countries most liable to suffer from the EEC enlargement.[103] The Spanish case was complicated by its authoritarian regime, with which member countries preferred to have little contact. The Israeli case was complicated by the fact that any concession to Israel appeared to be a political advantage subtracted from Arab countries. The contribution of France on the substance of the agreements came in the form of applying to Spain and Israel the same formula of "free trade" that had been applied to Portugal.[104] If Portugal, which was a case of an authoritarian regime, could establish privileged trade relations with the EEC, then the same could be possible with Spain and Israel, France argued. Two crucial conceptual blocs on which the Mediterranean region would be formed were thus forged from the parallel between Israel, Spain and Portugal.

"From that moment on the situation developed very quickly" (Tovias 1977, 70), as national representatives weighed up this approach and expanded on it. France formalized its ideas at COREPER meetings on May 16–18 and May 23–24, 1972 and Maurice Schumann presented them at the meeting of the Council of General Affairs on June 6, 1972. The Netherlands and Germany, traditional allies of Israel, reacted positively.[105] The Netherlands went even further, hinting at the possible inclusion of some other Mediterranean countries to avoid negative Arab reactions. Italy, for its part, raised objections, mainly linked to the inclusion of agricultural goods in the discussion.[106] Belgium was hesitant about generous offers to Spain (Tovias 1977, 71). As an outcome of the discussion, both the "old" and the "new" approach were retained. The Council thus entrusted the COREPER to continue the discussion about the old issue of selective changes, but it also asked COREPER to study policy options of a "global approach" (i.e., entailing free trade and cooperation) with the "various" countries of the Mediterranean.[107]

EEC institutions also played a part in developing the cognitive definition of Euro-Mediterranean relations. On June 12, 1972 the European Parliament enthusiastically, but also pragmatically, supported the French proposal.[108] The Commission sketched a Communication about the North African countries that combined its developmental approach with the joint geographical focus on the Maghreb and the free trade approach proposed by France for Spain and Israel.[109] The final goal at this stage was the creation of a single free trade area EEC-Maghreb with a joint Association Council.[110]

In parallel to the Commission's Communication, France upgraded its proposal to address the whole Mediterranean. Elaborating on the Dutch suggestion at the COREPER meeting on June 14–15, 1972, France envisaged the creation of a free trade area between the EEC and *all* the Mediterranean countries. France thus was suggesting "une approche globale avec un orientation commune"[111] for all Mediterranean countries, hinging on a free trade area for industrial goods and substantial concessions in agriculture, with the final aim of promoting economic development. In parallel, the Commission was insisting on aid being granted too.

A region—and a policy—were thus in the making. One of the key shifts which occurred was on geographical scope. From the early Spain-Israel parallel, France moved to equate all the Mediterranean countries, thus "calling" the Mediterranean region into being. The other member states, more or less, supported the project. The countries concerned were considered homogenous enough to be addressed in principle in the same way, so on that principle, all the delegations of national representatives agreed.[112]

The official birth of the Mediterranean for the EEC is thus dated June 26–27, 1972, when at a Council meeting member states decided to stress the option of the "global" (both in substance and in geographical scope) approach over the option of "technical adjustments," which remained on the table but with a lower profile. The Commission received the mandate to prepare a Communication on the global approach.

Within just over a month, the manner in which the EEC approached Euro-Mediterranean relations had thus changed completely. It was a sort of revolution. Beforehand, as per the criticism of the Rossi report mentioned earlier, the state of relations between the EEC and the countries around the Mediterranean was at a very low point. Things started moving when the Italians first pushed for a political initiative to resolve the situation. The Commission then lobbied for member states to focus on developmental issues. France's intervention was decisive and was based on EEC trade policy doctrine. Through their interaction, member states thus singled out the Mediterranean countries for a completely new project: the construction of a region with which to establish privileged trade relations.

The official coronation of the "global policy" came at the Paris Summit, on October 19–20, 1972. At the summit, organized by Pompidou, Heads of State and government of member states and applicant countries stated that the EEC attached "une importance essentielle" to the Mediterranean basin and they expressed the intention to establish new agreements within the framework of "approche globale et équilibrée."[113] The geographical creation of the Mediterranean as a region was thus codified, the EEC pledged to contribute to its economic development and to smoothen the international tensions that had plagued it. From that moment on, the word "Mediterranean," which I have adopted for the previous period but which was not used by the EEC, became part of the EEC's official repertoire of concepts and labels.

The EEC then embarked on the enterprise of specifying the content of the GMP, but this was a less successful endeavor. In September 1972, the Commission produced a plan for a global policy that was actually written along the lines of the debate in the Council.[114] What the Commission added was not only specific suggestions for aid, but also a timetable for implementing the "global policy." It asked for a mandate to negotiate agreements in 1973 and it set out a tentative timetable for the creation of the free trade areas. For the first time, a temporal perspective was envisaged, thus contributing to the contextualization of the "global policy."

The increasing presence of the United Kingdom after the Paris Summit, however, disrupted the consensus reached, as it made discussions of transatlantic relations unavoidable.[115] The United States had started in the autumn of 1972 to voice its criticism of the GMP. Formally, it objected to the idea of creating a free trade area between the European and the Mediterranean countries, which would have excluded U.S. goods (the so-called issue of inverse preferences and reciprocity).[116] In practice, despite assurances that the United States did not oppose the general principle of the GMP global policy for the Mediterranean, the issue at stake was the growing political profile of the Mediterranean region. How far did member states want to go in creating a "third pole" in international politics, by establishing privileged relations with the Mediterranean? As Nixon put it in a discussion about the GMP, what was to be avoided was a "Finlandization of Europe,"[117] and of the Mediterranean as part of such a project. All parties were well aware of the political stakes. The General Secretariat of the European Commission reported that the main U.S. fear was that the Mediterranean nonmembers might gang up with the EEC on political issues as well as in multilateral negotiations about trade.[118]

By October 1972 the United Kingdom began to raise the issue of U.S. objections and ask for a *political* discussion of the GMP which took place on November 6–7, 1972. The British representative urged fellow partners to consult with the United States before making final choices on the issue of reciprocity, mentioning the need to scrutinize how the EEC related to the wider world. The immediate effect was to pull Germany into a more pro-Atlanticist stance. France was completely opposed to such an approach and stressed that it was important "not to feel inferior" to the United States. Striving to steer clear of a debate about transatlantic matters, France refused a proposal to create a joint POCO-COREPER group to study the issue, as well as another one to charge the POCO with analyzing the political aspects of the GMP.[119] Italy, Belgium and the Commission supported the French position (Tovias 1977, 72).

Under heavy pressure from the United States, the issue kept coming up at COREPER and Council meetings, until the balance tilted in favor of the United States. At the meeting held on March 5, 1973, the United Kingdom gathered the support of Germany, Denmark, Ireland, and the Netherlands, while France received open support only from Italy. The Commission was split along national lines. The paradox was that the United Kingdom was arguing against free trade with the Mediterranean, while France and Italy supported it. At that meeting, member states found an economic and political compromise by bringing down their economic concerns to the core. If the EEC was not in a position to create a third, neutral pole at a time of détente, it could at least guarantee that the politics of Euro-Mediterranean economic relations did not reach the dramatic heights they had acquired during the period of nationalizations. The Council thus agreed to consider "different types" of reciprocal concessions by the Mediterranean nonmembers, among which member states mentioned the all important principle of protection of investments (Flory 1982, 116). Unfortunately, this principle was soon to prove too weak in the face of the oil shock.

The conclusion of the discussion about reciprocity and free trade signaled the end of the cognitive interaction process about the key aspects of Euro-Mediterranean relations, namely the geographical scope of the Mediterranean, the type of problems at stake and the contribution that member states could collectively make. After that, deprived of any great momentum, the discussion focused on more traditional bargaining negotiations, addressing costs, tariffs, deadlines, and who should pay what.[120]

Two issues turned out to be particularly divisive. One was the discussion about agricultural goods, which showed the absence of any automatic southern European/Mediterranean solidarity. Italy, despite supporting the general idea of the GMP, fought against concessions[121] and insisted on drawing a parallel between trade concessions and aid: the number of trade concessions (by southern European countries) was to be equated to the amount of aid provided (by northern European countries), in order to distribute the GMP's costs among all member states.[122] France proposed a progressive method of concessions, which however paved the way to a "policy of meetings" that exacerbated divergences.[123] The Commission failed to broker an early agreement and it took months of further discussions in the "agricultural" Council[124] before a compromise was reached on the basis that the reference price was to remain for all intents and purposes the European/CAP one.[125]

Cooperation too was contested, although less than reciprocity or agriculture. Apart from the linkage established by Italy between aid and trade, the question essentially centered on the countries that should receive the benefit. Spain was excluded, less for political reasons (that Belgium had raised) than because of its level of development. Israel benefited only from technical cooperation. For Greece and Turkey forms of aid were already in place. At first, only the Maghreb countries were offered financial aid, but the Machrek countries "let it be known immediately that an agreement which excluded financial cooperation was of no interest to them" (Cova, n.d., 10). Therefore, financial, economic, and technical cooperation, became one of the key elements shared by almost all Mediterranean countries.

This second stage, in which member states discussed the details of the GMP, thus reflected classical bargaining techniques, and the scope of the initiative was somehow diminished as a result.

Several principles were, however, established. First, the southern neighbors of the EEC shared enough similarities and issues to be addressed as a region. The equal treatment reserved for Israel and the Arab countries expressed member states' slow shift toward a more pro-Arab position, which was in turn expected to contribute to ease part of the tension of the Middle East conflict. Second, the main contribution of the EEC/EPC to Mediterranean problems was economic, linked to regional development, although this endeavor carried political overtones. By fostering economic development, the EEC could contribute to strengthen the nonaligned tendencies of countries in the area, although the discussion showed that a majority of member states were not ready to go all the way. Conditional economic development was also the way to protect economic relations across the region, thus eliminating a source of tension.

What do GMP negotiations demonstrate, for the purpose of this book's theoretical framework and more specifically for the *pars construens* of the proposed framework? First, there was a flurry of entrepreneurial activities, among which French initiatives were the most effective. Italy and the Commission provided entrepreneurial inputs, but while these were important contributions to the debate, they did not drive European foreign policy making toward the Mediterranean. Second, France's entrepreneurship was linked to the launching of a general initiative, rather than to a specific proposal, thus being closer to the "broker" than to the "believer" model. Its early suggestion of parallelism between Spain and Israel evolved in the course of the debate. The actual content of the initiative benefited from the inputs offered by Italy, the Commission, the Netherlands and Belgium, just to mention a few contributors.

Third, the style of the debate showed the existence of separate and parallel processes. In one process, taking place in EPC under the input of Italy, security aspects were addressed. In another, prompted by France in the EEC, the debate centered on the geographical scope to be addressed and on the type of (economic) solution to be provided. Within the EEC a discussion also unfolded about the type of economic issues that were raised by the Mediterranean countries. The Commission stressed the deadlines imposed by previous agreements and the enlargement process. It also contributed to define the key elements of the economic approach to be adopted. By piecing together these elements, a frame for Euro-Mediterranean relations began to emerge and to be translated into a concrete initiative.

The analysis of the negotiations leading to the GMP's implementation thus demonstrates a pattern of gradual change. From an initial readiness to talk due to cognitive uncertainty the debate turned into a framing process about broad perspectives and then into a classical bargaining negotiation over specific arrangements and funds.

Negotiations in the EPC Framework: The Euro-Arab Dialogue

Parallel to the late stages of the debate about the Global Mediterranean Policy, the European countries put forward another foreign policy initiative that included the majority of the Mediterranean countries, together with the other Arab members of the Arab League, under the name of the Euro-Arab Dialogue (EAD). The initiative was linked, as all commentators agree, to the oil shock and the need for industrialized countries to respond to it and place relations with the Arab oil producers on a more secure footing.

The initiative was not focused on the Mediterranean, and as such its analysis represents a slight detour from the object of this book, which I will keep short. It is however interesting, not only for the dynamics it unveils, but also and especially for the similarities between negotiations for the GMP and those for the EAD. As oil became a security matter, European member states had to frame the new reality and choose among different policy options. Similar to the GMP, the EAD had a strong cognitive component that characterized the early stages of negotiations, in the form of piecing together the relevant ideas into a frame. Here again, France acted as a policy entrepreneur, leading the debate in "broker" style, so that other members' contributions were accommodated as the discussion progressed. Finally, divergences with the United States, which had initially spurred cooperation between member states, became once again the stumbling block undermining the initiative.

The first outcome of the oil shock was not multilateral diplomacy. France, Britain and the other member states rivaled each other for the attention of the oil-producing countries, often offering arms-for-oil deals. "Faced with a united OPEC, the consuming governments were thoroughly disunited" (Sampson 1975, 261). It was not the finest moment in the history of Western cooperation.

After a few weeks of frantic activism to reestablish supply sources, however, multilateral cooperation restarted, and began to focus on the idea of a Euro-Arab dialogue. The literature generally indicates the genesis of this idea in the unexpected arrival of four Arab ministers of Foreign Affairs at the European summit in Copenhagen on December 14, 1973. There is, however, some evidence that similar ideas were around before then. For instance, in a meeting held in Paris at the beginning of December, Pompidou raised the idea with Bourguiba, the President of Tunisia.[126] On that occasion Michel Jobert, who was by then minister of Foreign Affairs, suggested "ce qui pourrait être la préparation d'une conférence euro-arabe, ses étapes et son calendrier"[127] (Jobert 1976, 277–789). Similarly, at a meeting with Brandt on November 26–27, 1973, Pompidou floated the idea of a Euro-Arab Dialogue between member states and the members of the Arab League.[128] At the beginning of December 1973, the Commission volunteered to examine economic, technical and financial measures for a policy toward the Middle East in general. This hint, which would have expanded the role of the Commission in the EPC was not pursued, although the Commission was eventually associated to the EAD. Moreover, within the Political Committee in early 1974, the Netherlands overcame its reluctance to address issues related to the Arab-Israeli conflict and suggested analyzing economic and cooperative aspects of future relationships with the Arabs.

The point was agreed in principle by the Political Committee (Langlois and Blanchi 1979, 207).[129]

There was thus a change in the way member states and EEC institutions looked at the issue of relations with the Arab countries. Once the key material bases of the relationship were secured through bilateral contacts, the efforts of the Europeans were directed at a cooperative, multilateral endeavor, aimed at smoothening over a long period possible areas of friction, and at establishing partnership measures. As a consequence of the visit of the ministers from Algeria, Tunisia, Sudan, and United Arab Emirates to Copenhagen, the issue of a Euro-Arab Dialogue was squarely on the agenda. Pressured by the "unexpected" visit, European chiefs of government issued a declaration that committed the Europeans to institutionalize a dialogue with the Arab countries.

The fact that the idea was adopted was a remarkable achievement given the sharp U.S. opposition to such a project. Immediately after the oil shock the United States made it quite clear that "its foreign policy would not be changed because of pressure from Arab countries exploiting their monopolistic position on oil" (Campbell 1975, 116). Therefore, especially in the short term, the attitude was rather to denounce Arab blackmail—and the European surrender to it.[130] The U.S. proposal was the creation of an Energy Action Group (later an International Energy Agency) representing the consuming countries in their negotiations with the producer countries, which would embody an approach of horizontal cooperation between consumers only.

The Europeans did not share this attitude. By adopting the idea of a Euro-Arab Dialogue, they expressed their preferences for vertical cooperation between consumers and producers. Moreover, by going in this direction, "the EC saw an avenue to achieve greater independence from the United States and U.S. foreign policy interests" (Ginsberg 1989, 167). Through the EAD, European countries attempted to secure closer relations with Arab countries, while at the same time distancing themselves from the U.S. conflictual approach.

Once these cognitive decisions were taken, and actors had chosen how to look at the phenomenon, the first stage of framing Euro-Arab relations ended, and a second stage began. It was characterized by tighter bargaining logics, which under the relentless action of the United States exposed contradictions in the European approach. The U.S. administration convened an international conference in Washington on February 11, 1974 to which they invited the main European countries (United Kingdom, France, Germany, Italy, and the Netherlands) as well as Norway, Canada, and Japan. The European invitees, however, demanded and obtained the participation of all EEC countries, together with the EEC itself and on the eve of the meeting consolidated their position of not alienating the Arabs with the creation of an exclusively Western organization.[131] However, once the conference began, the European position came unstuck as Germany embraced the American stance while France maintained its own approach and did not participate in the International Energy Agency that was eventually created (Lieber 1976, 20–21). The conference descended at times into a personal showdown between personalities holding opposite views about Arab affairs.

Disagreements in Washington did not put the EAD off the agenda. The issue of consultations between the allies prior to meetings of the Euro-Arab Dialogue became particularly relevant, as the United States demanded a say in the topics to be addressed. The solution was found in the first Gymnich meeting of European ministers of Foreign Affairs, at Schloss Gymnich in Germany on April 20–21, 1974, where it was agreed that the Presidency, at the request of member states and after discussion among them, would consult the United States before finalizing decisions. Thanks to this vague formula, which in practice made it impossible to tackle hot issues such as oil or the Middle East conflict, the U.S. opposition to the EAD was reduced and the EAD survived (Nuttall 1992, 90–93).

In the formulation of the EAD, then, France acted once again as the political entrepreneur, converting the passive concern of other member states into an active process of formulating a cooperative foreign policy initiative. The Commission mainly swam with the tide (Nuttall 1992, 96ff.). The process, thus, reflected a similar pattern to the GMP. France, having first reinforced its national position through consultations both with Arab countries and with EEC member states, led the debate through which member states and the Commission converged around the definition of a Euro-Arab Dialogue. In the face of strong U.S. opposition, however, the EAD lost political momentum, although it retained the symbolic message of a European overture toward the Arab countries. The expulsion of Egypt from the Arab League after the Camp David Agreements brought the EAD to a semipermanent standstill.

The Global Mediterranean Policy and the Euro-Arab Dialogue in Practice

At the heart of the GMP was a new generation of agreements, the main elements of which were to be the same for all participating Mediterranean nonmembers. Technical, financial, and institutional measures of cooperation accompanied the agreements.

The EEC concluded the agreements, generally called Cooperation Agreements, with each Mediterranean country between 1976 and 1977 (see table 3.3).[132] The exceptions were Greece and Turkey, which maintained their previous Association Agreements. Malta and Cyprus upgraded their Association Agreements to take into account concessions offered by

Table 3.3 The Association and Cooperation Agreements with the Mediterranean Nonmembers following the Adoption of the GMP

Country	Legal Basis	Type of Agreement	Date of Signature	Date of Entry into Force
Greece	Art. 238	Association Agreement (mixed)	9.VII.61	18.II.1963 (OJEC L26)
Turkey	Art. 238	Association Agreement (mixed)	12.IX.63	29.XII.1964 (OJEC L217)
Cyprus	Art. 238	Association Agreement (final stage, customs union)	19.XII.72	31.V.73 (OJEC L143)
		Additional Protocol (on duty-free access)	15.IX.77	1.I.79 (OJEC L340)
Malta	Art. 238	Association Agreement (extended)		27.III.76 (OJEC L81)
		Additional Protocol (duty-free access)	27.X.77	28.IV.76 (OJEC L111)
Algeria	Art. 238	Cooperation Agreement (mixed)	26.IV.76	27.IX.78 (OJEC L263)*
Morocco	Art. 238	Cooperation Agreement (mixed)	27.IV.76	27.IX.78 (OJEC L264)*
Tunisia	Art. 238	Cooperation Agreement (mixed)	25.IV.76	27.IX.78 (OJEC L265)*
Egypt	Art. 238	Cooperation Agreement (mixed)	18.I.77	27.IX.78 (OJEC L266)*
Lebanon	Art. 238	Cooperation Agreement (mixed)	3.V.77	27.IX.78 (OJEC L267)*
Jordan	Art. 238	Cooperation Agreement (mixed)	18.I.77	27.IX.78 (OJEC L268)*
Syria	Art. 238	Cooperation Agreement (mixed)	18.I.77	27.IX.78 (OJEC L269)*
Israel	Art. 113	Preferential Agreement	11.V.75	28.V.75 (OJEC L136)
	Art. 238	Mixed Protocol	8.II.77	29.IX.78 (OJEC L270)
Spain	Art. 113	Protocol**	29.I.73	30.III.73 (OJEC L99)

* The trade provisions in these agreements were implemented in advance by an Interim Agreement.
** In spite of the role Spain had in sparking a debate about the Mediterranean, it only formalized a Protocol of transitional measures before relations with the EEC were changed by the death of Franco. This Protocol was expressly meant to be transitional while a new Agreement along the lines of the GMP was negotiated. However, this second step gave way in the late 1970s to the debate about Spain's accession to the EEC.
Source: OJEC, various issues.

the GMP. With little exception the agreements were based on Art. 238, thus bringing a common legal basis to Euro-Mediterranean relations.

The new agreements were meant to create free trade areas for industrial goods and grant concessions in the agricultural field. The GMP was intended to harmonies different regimes, which had been in place until then. With the GMP, the EEC was to lower its tariff barriers to imports of industrial goods produced in Mediterranean countries and then finally phase them out by January 1, 1977. The issue of reciprocity, which provoked so much tension in transatlantic negotiations, was resolved by differentiating among Mediterranean countries. The EEC demanded reverse preferences from some countries,[133] while to others it offered the option of reverse preferences of a nontariff nature (Levi 1972, 809), or to grant them also to other countries such as the United States (Tovias 1977, 73) or even not to grant them at all. The final decision was left to negotiations[134] and, in the event, all Maghreb and Machrek countries rejected reciprocity of concessions (Tsoukalis 1977, 431). As a consequence, the GMP's main innovation for most of the countries involved consisted of free access for Mediterranean industrial goods to the EEC.

Nevertheless, this was an important innovation (Flory 1982, 116; Tovias 1977; Tsoukalis 1977). The underlying rationale was to create economies of scale for Mediterranean nonmembers, thus overcoming the limitations of their internal markets and encouraging development. Still, the EEC called for exceptions in some sensitive areas such as textiles, clothing and phosphate products, on which Mediterranean countries were highly competitive. Moreover, the introduction of strict European rules of origins de facto hindered the access of Mediterranean goods (Martines 1994, 124–125). Pending the decision on a common energy policy, oil was not addressed (Levi 1972, 804).

The EEC addressed cooperation in Financial and Technical Protocols, which were concluded in parallel with trade agreements. Technical cooperation centered on technological transfer and workers training, while financial cooperation foresaw soft loans and grants. Some agreements also included provisions for social cooperation, in the form mainly of social security provisions for migrant workers.[135] The Financial and Technical Protocols, different from the agreements, were not concluded for an unlimited duration. Their length of application was five years, after which the amount and type of cooperation was renegotiated. Moreover, the amount of money devoted to these forms of cooperation changed from country to country.

Finally, the GMP envisaged common institutions, which were a first embryonic attempt at a political dialogue. According to the provisions of the agreements, the EEC established bilateral Cooperation Councils and Committees with every Mediterranean nonmember. Representatives of member states, of the Commission and of single Mediterranean countries met regularly to manage and in some cases revise the Cooperation Agreement (Martines 1994, 37–53).

This wide array of provisions was however not going to achieve the developmental goals for which they were designed, although it contributed to ease economic and even political relations. Mediterranean exports to the EEC did not increase significantly, expect in a few cases.[136] Several factors contributed to the GMP's "lack of teeth." There was an effective bias in favor of European agricultural products. High inflation in the 1970s corroded financial provisions, while the recession in Europe in the same period played against increases in Mediterranean exports. There was opposition on the part of the United States. Most importantly, there was a mismatch between the approach implied by the GMP and the preferred economic policy of the Mediterranean nonmembers in this period. The GMP was designed to favor the export of goods from the Mediterranean producers toward the European market, thus suggesting an export-led process of development. The prevailing approach to economic development among Mediterranean nonmembers relied instead on a strategy of import-substitution, curtailing exchanges with foreign markets and broadening the range of internally produced goods, with little attention to their lack of competitive advantages. This "ideological" mismatch constituted a formidable obstacle to reaping any benefit from free access to the EEC, as demonstrated for instance in the case of Turkey (Pomfret 1986, 51). In other terms, the GMP approach was based on offering a new type of interdependence, when Mediterranean nonmembers were still trying to pursue independence.

There are grounds therefore for viewing the GMP as a rather "European" approach to the Mediterranean, in spite of its cooperative characteristics. The philosophy for economic development it enshrined can be easily traced back to internal EEC debates about the utility of free exchange of goods, comparative advantages and economies of scale, rather than any Mediterranean understanding of development. Still, for all this, the GMP was a cooperative endeavor. The overall conception of the Mediterranean as a single region was a qualitative leap vis-à-vis the previous bilateral conception. While the 1960s appeared to suggest a *divide et impera* interpretation of the EEC approach, the adoption of a regional scheme pointed to a more cooperative trend. Moreover, the institutional arrangements created a sound bridge for dialogue and communication, which was to presage stronger versions of cooperation in later years. And free access to industrial goods was a principle that continues to characterize Euro-Mediterranean relations nowadays, as Mediterranean countries have come round to seeing its benefits. It could also be argued that in the middle to long run it contributed to a certain change in the mindset of Europeans toward the Arab-Israeli conflict, which was evident by 1980. However, this point would need further research per se.

Whereas the impact of the GMP may be measured in the mid- to long-term, the relevance of the EAD is questionable on any basis. It took a long time to formalize, and the list of participants was controversial because it initially contained Palestinian representatives, until it was agreed that the Arab League would represent all Arab countries. The first meeting of the EAD thus took place on the July 31, 1974, between the Secretary General of the Arab League, the President of the Commission and the EEC Presidency, in the person of the French minister of Foreign Affairs. A spate of multilateral meetings ensued (Al-Mani 1983, 50). For one year, until July 1975, meetings focused on identifying a list of topics for joint working groups, whose subjects ranged from trade to agriculture to technological development, but carefully avoided any overt mention of oil and of the rights of the Palestinian people.[137]

Still, the EAD shares several characteristics with the GMP, and for this reason it is worth mentioning here. Both initiatives tended to reflect European concerns. The agenda, principles and organization of the two institutions derived from the European way of doing things and did not leave much space for the other participants to offer their own initiatives. In the case of the EAD, the Arabs were not only ready to address oil in the dialogue, but very eager to focus on the Arab-Israeli conflict and on Palestinians' rights. The Europeans, on the contrary, wrote both issues off the agenda as too controversial and sensitive, thus contributing to the initiative's failure. Moreover, both the GMP and the EAD introduced a strong multilateral and regional element. Both policies testified to the European intention to engage in long-term cooperative relations with their southern neighbors as a group. While the GMP included countries bordering the Mediterranean, the EAD addressed the wider Arab states. The EAD, in particular, adopted a cooperative, rather than conflictual approach to the Arab countries, at a time of strong conflict. It can be argued that both the GMP and the EAD "took for granted" the basic characteristics of the "region" with which they wanted to develop a dialogue, but they did not provide for concrete measures to construct such a region. Still, the principles of multilateralism and regionalism were there to stay, and more savvy initiatives adopted in the 1990s built on these conceptual blocs established in the 1970s.

Conclusions

In 1972, the Mediterranean was officially born in the eyes of the EEC. The GMP represents the first time the Europeans addressed their southern neighbors as belonging to the same region, thus emphasizing similarities over differences. This (metaphorical) sea change occurred thanks to the simultaneous presence of several factors.

In 1970, a policy window for the formulation of an EFP initiative toward the Mediterranean began to open. Terrorism and economic relations made the Europeans progressively aware of the need to search for new concepts for Euro-Mediterranean relations. The U.S. policy for the Middle East magnified the urgency of defining a specific European approach. UK accession and West Germany's Ostpolitik injected a need to maintain the internal and external cohesion of the EEC. The early and relatively weak policy window was thus strengthened by the existence of different perceptions across the Western area. By then, the Europeans were ready to concede that "something should be done" for the Mediterranean nonmember countries. Such a perception was further reinforced by the securitization of terrorism, in September 1972, and of oil, in October 1973. Through this open window the question raised was "what exactly could be done about these issues?"

The policy entrepreneur active throughout this period was France and its action came in the form of "brokerage." At the turn of the decade, France underwent a change in its foreign policy. Pompidou downgraded the Gaulliste project, while at the same time placing it on a sounder basis. The bedrock of France's international status was to be the Mediterranean, and especially the Western Mediterranean. Bilateral relations thus became the object of intense diplomacy and improved as a result of the substantial political effort that France invested in the issue. However, international recognition of its world role had to come from outside France and this justified French efforts to promote international initiatives toward the Mediterranean within the EEC. At the same time, France was relatively neutral about how to achieve this aim, as long as it did not entail a discussion of the Mediterranean and of the United States in the EPC framework.

The simultaneous existence of a policy window and of France's entrepreneurship led to a truly common debate among member states and

EEC institutions. Several leads converged in the initiatives championed by France. In the case of the GMP, the political efforts of Italy and the European Parliament coincided with the developmental concerns of the Commission and found an outlet in the geographical discussion about trade in the Mediterranean. In the case of the EAD, the unease of European parterns about the Middle East conundrum and tough U.S. negotiating techniques coalesced around the idea of vertical cooperation between European consumers and Arab producers.

How to interpret, then, the overall picture that emerges from this specific instance of EFP making toward the Mediterranean? The story presents some clear realist aspects, but at the same time it is a neat example of open ended, socially constructed, and ideationally motivated state behavior. France tried to bolster its own power, while the transatlantic and the northern/southern European split did develop along a balance of power logics. At the same time, the whole process took the cue from the changing perceptions of national policymakers. Without the background of cognitive uncertainty about Mediterranean challenges, there would have been no scope and no hope for entrepreneurial efforts. Contrary to rationalist expectations, deconstructed (rather than preformed) national preferences represented the crucial policy window. Moreover, the entrepreneurial behavior not only was more flexible than liberal intergovernmentalism would have suggested, but also it was inspired by an ideational aspiration to international recognition more than by the quest for specific material gains. While the two can not be easily divided, the rationale for European action exceeded the set of material benefits that France secured through national initiatives, to say the least. The interaction among European partners that developed in the cases of the GMP and of the EAD showed the recurrent patterns of frame construction, but also the open ended nature of the process. Whereas elements of realist explanations of EFP have thus emerged in this case, the way that concepts such as power politics and rational expectations have acquired their specific meaning is strongly connected to the context and to the dynamics among actors at the time.

CHAPTER 4

The Partition of the Mediterranean

Dogs that did not Bark

The 1980s were a decade of contradictions in Euro-Mediterranean relations. On the one hand, the EC went through a period of activism. The southern enlargement included Greece in 1981 and Spain and Portugal in 1986, thus shifting the EC's internal balance toward the South for the first time since its creation. Moreover, the negotiations and the adoption of the Single European Act (SEA) gave new momentum to the institutional framework while developing new decision-making rules. By the end of the 1980s, the EC was experiencing one of its most positive periods. On the other hand, these internal developments did not translate into new initiatives toward the Mediterranean. On the contrary, the 1980s witnessed a worsening of Euro-Mediterranean relations and of Mediterranean politics more generally, and deepening rifts across the region. Not only did the southern enlargement absorb most of the attention of member states, but also meant that the EC improved its self-sufficiency in several sectors. During the 1980s, the Mediterranean nonmembers became less relevant to their European neighbors despite their worsening domestic conditions. The few compensatory measures drafted by the EC did little to change the overall picture.

What explains this dichotomy of heightened activism inside the EC and on the Mediterranean border, but greater indifference toward its (now reduced in number) southern Mediterranean neighbors? Two reasons are particularly important in relation to the stasis of the 1980s. First, there was no policy window. European security perceptions were absorbed by two issues, one old and one new. The old one was represented by the second cold war, which began with the 1979 Soviet invasion of Afghanistan. It put an end to the time of *détente*. In the new international climate, the Europeans fell back into traditional cold war mindsets and behavior, although in a lower key. A second and new development consisted of the substantial attention the EC devoted to the stabilization of its three new members. While Greece, Portugal and Spain turned into "Southern European" countries, the other "Mediterranean" ones were left behind. Absorbed by "traditional" cold war problems and by new accession challenges, member states' foreign policy agendas did not focus on the Mediterranean nonmembers, despite the profound transformations that the Arab world was undergoing.

The second substantial reason for little EFP activity toward the Mediterranean nonmembers was the presence of a weak policy entrepreneur. The Commission during this period showed few distinct signs of entrepreneurship. Well aware of the costs of exclusion for Mediterranean nonmembers, the Commission mapped out and suggested alternative scenarios. However, the activities it undertook, while representing a first attempt at autonomous action, were not sufficient to prevent or soften the decline of Euro-Mediterranean relations—and the de facto partition of the region between "ins" and "outs."

The analysis of the 1980s up to the end of the cold war is therefore interesting for various reasons. It represents another case of "dogs that did not bark," which is useful to test *a contrario* several of the points I made in the approach adopted in this book. It confirms that the presence of a policy entrepreneur, and especially of a weak entrepreneur, makes little difference in the absence of a policy window. Moreover, the empirical evidence also demonstrates the importance of perceptions in creating a policy window. As domestic politics in the Arab world faced growing problems, the Europeans, trapped in a cold war mentality, did not take them up and devote even marginal attention to issues which would come back to haunt them in the following decade.

This chapter contributes furthermore to questioning two other hypotheses. First, the analysis of this period offers mixed evidence for supranational/neofunctional explanations. The schism between EC institutional developments and activism toward the Mediterranean questions the supranational/neofunctional tenet, according to which developments at the institutional level tend to translate into policy initiatives. The Single European Act added some new features to EPC (Nuttall 1992, 239–259), bringing it more squarely into the domain of "soft law" (Dehousse and Weiler 1991). The main product of activism in the EPC framework in terms of Euro-Mediterranean relations was the Venice Declaration on the Middle East, adopted in 1980. While it constituted an undoubted success (Moïsi 1980), it also was the end, rather than the beginning of something (Allen and Smith 1989, 100). The Commission's attempts at entrepreneurial behavior play instead in favor of supranational/neofunctional explanations. As we shall see, this was a clear case in which the Commission, in the face of largely disinterested member states, tried to promote an initiative for the Mediterranean. At the same time, its efforts did not succeed, for a variety of reasons that we shall explore.

Second, contrary to hypotheses cast from liberal intergovernmentalism and also realism, the analysis of this period will show that perceptions of security challenges can diverge quite markedly from "real" dangers, and that what matters for policy formulation among member states is the former. As it will be demonstrated, this period was fraught with problems within Arab countries, which would soon become explosive. Economic difficulties, social unrest, delegitimization of existing regimes, and the rise of radical Islam, all these problems attracted the attention of the EC *after* the end of the cold war, but bred unrecognized during the period under examination. Member states were in fact unable to see them coming and relied on a "cold war" reading of the area despite the transformations within the region that were going on under their eyes.

The chapter is organized as follows. First, I will analyze the lack of a policy window, as the cold war entered a new potentially "hot" stage. Second, I will focus on the unperceived dangers that spread around the Mediterranean in this period, emphasizing how they failed to command the attention of the Europeans. I will then examine the southern enlargement and its negative consequences for Mediterranean outsiders. Finally, I will describe the attempt of the Commission at pushing through foreign policy actions and I will emphasize its limitations.

The Absence of a Window of Opportunity

During the 1980s, the Mediterranean was not a European foreign policy priority. It did not present substantial dangers in the eyes of the Europeans and did not challenge their policy stance. The issues that arose during the early 1970s seemed to have disappeared or to have lost much of their urgency. Little attention was paid in Europe to the deep transformations under way in the Arab countries. Economic stagnation, worsening social conditions, alienation in political debates, all these phenomena, which emerged during the period under examination here, did not reach the European shore. Neither did the Europeans detect the potentially negative impact of these issues on Euro-Mediterranean relations. Their sightline was dominated by the cold war's new stage, which although markedly less dramatic than a decade previously was enough to distract the Europeans and to bring them back to well entrenched sets of concepts. There was no cognitive uncertainty during this period, as member states were content to follow established policy frames and as a consequence, there was no window of opportunity for formulating a new EFP initiative toward the Mediterranean.

The Second Cold War

The new international climate can be summarized as follows. The Soviet invasion of Afghanistan in December 1979 marked a new stage in the cold war, often referred to as the Second cold war (e.g., Halliday 1983). The Soviet military intervention was a watershed between the previous period of détente and the following years of containment and confrontation (Garthoff 1985, 887; Di Nolfo 1994,1258) The invasion of Afghanistan unleashed tensions accumulated in previous crises, triggering a period of renewed hostility and put down to any hopes of relaunching détente. When Reagan took office in January 1981, his description of the USSR as an "evil empire" set the tone of the age. Not only did SALT II disarmament negotiations come to a halt, but the Reagan Administration started developing the Strategic Defense Initiative (SDI), which contributed to the perception that the United States had abandoned any substantial policy of arms control (Smith 1989, 167). However, Reagan did retain an interest in dialogue (Dunbabin 1994, 334ff.). His main aim was to restore American confidence in order to achieve "peace through strength" in negotiations with the Soviets (Garthoff 1985, 1013). This new attitude which depended on confronting the USSR did not, however, achieve tangible results until Gorbachev replaced Chernenko as Soviet leader in July 1985. Negotiations were then resumed in November 1985, thus bringing to an end the longest period of the postwar era in which no meeting was held (Smith and Wertman 1992, 1). Following this, international politics entered a transitional stage which, with hindsight, could be seen as anticipating the end of the cold war, although at the time no such outcome seemed likely.

European states were less supportive of this second period of the cold war, although the global frame of reference remained the anchorage of Europe in the Western camp under U.S. leadership. In spite of strongly opposing the Soviet invasion of Afghanistan and martial law in Poland, the Europeans were reluctant to jettison détente and good relations with Eastern Europe that had proved so beneficial. European détente had "different origins, wider impact, and deeper roots than the American-Soviet détente of the 1970s" (Garthoff 1985, 977). Although the Europeans condemned the developments in the communist world, they also refused to impose sanctions along the lines agreed in the United States. Instead, they tried to do "business as usual" with East European countries and even with the USSR,[1] thus profiting from continued cooperation, to the dismay of the United States. Moreover, the Europeans maintained their distaste for U.S. unilateralism. Most U.S. acts of disruption, from the imposition of sanctions to the launching of the Strategic Defence Initiative (SDI), took the Europeans by surprise, thus triggering a negative response.

European countries did, however, acknowledge the fact that European détente could not be divided from the United States-USSR confrontation, while they obviously supported the United States against the USSR. In European affairs, the debate was dominated by the deployment of intermediate-range nuclear missiles (INF). The deployment had first been demanded in the late 1970s by the Europeans, especially the United Kingdom and West Germany, to match Soviet conventional and nuclear superiority while strengthening the link between conflict in Europe and use of the U.S. nuclear arsenal (Smith 1989, 172). But then European leaders hesitated in the face of opposition from large sections of their populations and demanded an emphasis on arms negotiations. The United States helped to broker a compromise (deployment plus negotiation with the Soviets on the zero option) which, if not solving the latent tensions among Allies, did shape NATO credibility for the early 1980s (Di Nolfo 1994, 1265–1266). In international affairs too, the Europeans had little leeway and made little attempt to increase it. The few times that member states achieved a common agreement on the substance of an issue, they found it too difficult to maintain an autonomous position vis-à-vis their internal differences and the opposition of the United States.

In the Middle East, which is "the longest standing focus of European-American interaction outside Europe itself" (Allen and Smith 1989, 99), the 1980s marked a period in which transatlantic relations swung between confrontation and cooperation on the various crises of the area. From the outset, the decade seemed to be heading for confrontation, with the Venice Declaration, which sought to widen the basis for any future settlement of the Arab-Israeli conflict, by stressing the importance of a comprehensive agreement (in contrast with the bilateral approach prevailing with Camp David) and the inclusion of the Palestinians in the negotiations. It thus went against the central tenets of U.S. policy toward the area, including the increasing drift toward a harder line against terrorism. The negative reaction of the United States and of the Israelis was immediate and to be expected. Reagan's election further widened the distance between the Allies on the issue. However, if the Venice Declaration was a landmark in the development of European cooperation in foreign policy, it soon fell short of expectations as follow-on documents and missions sent to the area failed to accomplish any of their substantial aims (Garfinkle 1981, 635).

Shortly afterward, when Lebanon plunged again into a civil/regional war in 1982, transatlantic cooperation prevailed, especially in the early stages of the crisis. Having at first relied on Israel to deal with the regional turmoil, the Reagan Administration became directly embroiled in the area in an attempt to restore peace, sending peace forces while at the same time trying to reach an agreement, both to no avail, A number of European countries responded to U.S. requests for a European contribution and sent troops to the multinational force in Beirut, thus expressing their support. They acted in a similar manner in 1981 in the Sinai, and then again in 1984 in the Red Sea, and in 1987–1989 in the Gulf.

In all these cases, the Europeans intervened to support a strategy basically conceived in Washington, but lacked their own autonomy. The U.S. strategy contained flaws, the EC support was not decisive and the outcome was the eventual alienation of Western powers from the local conflicts, as well as bickering among allies. But this could not change the fact that the new stage of the cold war did not witness any independent move by the Europeans, as was particularly apparent in the Mediterranean. Against the backdrop of the new cold war, the decade marked the de facto renunciation by the European countries of the aspiration to play an autonomous role in the Mediterranean region (Guazzone 1991, 310), and fell in with the broad framework of U.S. leadership.

The passivity of the Europeans was exacerbated by the fact that previous challenges perceived as originating from the Mediterranean tended to diminish in importance during this period. The cold war itself lost much of its salience during the 1980s in the Mediterranean (Sayigh and Shlaim 1997, 5). The main region of superpower confrontation moved toward the Gulf and away from the Mediterranean. The Soviet invasion of Afghanistan seemed to indicate a new USSR interest in the northern Tier of the Middle East, a change to which the U.S. was quick to respond with the Carter doctrine. For the Arabs, the invasion of a Muslim country by Soviet troops marked another stage in the process of disillusion that the Arab countries had started experiencing. Given the lack of any manifest interest of the USSR in the southern Tier, its former clients gradually ceased to consider it a relevant player and a source of influence in the region. While at the same time recognizing the importance of the United States in the area, Arab states were also aware of the limits of the U.S. influence on Israel (Brown 1991, 10). Therefore, during the 1980s, not only did the cold war shift the focus of international attention onto a different part of the region, but also Mediterranean countries increasingly detached themselves from the dynamics of superpower confrontation.

At the same time, oil, which had represented a main European security concern in the 1970s began to lose its importance as availability increased and crude prices fell (Richards 1994). The sharp increases in oil prices that followed the two "oil shocks" of 1973 and 1979 made it profitable to exploit sources that would have otherwise been too expensive, including in the United Kingdom and in Norwegian sectors of the North Sea. Increased world competition squeezed the percentage of oil produced by OPEC countries. By 1986 OPEC was forced both to raise production ceilings and accept a lower price (Richard and Waterbury 1990, 67–68). This solution fitted nicely with European interests. All in all, "in the new circumstances the perceived political-strategic value of the southern Mediterranean neighbors to some of the Community's member states was rapidly decreasing" (Grilli 1993, 202).

As a result of this twist to a long standing problem and of the low profile of the Mediterranean in international security politics, the Europeans were content with existing policy directions and saw no uncertainty which required them to reexamine their policy goals and the means to achieve them. The elements described earlier did not challenge their understanding of world politics of Euro-Mediterranean relations or of Europe's role in them. On the contrary, the defining traits of this period drew on patterns of relations that were familiar to the Europeans. There was no questioning, no self-doubt about policy stances, no cognitive uncertainty. In other words, there was no policy window for the definition of an innovative EFP initiative toward the Mediterranean.

This is particularly striking because if we put aside the "traditional" European considerations about the cold war and oil, the southern Mediterranean and the Arab world more generally were fraught with dangerous changes. Not only did the improvement the Europeans perceived in the regional situation actually represent a worsening for the

Arab countries, but new issues also emerged, which would grow in significance during the 1980s. Looking at the world through old glasses, member states failed to spot the perils that were building across the Mediterranean. Adapting what has been said about the United States and the Iranian revolution, the Europeans looked at the Mediterranean only through cold war lenses. They seemed more concerned in "looking for the hand of Moscow"[2]—and were relieved not to find it.

Unnoticed "Real" Problems

The downgrading of the cold war and the oil crisis represented an improvement for European security, but it constituted a negative development for the Mediterranean and especially the Arab Mediterranean countries, foreshadowing bigger problems to come.

The main problem was economic. The 1980s were a "lost decade for development" (Perthes 1992, 37) for all the developing countries, Arabs included. After a period of growth and rising living standards, economic stagnation and worsening social conditions spread across all the Arab Mediterranean countries, regardless of their proclaimed differences in regime orientation. As it was written in 1984, "[c]ertainly, for the moment, the great Mediterranean boom is over."[3]

There were several reasons for this Arab stagnation. In part it was due to domestic reasons, as the ability of governments to manage their economies, and societies more generally, was severely tested (el-Malki and Santucci 1987, 3). However, the problems that all the Arab Mediterranean countries encountered were exacerbated by international economic conditions. First, the fall in oil prices, which so pleased the Europeans, represented a sharp loss of revenues for the oil-producing countries. It affected governments' spending and worsened their fiscal crisis (Luciani 1994). It also triggered a sharp decrease of aid, especially from oil-producing countries to the other Arab countries. Second, diminishing revenues were matched by a sharp increase in interest rates on the debt accumulated by all Arab Mediterranean countries in previous years. From the early 1980s, growth rates languished while debt servicing costs continued to rise (Camdessus 1984), absorbing high percentages of export revenues.[4] In the shift from the "oil decade" to the "finance decade" (Bressand 1984), the Arab Mediterranean countries largely crossed from the winning side to that of the losers. The result was that, for instance, the average GDP per head was in 1985 lower than in 1970s.[5] The recession that struck both developed and developing world at the turn of the decade made things even worse.[6]

The difficult economic situation had a significant impact on the domestic political consensus within Mediterranean countries. International economic constraints demanded tough economic choices from the regimes. These in turn were made more difficult by falling GNP and more urgent by the declining performance of state-run economies (Clawson 1992, 214). One by one all countries enacted some form of structural adjustment. Some of them had already experienced serious disequilibria in their balance of payments during the 1970s and continued to be under heavy strain in the 1980s. But by the mid-1980s, most of the Mediterranean countries attempted to restructure their economies, either as part of an IMF framework or outside of it. Turkey, Syria, Egypt, Tunisia, Algeria, Morocco, even Israel, all Mediterranean nonmembers wrestled with very similar structural adjustment programs, in spite of their diverging political foundations (Richard and Waterbury 1990, 228 ff.).

This reversal of economic fortune led to widespread social unrest and to the emergence of Islamist parties as the main opposition to the regimes in power. Street riots punctuated government attempts to cut public investment, springing from the deteriorating social conditions experienced by the population. Having previously based their ideologies largely on economic development, governments needed to address the issue of political consensus, and how to maintain or partially reform the relationship between state, society, and economy (Payne 1993, 143).

As a result of the protests and of the regimes' need to consolidate their position, Islamist movements in the Arab world gained new strength. Since the Iranian revolution of 1979, radical Islamist movements constituted a clear example of a quest for a different type of state (Kepel 2000, 123).[7] Their program questioned not only the secularity of the regimes, but also their inability to achieve social justice and welfare for their populations. As Algeria came to symbolize, the 1980s witnessed the parallel deterioration of the economic situation and the rise of Islamist protests (Vandewalle 1997). To this challenge, the Mediterranean governments were unable to respond effectively, and they oscillated between repression and collaboration with Islamist forces and Islamist themes. Moreover, the early 1980s saw the emergence of terrorism motivated by extreme Islamist movements (Wilkinson 2001), another issue that was later to concern European countries, once the cold war was over.

In the second half of the 1980s, therefore, while the international profile of the Mediterranean countries showed an improvement in terms of Western European security vis-à-vis the previous decade, the *domestic* situation of those countries already bore the seeds of problems the Europeans were to perceive acutely after the end of the cold war: economic crisis and social unrest, increasing delegitimization of Western-like policy styles, and a growing preponderance of Islamist movements in domestic politics. In this period, the "apparent paradox of stable and enduring regimes in deeply disturbed societies" (Hourani 1991, 448) ought to have been worthy of concern, but this was not the case. The Islamist opposition, which was later to become a primary issue for the Europeans, did not attract much concern. On the contrary, the support that Islamist parties lent to the fight against communism was seen as a positive element, suggesting that Islamist movements should be supported, as was indeed the case in Afghanistan.

This split between changes on the ground and European understandings of the situation serves to support my explanation of EFP making. What mattered most for the opening of a policy window was European understanding of new challenges originating from the Mediterranean, just as other challenges diminished in importance. During the 1980s, the cold war once again attracted the attention of the member states. They saw in it not only an international issue, but also an interpretative framework through which to analyze foreign affairs and, for our case, Mediterranean politics. Seen in this light, the Mediterranean posed very little challenge, and nor indeed did oil. Changes on the ground in the form of structural economic imbalances, social unrest, and increasing support for Islamist parties could (and should) have represented a cause for concern on the part of member states. But because they did not fit within the ideational framework adopted by the Europeans at the time, they went largely unnoticed. So just when it should have, no policy window opened up. Such a conclusion is difficult to understand from a materialist explanation, grounded in realism or liberal intergovernmentalism. Only by highlighting the ideational mindset that prevailed in Europe at the time can the lack of action during the 1980s be explained.

The Southern Enlargement and Its Negative Effects on Outsiders

The main contribution of member states to stability in the Mediterranean in the period under examination came in the form of the accession of Greece, Spain and Portugal, the consequences of which were particularly harsh on Mediterranean nonmembers. As regime change in the three countries cleared the political obstacles to membership, member states considered their entry into the EC as the best strategy to consolidate the area and reduce cold war tensions in the Mediterranean. However, this endeavor, which absorbed much European resources for most of the 1980s, had negative repercussions on Mediterranean noncandidate countries. Not only did the Europeans fail to acknowledge southern Mediterranean problems, they indirectly contributed to the crisis into which their southern neighbors were plunging, as they planned the southern enlargement with little attention to the countries left outside. The southern enlargement being a very positive development for both the EC and the countries involved, it led to the de facto partition of the Mediterranean because of the absence of a bridging mechanism between the "ins" and the "outs." The lack of a window of opportunity for the formulation of an initiative in this direction meant that no real compensatory measures were crafted, and a rift opened in the region.

Changes in the domestic regimes of Greece, Portugal, and Spain occurred almost simultaneously, triggering a process which culminated in EC accession. The fall of the Greek dictatorship in the summer 1974, which ended seven years of the regime of "the Colonels," paralleled the end of Salazar's dictatorship in Portugal and was followed, in November 1975, by the death of Franco in Spain. All the three countries eagerly sought EC membership as a stabilizing factor in the processes of democratization and economic modernization (Pridham 1991) into which they suddenly plunged. The EC soon realized the importance of the anchor that membership would offer to southern European transition processes. It thus engaged constructively in the accession talks. European policy makers, once the discussion about the utility of enlargement was over, began to consider its immediate implications for the EC, especially in terms of competition in agriculture in the case of Italy and southern France. Accordingly, the negotiations about the southern enlargement contained a bizarre mix of references to Greek culture with expressions of fear about peaches and courgettes (Tsoukalis 1981, 142). Perhaps unsurprisingly therefore the negotiations turned out to be long, complex, and far-reaching. Greece formally became a member by January 1, 1981, but with a transitional period of five years, while Spain and Portugal acceded by January 1, 1986, with a transitional period which varied from six to ten years according to the issue (Williams 1991, 69). Thus, during the 1980s, the "Northern Mediterranean" countries became "Southern European," and their economies, societies, and polities intermingled with the other member states.

The southern enlargement widened the cleavage between members and Mediterranean nonmembers in two ways. First, it provoked a loss in trade revenues due to trade diversion (Grilli 1993, 199).[8] Economies across the Mediterranean were (and still partly are) quite similar, both in type of industrial development (textiles, footwear, chemicals, and so on) and of agricultural production. The entry of the new members increased EC self-sufficiency in key areas of typical Mediterranean production up to 100 percent for products such as tomatoes, potatoes, olive oil (Ginsberg 1983, 160). Moreover, given the unused potential of Spain, the detriment suffered by nonmembers would only rise over time as Spanish agriculture blossomed (Swinbank and Ritson 1988). Furthermore, in the industrial field, nonmember Mediterranean countries had already suffered in 1977 and again in 1978 from restrictions imposed by the EC on imports of textiles. The entry of three south European competing economies, in the EC, was bound to worsen the situation in this domain, which was important for Turkey (73 percent of its nonagricultural exports to the EC in 1983), Cyprus (43 percent), Tunisia (28 percent), and Morocco (24 percent).[9]

The second disadvantage of Mediterranean nonmembers vis-à-vis the new "Southern European" members consisted of the positive measures enacted by the EC to increase the level of development of the new members and cushion the effects of new intra-EC competition (Tovias 1996, 19; Commission 1984, 53–54). Greece, Spain, and Portugal gradually became recipients of the benefits of the CAP. This was particularly important for Spain, as Spanish prices for "Mediterranean agricultural goods" were lower than the CAP reference prices, thus constituting an incentive for an increase in Spanish agricultural production (Hine 1988, 16ff.). Moreover, the EC agreed on "payments to existing members likely to suffer economically as a result of enlargement, and financial aid to the entrants designed to strengthen their economies and bring them closer to EC norms" (Featherstone 1989, 192). Italian and southern French farmers strove to use the opportunity to increase the substantial support of the CAP to southern European production, with a fair amount of success. Greece, having become a full member before Spain and Portugal, made its assent to their accession conditional on the adoption of the Integrated Mediterranean Programmes (IMP), which aimed at financing the medium term structural adjustment of the EC's southern regions (thus no relations with Mediterranean nonmembers) most affected by the accession of Spain and Portugal (Yannopoulos 1989; Devret 1986, 195ff.). Portugal received a special provision within the EC budget as preaccession aid. Other EC policies (regional policy, social policy, investments in agriculture) allocated a greater amount of funds to all the new entrants (Featherstone 1989, 192–195).

More broadly, during the 1980s, the member states succeeded in formulating an *active* redistributive policy toward least-favored regions. The process matured with the Single European Act, which proclaimed the aim of "strengthening the economic and social cohesion" of the EC. It led to the establishment in 1988 of the structural funds, mostly to the benefit of the southern European countries.

Therefore, while the southern enlargement fitted the cold war logic of stabilizing that part of the Mediterranean, the absence of a policy window for a broader initiative in the area meant that a rift was opened between the EC and its new members, on the one side, and the Mediterranean nonmembers on the other. The entry of Greece, Spain, and Portugal downgraded the importance in economic terms of the other Mediterranean countries in the eyes of the EC, while their political importance was also eroded by the shift toward Asia as the cold war's main theatre. While the northern Mediterranean profited hugely from accession to the EC, its consequences were partly paid for by the southern Mediterranean left outs.

Early Entrepreneurial Attempts of the Commission

The Commission was aware of the difficulties that an enlarged Community was bound to have for the Mediterranean and therefore acted in various ways to seek out a solution. This was the first time that the Commission consistently sought a solution to a foreign policy problem, by drafting documents and trying to put the issue onto the agenda. However, the absence of a window of opportunity, together with a weak entrepreneurial action on the part of the Commission, prevented any substantial initiative from being adopted.

The Commission engaged various fronts in order to determine the nature of the problem and the policy options. It commissioned a report from a team of experts, which was completed in 1984.[10] The report focused on the consequences of enlargement for the Mediterranean states and for the EC itself, and on the conditions for a forward-looking European policy toward the Mediterranean basin. The Commission drafted some proposals,[11] and on their basis, authorized by the Council on January 24, 1983, it held exploratory meetings with both applicants and nonapplicant Mediterranean countries.[12] The European Parliament too showed an interest in developments in the region.[13]

These reports drew a vivid description of the risks that enlargement was creating and of the GMP failure to avert them. In the experts' report written for the Commission, the root problem was identified as economic recession in Europe (1984, 52), which made it difficult to honor agreements taken during a period of rapid growth. The interpretation put forward by Mediterranean nonmember countries, and voiced during the Commission's exploratory talks highlighted a contrary explanation: that it was the EC reaction to recession, and the adoption of protectionist and inward-looking practices, which had soured relations. Their definition of the European space had included the applicant countries, but not the southern Mediterranean countries, which were thus excluded from EC attempts to fight recession.

From these analyses five possibilities emerged as to how to define a Mediterranean policy for the newly enlarged Community.[14] First, an open policy entailing free trade of all type of goods between the EC and partner countries, including the Mediterranean states. The EC would have coped with the consequences of more or less free imports from its Mediterranean partners and elsewhere through an active set of internal industrial policies. But this strategy was fraught with political obstacles. A second strategy would have been to offer more concessions to Mediterranean nonmembers, along the lines of the GMP, thus deepening Euro-Mediterranean relations. Clearly, this option was favored by Mediterranean nonapplicant countries. A third, pragmatic strategy would have relied on compensations to Mediterranean countries for increased EC protection. This would have meant northern European countries bearing the cost of the protectionist approach advocated by southern European member states. Fourth, the European countries could have chosen to encourage and pay for the diversification of southern Mediterranean production toward areas where there was no overlap with the EC's southern member economies. Finally, the Europeans could have simply left it to the Mediterranean countries to adjust to enlargement.

The strategy eventually adopted by the EC centered on the three less generous options, as free trade and a strengthening of Mediterranean preferences were clearly ruled out. Formally, the EC adopted Additional Protocols[15] to amend trade terms enshrined in the Cooperation Agreements signed in the 1970s, and Financial Protocols[16] renewing for the third time aid granted to Mediterranean states under the Global Mediterranean Policy. In revising the terms of trade, some temporary concessions were made on traditional exports that were competitive with southern European production and compensations were offered for trade in goods that were not competitive (Grilli 1993, 201–202, Tovias 1996, 12). In the Third Protocols on financial and technical cooperation, the emphasis was placed on the option of "complementarity and diversification," which the Commission promoted as a way of combating the food dependence of the Mediterranean countries.[17] Aid was primarily to be used for operations to develop and diversify agricultural production with a view to increasing the complementarity of the different regions around the Mediterranean sea. The total amount allocated to Third Protocols was, at first sight, greatly increased vis-à-vis the previous generation of protocols, rising from about 1 billion ECU to 1.6 billion ECU. However, on a closer look, this improvement merely offset the effects of inflation on the amounts of aid offered while taking account of the accession of Spain and Portugal (Tovias 1996, 12). Apart from these two aspects, Mediterranean nonmembers had to make their own adjustments.

Ultimately, the EC approach recalibrating Euro-Mediterranean relations to the southern enlargement did not constitute a coherent strategy (if indeed it was a strategy at all). It marked an attempt to stop the erosion of preferences and to return to both "the spirit and the letter" of the GMP. It did so by restating some of the principles already addressed in the GMP, including agricultural and industrial concessions and cooperation policies (Pierros et al. 1999, 105). Other suggestions and strategies, which would have entailed a radical change in Euro-Mediterranean relations, such as the free trade option or the strengthening of relations, received little attention. The burden of adjustment was, in fact, left to Mediterranean nonmember countries while the EC was more concerned with bringing the enlargement to a successful conclusion for member states and with the achievement of the Single Market by 1992 (Grilli 1993, 203; Tovias 1996, 12).

Conclusions

The 1980s witnessed the "construction of a rift." Rather than shrinking the distances between the EC and its southern neighbors, the accession of Greece, Spain, and Portugal created a new set of legal, political, and economic borders of the EC, and in its wake crystallized a North/South split. The GMP and the EAD launched in the 1970s aimed at defining a common economic and political space across the Mediterranean. However, the instruments devised were neither robust nor effective enough to stand the test of difficult times. Grounded mainly in economics, they offered neither the time nor the means to tighten overall links between the EC and Mediterranean nonmembers. Thus, as Greece, Spain, and Portugal applied for EC membership, their newly acquired status resulted in a rift in the Mediterranean between the "ins" and the "outs."

The Europeans were unable to conceive a new vision for an enlarged EC in the Mediterranean because they looked at the area through the old lenses of the cold war, which entered a second "hot" stage during this period. Moreover, nothing occurred to challenge their thinking. While the United States behaved along conventional cold war lines, expecting European solidarity particularly in the crises that beset the region, with the exception of the Venice Declaration member states mainly ended up following both a U.S. mindset and leadership in the region, whatever the mumbled criticisms they voiced against American policy. Moreover, this cold war reading meant that despite the signs of disintegration from the USSR to the Arab states the Europeans failed to detect any real problem in the Mediterranean. Even the oil weapon, which had been so effective in the previous decade, lost its edge under pressure from an increasing number of free riders. As a result the Europeans failed to spot emerging challenges in the shape of economic underdevelopment, social unrest, the loss of regimes' legitimacy, and the ascendance of Islamist opposition, and continued to regard the area as relatively secure. The Commission was the sole actor to perceive the difficulties of the Mediterranean nonapplicant states in relation to southern enlargement (but not to the other issues explored here). Its weak entrepreneurship did not, however, allow it to produce significant innovation.

Therefore, this was a case of "dogs that did not bark." It showed that in times of no newly perceived challenges, the European member states did not rouse themselves to develop a common vision for the whole Mediterranean. The presence of a weak entrepreneur made no difference given there was no policy window. The initiatives finally adopted did not amount to a coherent strategy and simply replicated in a "lighter" version principles already enshrined in the GMP.

This chapter contributes to the clarification of two analytical and theoretical points. First, the opening of a policy window is linked to the Europeans' understanding of Mediterranean challenges, rather than to changes on the ground. This counters materialistic explanations that would have expected a more active concern by Europeans for the domestic situation in Mediterranean nonmembers. While the relevance of the cold war might seem to lend support to realist explanations, I argue that instead what mattered most was the framework of ideas represented by the cold war, as those lenses distorted the Europeans' understanding of the Mediterranean. Second, the analysis of this period shows that without a policy window, little could be achieved. As member states were more interested in planning the southern enlargement and finding a position in the international context of the "second" cold war, they were not available to discuss Euro-Mediterranean relations. Therefore, the activism of the Commission failed against the passive disinterest of member states, in contrast to the passive availability that characterizes a policy window. Finally, the Commission's entrepreneurial efforts conformed to supranational/neofunctional explanations of European integration. The Commission did attempt to raise the issue of Euro-Mediterranean relations and managed to have the Financial Protocols updated. What it failed to do was to launch a process leading to new understandings of Euro-Mediterranean relations. Its entrepreneurship was instead confined to restating existing principles. Still, these entrepreneurial traits were to resurface shortly afterward, and thanks to the demise of the cold war, they were to have more significant effects the next time around.

CHAPTER 5

The New Post–Cold War Activism

Introduction

The end of the cold war opened a new period of EC/EU activism toward the Mediterranean. After neglecting their relations with the Mediterranean nonmembers during the southern enlargement of the EC, European countries and EC/EU representatives began to devote more attention to their southern neighbors. More importantly, they started to debate the utility and the feasibility of a new EFP initiative. New ideas were circulated, new options considered. The overall process of policy formulation lasted longer than in the previous episodes of the GMP and of the EAD. It began with an interesting but limited policy initiative, the Renovated Mediterranean Policy (RMP),[1] adopted in 1990. It then tentatively focused on a more imaginative partnership, which was however limited to the Maghreb. Finally, the idea was expanded to the whole Mediterranean, and the EU launched the Euro-Mediterranean Partnership (EMP) in November 1995, in Barcelona, in the presence of 27 ministers of Foreign Affairs.[2] Since 2004 a debate has evolved over the European Neighbourhood Policy (ENP), which is supposed to complement the EMP.

What triggered and then sustained the process of policy formulation between the end of the 1980s and 1995? How are we to understand why, following a long period of neglect, the EC/EU once again put the Mediterranean at the top of its foreign policy agenda? What conditions made the launching of the RMP and then the EMP likely and possible? Which policy entrepreneur(s) contributed to push the Mediterranean up the European agenda, and what kind of negotiations among partners led to the adoption of the EMP and then of the ENP?

It is a truism that the window of opportunity which opened at the end of the 1980s was a direct consequence of the ending of the cold war. The idea that existing patterns of Euro-Mediterranean relations could be improved arose out of the overall attempt to rethink world order and Europe's role within it. The analytical challenge lies in understanding exactly why and how the end of East/West confrontation came to affect North/South relations in the Mediterranean. The policy window opened as the Europeans came to perceive new security challenges, namely migration, Islamic fundamentalism, and a new form of terrorism as the cold war faded into history. European governments and EC/EU representatives were uncertain about how to frame these new phenomena and, as was the case in the early 1970s, they shared a situation of cognitive uncertainty.

Within this structural context, Spain was the most central entrepreneur, as it sought to have its new status of "democratic middle power" acknowledged by the other European countries. Supporting Spain in sparking a process of interaction among member states was France, the Commission, and at times Italy, all playing different roles. Together they were better at coordinating their actions than in the 1970s and they operated over a longer time span than in the 1970s. This provides an interesting test of the approach sketched in chapter 1. I will show that states have been stronger entrepreneurs than the Commission, but their activism has been linked to ideational reasons more than to material interests. The analysis of the role played by national entrepreneurs is also quite distinctive, because it stresses how this came to potentially have supranational effects.

Moreover, the final product was the outcome of a collective effort among member states and EC/EU institutions, which I have aimed at capturing under the label of cognitive interaction. Several principles converged to produce the final shape of the EMP and the process addressed cognitive aspects, through framing, before turning into a more traditional style of bargaining.

The analysis of these years and of the process leading to the EMP and of the ENP thus develops along the line of the conditions I have put forward in chapter 1. The articulation of new political and security perceptions pushed the region up the EC/EU agenda in the early 1990s. The most effective entrepreneurship was provided mainly by a single member state, though working in conjunction with the Commission and other member states. The debate evolved by contextualizing ideas, elaborating new concepts, and establishing conceptual parallels.

The question that will remain open at the end of this chapter is about the ENP, which is a policy still in the making. It was conceived and framed in the context of the run up to the 2004 enlargement, and has included the Mediterranean almost as an afterthought. Whether the ENP possesses the potential to change the main tenets of the EMP is a matter that only time will tell. Its impact seems to be a watering down of the EMP framework and a partial redirection of the EU's efforts, without amounting to a "new" initiative as defined in this book.

The chapter is divided as follows. In the first section, I analyze the conditions that led to the opening of a policy window, focusing on the politicization and securitization of migration, as well as the parallel politicization of Islamic fundamentalism, and of forms of terrorism connected to it. I then examine divergences in perspectives between the Europeans and the United States, on the one hand, and among the Europeans, on the other. In the following section, I focus in depth on policy entrepreneurship, analyzing the limits of the Commission's efforts and the meaning of Spain's entrepreneurship. The chapter then analyses the debate within the EC/EU leading to the adoption of the EMP and it outlines the main elements of the EMP. The chapter will then briefly assess the genesis and potential significance of the ENP.

Geography and the End of the Cold War: New Perceptions or New Dangers?

The end of the cold war and the fading away of the Soviet threat from the second half of the 1980s deeply affected Euro-Mediterranean relations and triggered in various ways a new period of activism by European countries toward the Mediterranean nonmembers. This culminated in the launch of the Euro-Mediterranean Partnership. The most direct consequence was a radical transformation of the European definition of security vis-à-vis dangers and challenges emanating from the southern neighbors at the beginning of the 1990s and a change in European security perceptions toward the Mediterranean nonmembers. As the veil of the cold war was lifted the Europeans became aware of the problems that plagued the area and fretted at the risk they posed to European security.

The relative importance and urgency of oil and terrorism had diminished since they had reached the top of the political agenda in the early 1970s. Twenty years on European attention focused on different issues. Migration, Islamic fundamentalism and terrorism linked to Islamic fundamentalism were the three themes that monopolized the debate about Euro-Mediterranean relations at the turn of the decade. The military and economic dimension of security thus dropped to the bottom of the agenda while societal security (migration) and political aspects of security (Islamic fundamentalism and its terrorist spin-offs) climbed to the top. The cognitive uncertainty about the newly perceived challenges and how to tackle them created a window of opportunity for redefining policy options toward the Mediterranean.

In this section, I will explore the changes in European perceptions and how the changing definition of security in the period between late-1980 and 1995 affected the formulation of EFP toward the Mediterranean countries. Usually there was a time lag between the appearance of the underlying phenomena and their perception in the European public sphere. There was, in other terms, a split between the emergence of a phenomenon in Mediterranean nonmember countries and its reception in ideational terms by Europeans, which at times was particularly acute. This will confirm the hypothesis I have drawn about the ideational side being the most important for explaining European foreign policy making.

Desecuritizing the Military

The most evident desecuritization process of this period occurred in the military sphere. The years following the end of the cold war saw a tremendous change, in terms of reorganizing and downsizing all armies in Western Europe. As a first step, all governments cut military spending, cashing in on the "peace dividend." This did not lead, however, to a complete dismantling of military apparatuses. The new world ushered by the end of the cold war still presented challenges, which had the potential to escalate into crises. But the nature of those challenges tended not to be primarily military. While the military sphere was thus desecuritized, some military means were put in place to cope with nonmilitary crises. As a consequence, the reorganization of (diminished) forces was designed to create more flexible units. The Mediterranean epitomized this trend. Western European capacities remained vastly superior to the limited regional strike capacity by southern Mediterranean countries, which could no longer count on Soviet backing. Still, the area appeared as a source of instabilities for Europe. The early 1990s is thus a period in which the Europeans cut their military forces while establishing multilateral reaction forces that could be deployed if necessary to face southern nonmilitary challenges.

The U.S. military presence in the Mediterranean, while downsized, remained impressive, with the maintenance of most of its bases in the region and the presence of the Sixth Fleet. The Soviet presence collapsed along with the political upheavals of the country and its satellites.

NATO entered in 1990 a period of profound rethinking of its mission, which included a redefinition of security contained in the 1991 new Strategic Concept and the identification of new types of dangers.[3] The reorganization of NATO took in the rebuilding of the Allied Forces Southern Europe (AFSOUTH), which had among its tasks containment toward the South (Gama 1995, 189). Less effectively, NATO also launched a Mediterranean initiative in 1994, intended to explain to southern countries the meaning of the new NATO profile.

All Western European countries carried out comprehensive military reviews, cutting defense spending, while modernizing part of the weaponry.[4] France entered a period of upheaval of its military organization. Since 1991, it began a process of reapproachment to NATO institutions. It also published a White Book on defense in 1994, an exceptional sign of soul-searching on the part of French policy makers.[5] Its ground forces were to go from 290,000 in 1991 to 225,000 in 1997. Belgium abolished conscription in 1994 and reduced its armed forces from 85,000 to 47,000. It partially modernized its weaponry, while selling off large quantities of arms. Denmark began in 1989 a comprehensive modernization plan, which also included a reduction in strength. Germany, also as a consequence of reunification, underwent a massive reorganization and a substantial reduction of manpower. As agreed in the Two-plus-Four talks that accompanied reunification, German forces went from a total (East and West Germany) of 620,000 to 370,000 in 1995 (Schmitt 1993, 53). Italy planned a cut of 25 percent of its armed forces within the framework of a broad reorganization plan that also abolished conscription. The Netherlands too announced in 1991 a reduction of armed forces by 30 percent by 2000, and ended conscription in 1997. Similarly, in 1990 Portugal announced a program of reorganization and downsizing. Slightly later than the other European countries, Greece and Spain underwent similar sweeping changes, which in Spain entailed a 40 percent cut in manpower of armed forces. In the United Kingdom, the "Options for Change" program was completed by September 1994. As a consequence, the Armed Forces manpower in June 1994 was down to 254,000 compared with 306,000 in 1990. While manpower had been reduced, weaponry was however much improved.[6]

In southern Europe joint initiatives such as EUROFOR and EUROMARFOR emerged, and part of the military arsenal previously directed at the Soviet menace was redirected against the southern "arc of crisis" (Lesser 1995, 22). However on the whole, southern Mediterranean countries, although constituting the perfect seedbed for spreading weapons of mass destruction and unconventional armaments, did not represent a structured threat to European countries, nor were their military capabilities perceived as a serious military challenge. In fact, despite the military initiatives, southern European countries shared a sense of superiority vis-à-vis their southern neighbors (Gillespie 1999, 162; Aliboni 1992, 8). One of the few certitudes amid the transformations of this period was "la disparition de toute menace [militaire] continentale majeure"[7] (de la Gorce 1993, 15). Problems were expected to come from "crises économiques et sociales, avec leurs prolongements ethniques ou religieux,"[8] and this might affect an area stretching from Morocco to the Indian Ocean (de la Gorce 1993, 15).[9] The main military risks in the Mediterranean did, in fact, remain South/South, rather than North/South, although regional rivalries could indirectly affect Europe. On this point, the literature is unanimous (e.g., Khader 1994; Aliboni 1996; Tanner 1996). The general opinion in military circles was that there was little military threat in the world after the end of the cold war, and especially so in the Mediterranean.[10]

The Challenge of Migration

Migration was, on the contrary, the hot new topic in Euro-Mediterranean relations. In the early 1970s migration was considered to be instrumental to economic development in northern European countries and it did not raise any specific concern.[11] Between the end of the 1980s and the beginning of the 1990s, a radical change took place in European perceptions. Framed in new terms, it was portrayed as a threat to the security of European citizens. Migration made it to the front pages of newspapers, and warnings of a "flood" of immigrants appeared to feed a collective sense of insecurity. Policy makers faced the task of keeping the situation "under control." The increasing unease of Europeans toward migrants is thus interesting in terms of security and of the cognitive uncertainty that the change entailed. It formed part of the puzzles that brought European policy makers to the EU table to discuss initiatives for the Mediterranean. I will illustrate this *destruens* process by making use of three indicators: (1) the relative increase in the numbers of migrants from Mediterranean countries; (2) the heated domestic debates about migration; (3) changes in legislation about migration and about powers entrusted to the police and the army to deal with it. The focus will be mainly on France, Germany, Italy, and Spain, which represent cases of countries where immigration is "traditional" and new in type. The section concludes with a focus on European debates about migration and the Mediterranean, to contextualize the parallel discussions about European foreign policy initiatives toward the area.

An analysis of Mediterranean migrants, in other words citizens of Mediterranean nonmember states resident in the EU, shows that in certain countries there was a long wave upwards, which culminated in the early 1990s and then began to diminish (tables 5.1, 5.2, 5.3, 5.4).[12] This curve was visible in the case of Germany, France, and Italy. Exceptions to this trend were migrants from Turkey and Moroccans settling in Spain.

Table 5.1 Germany, Stock of Foreign Population from Mediterranean Nonmembers and Total, by Nationality (Thousands)

	1985	1986	1987	1988	1989	1990	1991	1992	1993	1994	1995
Turkey	1,401.9	1,434.3	1,453.7	1,523.7	1,612.6	1,694.6	1,779.6	1,854.9	1,918.9	1,956.6	2,014.3
Morocco	48.1	52	47.3	52.1	61.8	69.6	75.1	80.3	82.2	82.4	81.9
Tunisia	23.2	23.6	20.6	21.6	24.3	26.1	27.2	28.1	28.1	27.4	26.4
Algeria	5.3	5.4	4.7	5.1	5.9	7.4	9.1	13.4	23.1	19.1	17.7
Lebanon	13.2	21.9	18.8	22.3	30.1	47.1	50.9	53.5	55.1	54.3	54.8
Total extra EU	2,839.9	3,148	3,000.1	3,213.2	3,520.5	3,709.9	4,395	4,982.1	5,342.5	5,214.2	5,362.2

Source: SOPEMI, various years. Data from 1987 to 1989 have been adjusted, taking into account results of the population census in 1987. Population counts cover Western Germany are only up to 1990 and Germany as a whole from 1991 on. Ethnic Germans are considered as nationals in statistics on migration.

Table 5.2 France, Stock of Foreign Population from Mediterranean Nonmembers and Total, by Nationality (Thousands)

	1982	1990	1999
Algeria	805.1	614.2	477.5
Morocco	441.3	572.7	504.1
Tunisia	190.8	206.3	154.4
Turkey	122.3	197.7	208
Total extra EU	2,119.4	2,284.7	2,067.7

Source: SOPEMI, various years, from Population Census.

Table 5.3 Italy, Stock of Foreign Population from Mediterranean Nonmembers and Total, by Nationality (Thousands)

	1985	1986	1987	1988	1989	1990	1991	1992	1993	1994	1995
Morocco	2.6	2.9	15.7	23.5	26.8	78	90.6	95.6	97.6	92.6	94.2
Tunisia	4.4	4.9	12	14.6	14.1	41.2	47.6	50.5	44.5	41.1	40.5
Egypt	7	7.2	11	12.6	10.2	19.8	22.7	23.5	24.6	21.2	21.9
Total extra EU	*423*	*450.2*	*572.1*	*645.4*	*490.4*	*632.5*	*751.4*	*776.8*	*834.4*	*781.1*	*827.4*

Source: SOPEMI, various years.

Data are adjusted to take account of the regularizations, which occurred in 1987–1988 and 1990, explaining the dramatic increases in those years. The decreases observed for 1989 and 1994 are partially a result of a clean-up of the register of foreigners. The trend is thus more linear than it is possible to render.

Table 5.4 Spain, Stock of Foreign Population from Mediterranean Nonmembers and Total, by Nationality (Thousands)

	1985	1986	1987	1988	1989	1990	1991	1992	1993	1994	1995
Morocco	5.8	8.6	11.2	11.9	9.1	11.4	49.5	54.1	61.3	63.9	74.9
Total extra EU	*98.5*	*122.2*	*141.4*	*151.5*	*104.7*	*114.2*	*202.6*	*220*	*238.3*	*251.2*	*264.2*

Source: SOPEMI, various years.

Numbers of foreigners with a residence permit. Permits of short duration (less than six months) and students are not included. The decrease in 1989 is the result of a clean-up of the register of foreigners. In 1991 data includes 108,372 permits delivered following a regularization program.

The overall number of migrants coming from outside the EU to settle in Europe underwent profound changes at the end of the 1980s. Legal migration increased first and then slowed in the early 1990s, with the notable exception of Germany. The number of asylum seekers however continued to rise, as the EU attracted large numbers from the countries of the former Yugoslavia, from Eastern Europe, and from the former Soviet Union, a trend which was most marked in Germany. Therefore, the debate about Mediterranean migrations was entangled in a much wider debate about migration and asylum.

These elements led to heated debates and in time to increased security measures. The terms of the debate differed according to the traditional immigration trend of immigration in each country. The problem in northern European countries with a long tradition of immigration, such as France and Germany, consisted of how to address the increased presence and visibility of settled migrants, while blocking the arrival of new immigrants. Southern European countries experienced a true revolution, as they shifted from witnessing net outflows to net inflows of migrants (Montanari and Cortese 1993, 218–223; King 2000, 8). In the latter case, while the ratio of flows and stocks of migrants to the population as a whole was lower than in other member states,[13] the change entailed a rethinking of southern European societies.[14] The outcome of domestic debates was however very similar, and advocated tighter border controls and measures to maintain internal order (Brochmann and Hammer 1999, 12). The usual reaction of member states was to step up external and internal security measures, in successive waves, in an attempt to appease nervous public opinion.

Germany exemplified this dilemma very well. Migrant numbers increased, though generally not from the Mediterranean, but due to a surge in flows from the former communist block.[15] Between 1990 and 1995, the number of German residents from the former Yugoslavia rose from 662,700 to 1,298,800, while the population from Eastern Europe (e.g., Romania, Hungary, Bulgaria, and former Soviet Union) doubled in size. At the same time, the fall of the Berlin Wall led to an open door policy for ethnic Germans living in Eastern Europe. These various factors took a toll on German society. During the early 1990s, police reports indicated a daily average of 50–100 antiforeigner incidents (Martin 1994, 189). Among them, the infamous arson attacks in November 1992 in Mölln, and in May 1993 in Solingen in which eight Turks died. The arguments, in fact, often unfolded in the streets, where broad antiracist demonstrations and xenophobia challenged the public discourse of civilized welcome. Meanwhile, extreme right-wing parties managed to obtain representation in European, Länder, and local elections, between 1989 and 1990 (Del Fabbro 1995, 139–141) and by the early 1990s immigration had become "perhaps the major social issue in Germany" (Martin 1994, 190).

The result was an ongoing process of ever tightening legislation. One of the first reactions to the fall of the Berlin Wall was the strengthening of border controls and restrictions or the dismantling of cooperation program toward Eastern European countries (Thränhardt 1999, 30). Similarly, Germany negotiated a series of tougher regulations of migration from Turkey, while at the same time opposing Turkey's membership of the EU on the issue of movement of people (Martin 1994, 207). In 1993, Germany changed its Aliens Law and reduced access to asylum seekers, while striving to neutralize at least a proportion of long standing Turkish residents.

In France too, restriction and control of foreign entries was a significant issue. Between 1984 and 1993, the debate was often framed as a police more than a policy matter (Hollifield 1999, 68). Charles Pasqua became the symbol of this approach, because of the two laws he passed, one in 1986 and then again in 1993 as minister of the Interior. In 1986, he granted new powers to the police, especially to the *Police de l'Air et des Frontières* in charge of border controls. In June 1993, he announced "zero immigration," thus expressing the desire to stem completely the flows of population especially those arriving from North Africa (Hargreaves 1995, 1).[16] As part of the law on immigration approved in August 1993, he strengthened police powers to carry out identity checks on foreigners (Horton 1995, 46, 51). All applications for residence were now "examined in terms of the threat to public order" (SOPEMI 1996). In April 1994, new provisions were agreed with Algeria, the traditional country of origin of immigrants in France. These restricted the access and stay of Algerians in France, including for family reasons. The new agreement apparently also included a readmission clause, by which Algeria agreed to take back illegal immigrants coming from its territory (Collinson 1996, 60). Even in the case of the "most mature immigration relationship" (Papademetrious and Hamilton 1996, 30) and in spite of falling numbers of Algerian residents, therefore, border restrictions were imposed out of security concerns.

Migration became a major factor in Italian politics in late 1989 and early 1990 (Bonifazi 2000, 241; Trasdanidis and Guerra 2000, 332), when violence against African immigrants increased sharply, paralleled by political clashes about how to address the issue. The sense of crisis became particularly acute in 1991, when two consecutive waves of Albanian immigration brought around 40,000 people to the shores of Apulia, demonstrating how vulnerable the Italian coast was to the unexpected and unwanted arrival of foreigners from the Mediterranean sea (Papademetriou and Hamilton 1996, 41). Populist discourses, such as those proclaimed by Lega Nord and by the Italian Social Movement (MSI—later Alleanza Nazionale), stoked the political debate. In this period, the Lega Nord repeatedly threatened to overturn the government on migration issues. Laws were tightened in 1990, with new provisions being approved and visa requirements introduced for potential migrants from Maghreb countries.

Moreover, the reaction was increasingly cast in security terms. The second wave of Albanians was forcefully repatriated and since then the Italian government has regularly called on the army and the navy to patrol borders against migration from Albania, Tunisia, and other countries (Sciortino 1999, 245; Barravecchia 1996, 215). Extended powers were also granted to the police force which was also granted an increase in its numbers (SOPEMI 1996, 122). While pursuing a complex process of integration of migrants into Italian society, in the crucial years under examination Italy approached migration on the basis of emergency measures and of a crisis mentality (Bonifazi 2000, 242). As emphasized by several participant observers, the government filed the issue under the label "public order and security."[17]

Spain was the only country where migration from Mediterranean nonmembers continued to increase at a steady pace after 1993. Migration from Morocco seemed to follow a similar pattern to Franco-Algerian and German-Turkish relations. Violence against migrants or tragic deaths among those who attempted to cross the Straits of Gibraltar focused attention on the numbers arriving and on the vulnerability of borders and internal order (Arango 2000, 270), demanding an instant response from the state. Mandatory visas for migrants from North Africa were introduced in 1991. Moreover, Spain negotiated a readmission treaty with Morocco in 1992. It was accompanied by high-level consultation and a beefing up of Moroccan surveillance on its northern shores (Collinson 1996, 58–59). Quotas were introduced in 1993 for foreign workers originating from outside the EU, while in the same year family reunification was made more difficult. In 1994, the law on asylum was amended, in an attempt to bring legislation into line with international standards before the phenomenon could increase further. Also, pressure was applied to the employers of illegal workers, leading to a substantial clamp down on some sectors of the black economy (SOPEMI 1996). From 1995 onwards, Spain aimed to create an effective barrier to protect its enclaves on Moroccan territory, that is, Ceuta and Melilla, to stop entry of illegal immigrants from there.

Therefore, the early 1990s were undoubtedly a time in which policy makers pored over the question of what to do about migration. From early efforts in France in 1986 to the waves of reforms introduced in the 1990s, laws changed, regularization processes were introduced and party politics reflected heightened societal sensibilities about foreigners. It could be argued that governments were implementing an effective plan, which in fact led to a decrease in numbers, at least in the case of the Mediterranean. However, if we view what took place in terms of public opinion, the issue remained far from settled.

In other terms, the shift change of migration from a rather private issue to the political and, more often than not, security arena, led European governments and more generally policy makers to experience cognitive uncertainty. National preferences were questioned and deconstructed as migration acquired new dimensions. The domestic process of formulating new preferences (understanding of the problem, definition of preferred outcomes, and the means to reach it) did not proceed smoothly. National preferences on the migration issue continued to be deconstructed and tentatively reconstructed over a few years. In this period, member states were uncertain about how to conceptualize the phenomenon and what to do about it. Thus, the politicization and at times low securitization of migration opened a window of opportunity for a common debate about the phenomenon and its causes.

Where and how could a common debate develop? The issue could be dealt with in a number of policy arenas, such as immigration/interior affairs, or more of interest to us here, foreign policy. The first major step in the direction of a common European debate came with the signature of the Schengen agreement, in June 1985, initially agreed upon by France, Germany, and the Benelux countries (Geddes 2000, 80ff.). In the run up to its entry into force, the agreement in practice entailed yet another reinforcement of security and internal control systems to compensate for the waiving of intra-EU controls (Brochmann and Hammer 1999, 308). In parallel, the creation of a third pillar devoted to Justice and Home Affairs with the Maastricht Treaty gave new scope to the EU to regulate the issue. The Council in fact aimed to construct a readmission zone around the EU, thus shifting part of the control burden onto neighboring states (Lavenex and Uçarer 2002).

The debate developed also in international fora such as the G7, the OECD and the Council of Europe (Cagiano de Azevedo 1994, 5). The Western European Union (WEU) too included migration in the list of "general [security] problems" in Euro-Mediterranean relations to which attention had to be paid.[18]

The link between security and migration was particularly clear in EU documents referring to the Mediterranean. Migration was perceived to open the door not only to people, but also and especially to all the problems which were associated with Mediterranean societies. In May 1991, the European Parliament passed a resolution on Europe's role in Mediterranean security,[19] which mentioned population explosion and increasing migration among the causes of insecurity. In October 1991, the Commission joined the debate, elaborating on the issues of demographic pressure, controls, restriction, and the integration of resident migrant-origin populations.[20] It pointed to European foreign policy as a key instrument to ease "migratory pressures." Mediterranean migration was included as a security problem also in a document about the future of the EC/EU, issued in 1992.[21] In the same year, the Economic and Social Committee emphasized the need to step up economic cooperation with the Maghreb countries to avoid consequences in terms of migration.[22] By then, migration had become a strong motivation for addressing the Mediterranean.

Islamic Fundamentalism, Terrorism, and other European Fears

Migration came to be seen as a security concern also because it was linked to an issue which was also moving up the political agenda: Islamic fundamentalism. European debates depicted Islamic fundamentalism as posing a threat not only in the form of Islamic fundamentalists in Arab countries challenging the West and Western-friendly regimes, but also by creating a dangerous "fifth column" of radical Muslims at Europe's core.[23] I will show the increasing salience and politicization of Islamic fundamentalism by making use of three indicators: (1) France's reaction to the 1991 Algerian elections; (2) a mention of the academic debate on the "clash of civilizations"; (3) NATO's strategic concept presented in 1991.

The external dimension of the perceived danger surfaced at the time of the Gulf War in 1991, which showed strong support even among some Arab countries for Saddam Hussein against the U.S.-led coalition (Moratinos 1999, 40). Many, for instance, interpreted the refusal of Algeria and Tunisia to join the coalition as "another sign that Islamic fundamentalism was gaining ground in North Africa" (Pierros et al. 1999, 150). For many in Europe, as well as in the Arab world, the conflict was a "struggle over values" (Kelsay 1993, 26–27). In Western Europe, the Gulf War entrenched anti-Arab and anti-Islamic attitudes (Collinson 1996, 42), thus contributing in Europe to establish a (false) equation "Arab = Islam = Islamic fundamentalism."

The prospect of a confrontation between Islamic fundamentalists and Western Europe seemed to materialize when the FIS (*Front islamique du salut*) won the first round of elections in Algeria in December 1991, thus paving its entry into government. Algeria seemed on the verge of becoming an Islamic state, a possibility that shocked European public opinion. The military coup, which occurred shortly afterward to put an end to the democratic experience, was greeted in most of Western Europe as the ultimate way to stop the fundamentalists. The issue refused to go away, however, as Islamic fundamentalists waged a war of terror against the Algerian civil population and against Western citizens regarded as supporting the regime.[24]

Governments in Western Europe strove to limit the danger of the Algerian civil war spilling into Europe. France declared fundamentalism a domestic threat and arrested Islamic militants suspected of supplying arms to Algerian Islamists (Esposito 1999, 98). Moreover, for fear of a radicalization of its Muslim communities, the French government drastically reduced the number of visas granted to Algerians of all political inclinations. It also fought any open expression of support for the FIS and quarreled with Germany and the United States over their admission of FIS representatives. Moreover, French officials entered into discussions with their counterparts in Italy and Spain to draft emergency plans in case of a sudden exodus of refugees (Collinson 1996, 46).

The Algerian crisis was the most pressing issue, but not the only one raising the question of relations between the West and Islam. Why was this apparent rift opening between the two? What did it mean for Western countries and societies? How should the West react? These questions, typical of a period marked by cognitive uncertainty, received an academic answer in Huntington's thesis of the "clash of civilizations." The approach advanced by Huntington (1993, 1996) suggested that the enmity between the West (or Christianity) and Islam was in fact a constant element of international politics. "Each has been the other's Other" (Huntington, 1993, 209) and this he claimed was particularly true of the early 1990s (see also Lesser 1995, 22–24; Tibi 1998, 43; Ahmed 1992, 264; Buzan 1991).[25]

It might have remained a purely scholarly debate, if it had not found an echo in other quarters. Probably the strongest indication of securitization, if only partial and at a low level, is NATO's Strategic Concept, presented in November 1991. While downplaying purely military aspects, it emphasized a "broad concept of security," including ethnic and religious factors. In the case of the Mediterranean, Secretary General Manfred Wörner was reported to have identified the key threats as overpopulation, religious extremism, migration, terrorism, and proliferation of arms of mass destruction.[26] Experts began to talk about NATO's southern "front," instead of the southern "flank." NATO underwent a partial reorganization, which revised some security structures (Gama 1995, 192) with the creation of confidence-building measures such as the Mediterranean Dialogue, launched in February 1995. At the press conference that launched the Dialogue, the new Secretary General, Willy Claes, claimed that following the collapse of the Soviet Union, Islamic fundamentalism now posed the major threat to the Alliance.[27] In his view, this was the main rationale behind the launching of the Mediterranean Dialogue (Aliboni 1998, 118).[28] In spite of the negative reactions that such statements attracted from inside and outside NATO, it did indicate the extent to which Western policymakers applied the concept of security to Islamic fundamentalism, migration, and terrorism.

In the early 1990s Islamic fundamentalism was, therefore, perceived as a challenge to political order inside and outside European borders. It did not raise the same level of heated debate as migration did in the same period, and full securitization of the phenomenon was to come only much later, with 9/11. It was perceived in different ways across Europe, with some parts of societies being more concerned about it than others. Moreover, there was no deconstruction of previous national preferences, as the issue was relatively new to political debates in Europe. It is thus even more difficult than usual to record the level of uncertainty that existed at the time. More than elsewhere in this book, the definition of cognitive uncertainty about Islamic fundamentalism is indirect and it relies on indicators of politicization and low securitization. Still, it was part of a growing trend of concern toward the Mediterranean and of the debate about "what to do" with it.

Immigration and Islamic fundamentalism were linked to a third aspect that, although not new in European security perceptions, acquired a new momentum in the early 1990s: terrorism. The problem came to public attention in the early 1970s when the Israeli-Palestinian conflict struck on European ground.[29] By the end of the cold war, armed Palestinian resistance and state-sponsored terrorism on behalf of Palestine had more or less collapsed (Joffé 1996, 142). More generally, since the late 1980s, terrorism had declined steadily (Deutch 1997, 10). However, in the early 1990s, it resurfaced in European debates, in the form of a possible attack by Islamic fundamentalists on European soil. The aspiration of fundamentalists to spread Islam "from below" constituted the perfect seedbed for terrorist attacks, as demonstrated by the cases of *Hamas* in the Gaza Strip, the FIS in Algeria, and the *Jama'at Islamiyya* in Egypt (Joffé 1996, 154). The networks created by migrants, especially if socialized to radical Islam, potentially expanded the scope of attacks to European ground. Therefore, European governments began to fear Islamist terrorist attacks linked to political instability in the Mediterranean.

This fear appeared to be justified by the campaign that the GIA (Armed Islamic Group) launched against French and Western citizens in 1993, to punish Western support for the Algerian regime. Moreover, in December 1994, the GIA hijacked an Air France airbus and threatened to blow it up with its 283 passengers over Paris, before the GIGN[30] managed to storm the aircraft (Wilkinson 2001, 162). Algerian extremists conducted a terrorist campaign again in Paris in August 1995.

While the broad phenomenon of terrorism was not new, this new format fed member states' uncertainty about how to fight terrorism at its roots. Police tactics were already in place, but it was not clear how to counter the ideological dimension. Even if the final political aims of terrorism throughout Europe had shifted from a secular to a religious ideology, the strategy to counter it in practical terms did not. Terrorism remained one of the reasons behind European police cooperation and the institutionalization of the EU sector of Justice and Home Affairs (Walker 1998, 176). In particular, terrorism evoked issues of migration when Europeans addressed the Mediterranean (King 1998, 120), and that, together with Islamic fundamentalism, constituted a strong drive toward the adoption of a new initiative toward the area.

Few other issues, apart from migration, Islamic fundamentalism and terrorism, deserve a mention in the analysis of European security perceptions in the early 1990s. Economic exchanges did not attract much attention, as the Europeans maintained the upper hand in the balance. In 1994, Mediterranean exports to Europe represented roughly half of the Mediterranean total, but only 5.6 percent of European imports. Moreover, as European exports totaled 7.6 percent of the European total, the balance of payments remained in favor of the EU (Aghrout and Alexander 1997, 311; Bensidoun and Chevalier 1998, 28, 52 fn.3). No risk was perceived—nor any real opportunity for trade and investment. Similarly, oil, while remaining a key determinant of European economic health and a salient political issue, was acquiring the characteristics of "normal goods" (Adelman 1991).[31] The oil market was substantially open (Fuller 1995, 88) and there was no need for "special energy relations" to be institutionalized in a foreign policy initiative (Chatelus 1997, 25).

For a period it seemed as if environmental concerns were to enter the security discourse as Europeans feared being geographically united with southern Mediterraneans' pollution of the sea (Haas 1993). It would have been a legitimate security concern and certainly a noble goal. However, the issue never really took root in public debates nor in governmental practices. The problem was not genuinely Euro-Mediterranean in nature and the main causes of concern were to be found rather on the northern shore (New Scientist, 4.II.95).

The analysis of this period shows just how much had changed in terms of the new demands placed on public authorities. In the late 1980s and early 1990s, the map of European perceptions, vis-à-vis Mediterranean challenges and threats, was redrawn to take in migration (securitized at a low level), Islamic fundamentalism (politicized and at times even securitized at low levels) and terrorism, of a different kind than the one prevailing in the early 1970s. Together the escalation of these issues on the political and security agenda fuelled insecurity across

Europe. Previous national preferences were questioned and deconstructed. New understandings and new policy instruments were debated. The early 1990s were thus marked by cognitive uncertainty in relation to the Mediterranean, as governments in member states tried to frame the right policy answer. The public and political debate about how to frame these phenomena represented the main condition for the opening of a policy window in the early 1990s. Therefore, when Spain promoted a debate about the Mediterranean to address the new challenges, its proposal touched a chord with the other European countries for a whole variety of reasons. As put forward in chapter 1, cognitive uncertainty triggered a passive availability across Europe to debate commonly perceived problems in relation to the Mediterranean.

The importance of cognitive uncertainty was also magnified by an intervening variable, in the form of diverging perspectives between the EU and the United States on the Middle East, on the one hand, and between member states themselves, on the question of EU enlargement to the East.

Diverging Perspectives I: Europe, the Middle East and the United States

The opening of a policy window because of cognitive uncertainty was reinforced by the marginalization of the EC/EU in the Middle East peace process, which prodded the Europeans to establish a Mediterranean policy as a Middle East policy by proxy. After the cold war and the Gulf War, the United States emerged as the sole superpower in the Middle East.[32] In October 1991, the United States, with the formal support of the USSR, made a fresh attempt to resolve the Arab-Israeli conflict, with a multilateral conference in Madrid in which all the key participants in the conflict took part, including a joint Palestinian-Jordanian delegation (Rubin 1994, 187–190).

Apart from providing the venue for the conference neither the EC/EU nor the member states contributed much to the process (Quandt 1993, 404; Khader 1997, 158; Aguirrebengoa 1998, 35). The EU was invited to attend but not to participate,[33] an odd situation which reflected a compromise between Israel, which was in favor of total exclusion (Quandt 1993, 399) and Syria, which pleaded for the EU's full participation (Bregman and el-Tahri 1998, 211).[34] The Europeans coordinated one multilateral forum, the Regional Economic Development Working Group (REDWG). Within this framework, the EU planned to finance several activities such as civil society networks, cross-border cooperation, projects on water, and so on.[35] The only other form of EU participation was its attendance as a special witness to the signature of the "Interim Agreement" on September 1995 in Washington (Aguirrebengoa 1998, 39).

With the United States taking the centre stage in Middle East diplomacy, European frustrations with the United States were at times tangible. As it has been aptly put, "the dominant feeling on the continent remained that Europe had not been given a satisfactory share in the process—in its concept, in the bilateral talks, nor in the committee on arms control—but was being asked to eventually bear a potentially substantial share of any cost needed to rebuild and develop the area." (Salamé 1994, 231). The United States perceived Europe as having "little to offer beyond economic assistance" (Haass 1996, 61).[36]

For member states, this situation might have been acceptable so long as the peace process was going in their preferred direction. They wanted rapid progress, taking full account of Palestinian rights and if necessary putting Israel under pressure, a stance that the United States was not prepared to take. In more fundamental terms, the transatlantic partners disagreed about their respective roles in the post–cold war Mediterranean (Fenech 1997, 161). Where the EC/EU saw the region as its immediate neighborhood and tried to shape its political development through economic and multilateral means, the United States pursued its own strategic aims (Gordon 1998, 23–32).

Unilaterally, the EU was more active, especially toward the Palestinians, but still found it difficult to translate its economic power into political influence. It allocated $80 million aid in the summer 1992 to relieve the negative effects of the Gulf War on the countries of the region. At the conference of donors in October 1993 in Washington, following the signing of the Israeli-Palestinian Declaration of Principles, the EU committed $573 million out of the $2 billion gathered from international donors for the period 1994–1998, and it increased its contribution in the following years (Hollis 1997, 22). It was the major financial supporter of the UN Relief and Works Agency (UNRWA), which brought together the bilateral contributions of single member states. Total EU aid to the Palestinians, including UNRWA (but not national contributions), for the period 1994–1998 was $2.3 billion (Salamé 1994, 231). However, even in the economic and financial domain, some of the credit went to the United States, which organized a series of Middle East–North Africa economic conferences (the so-called MENA summits), bringing together private investors from all over the world.

Member states strengthened the political framework for their economic contributions to the peace process, emphasizing its uniqueness. The Commission issued two communications in September 1993,[37] underlining how the European model of peace-through-free trade could also be followed in the Middle East (Pierros et al. 1999, 138–139). Moreover, in April 1994, the European Council agreed on a Joint Action in support of the peace process, according to the new procedure established by the Maastricht Treaty.[38] In it, member states specified a number of actions to be undertaken in the region, among which were strengthening of the relations with the countries of the area, monitoring Israeli settlements in the occupied territories and working to lift the Arab boycott (Soetendorp 1999, 111).

Still, the issue of how to express a European vision about the Middle East remained unresolved and fed a debate about alternative avenues for action. The Mediterranean was an obvious candidate, offering the possibility to conduct a Middle East policy in parallel to a more general policy in the region.[39] With the Euro-Mediterranean Partnership launched at the Barcelona Conference in 1995, the Europeans could thus claim to carry out a "European exercise"[40] in peacemaking and contributed to the Middle East peace process. It also helped raise the European profile vis-à-vis the United States.[41] An EU-U.S. "open channel" of consultation was activated in July 1996, within the framework of the Transatlantic Dialogue launched in Madrid in December 1995, between Assistant Secretary of State and the Director of the Middle East Department of the Ministry of Foreign Affairs of the European country holding the presidency in order to ensure a better functioning of the transatlantic partnership in the Middle East peace process (Aguirrebengoa 1998, 42).[42]

While the peace process in the Middle East helped pave the way toward a global initiative involving the Mediterranean countries it also served to redress the monopoly the United States exercised in the region and restore self esteem to Europeans who felt that they were being asked to be politically silent and economically active in the Middle East. They willingly contributed to finance the process and the region's future development thus acquiring political influence "by stealth" through economic weight (Hollis 1997, 29). At the same time, however, they expressed their views by merging the issues of the Middle East peace process into a broader framework, that is, the Mediterranean policy, which became, in large part, a Middle East policy by proxy. Once again, therefore, diverging perspectives between the United States and the Europeans about the Middle East led the Europeans to envisage a common policy toward the Mediterranean, in order to achieve what was impossible to achieve through national foreign policies.

Diverging Perspectives II: Europe, East and South

The third and final way in which the end of the cold war affected Euro-Mediterranean relations was through changes in Central and Eastern Europe which culminated in a new round of EU enlargement in 2004. Germany and other countries, especially from northern Europe, quickly reoriented their national foreign policy toward the Central and Eastern European countries (CEECs). They also urged fellow EC/EU partners to strengthen links with the CEECs and contribute to their transition. The increase in saliency of Eastern Europe and the importance attached to the CEECs by a number of member states opened a rift within the EC/EU. Southern European countries believed that neglecting the Mediterranean in favor of Eastern Europe would have serious consequences for European security. Spain was particularly outspoken on this. With the help of France and the other southern European countries, it managed to establish the EU's activism in the East as the benchmark for a "successful" EFP. In more analytical terms, member states "framed" external relations in terms of balance between the East and the South. Relations with the CEECs thus represented an intervening variable in the opening of the policy window, which I will describe here together with the use made of it by Spain, alongside the Commission and the other southern European countries.

From the point of view of the southern Mediterranean countries, the "heroic mission of reuniting Europe," which kept the EC/EU busy in the early 1990s, represented a serious setback, which challenged the traditional position of the Mediterranean countries in the EC/EU's pyramid of privilege in external relations (Barbé and Izquierdo 1997; Edwards and Philippart 1997, 469; Khader 1997, 80).[43] With the CEECs receiving such special treatment, the preferences granted to the Mediterranean countries came to pale in comparison. While the debate about the CEECs began to centre on enlargement, the daily relations with the Mediterranean remained relegated to issues of trade and aid. In substantial terms too, the competition for EU's resources became stronger. Although it was suggested that the opening up of the CEECs' markets should not have led to automatic diversions of funds, their attractiveness was in several respects much greater than that of the Mediterranean markets, especially for foreign direct investments (Hoekman 1995, 21; Michalet 1997; Pierros et al. 1999, 147–148).

This gave rise to a self-reinforcing mechanism, according to which the EU formulated political solutions that attracted economic investment, which in turn justified deeper political involvement.

Southern European countries perceived the need not to abandon the Mediterranean, if only to avoid the marginalization of their own national foreign policies. The predominant opinion in Spain was, in the words of Prime Minister Gonzalez, that "the priority accorded by the EC to Eastern Europe raises problems for our foreign policy as well as for our economic development."[44] Already in December 1989, Gonzalez had warned Morocco of the possible diversion of funds toward the East to the detriment of the South (Barbé and Izquierdo 1997). From 1989 until 1995, Spain conducted a campaign both in the EC and in the Maghreb countries to establish a link between the Eastern frontier, the southern frontier, and European security.[45] The Spanish concern was particularly acute during 1993–1994, as negotiations for EC enlargement were taking place with Austria, Finland, Sweden, and Norway. In the course of the negotiations, Spain expressed its fear that the "Mediterranean front" (and the importance of southern European countries) would be diluted if the blocking minority was raised from 23 to 27 votes (Granell 1994[46]). A compromise was reached at the Ioannina summit in March 1994, when Cyprus and Malta were included among the candidates for future EU enlargement. Although supporting the EU's opening to Central and Eastern Europe for political reasons, the Spanish government struggled to tie the issue of the Mediterranean to the bonding of relations with the East.

The other southern European countries also emphasized, though to a lesser extent, the need to rebalance East and South. While obviously concerned, France was internally torn between devoting its attention to the South, on the one hand, and competing for leadership in policy initiatives toward the East, on the other. Mitterrand insisted on the need for comparable attention and resources to be directed to the Mediterranean (Aghrout and Alexander 1997, 308). At the same time, France maneuvered to remain in the driving seat of Eastern European policy, on a par with Germany and the United Kingdom, thus leaving the role of championing the South to Spain. Italy too was divided in its foreign policy allegiances between the East and the South. While wishing to see the formulation of a new Mediterranean policy, both France and Italy remained unable to reconcile their national position with promotion of the Mediterranean interest (Khader 1997, 28).

The Commission also supported the linkage between East and South. Comparisons between relations with the CEECs and with the

Mediterranean countries began to surface in Commission documents. The comparison soon became a leitmotiv in texts about Euro-Mediterranean relations. At the most formal level, the two regions tended to be mentioned together, although without an explicit link. For instance, the Lisbon summit, in June 1992, listed the criteria according to which CFSP was to develop and explicitly specified Central and Eastern Europe, and the Maghreb and the Middle East as the two regions in which joint action would be "particularly beneficial" for the EU.[47] In Commission documents not addressed to the public the link was more substantial. The EU had "special responsibilities" both for Central and Eastern Europe and for the Mediterranean region[48] and the Commission advocated a policy initiative toward the latter on the grounds that the broadening and deepening process the EC was embarked on risked making other countries, such as the North African ones, feel excluded.[49] A new initiative toward the Mediterranean would demonstrate that "the pre-accession strategy the Community is pursuing with countries in Central and Eastern Europe in no way interferes with its commitment to developing closer ties with its Mediterranean neighbours."[50] The Commission often compared relations between the EU and the CEECs with those between the EU and the Mediterranean countries, in terms of population (current and foreseen), trade, GDP, migration, and so on. The comparison showed a yawning gap between the East and the South in terms of relations with the EU, thus justifying the Commission's pledge to strengthen Mediterranean policy. The European Parliament also called on the EU to develop an agenda for cooperation with the Mediterranean "comparable to the PHARE and TACIS programmes."[51]

The comparison with the East was thus useful in (re)framing and in cognitively defining EU policy to the Mediterranean. While previously the yardstick to measure the achievements of the Mediterranean policy had been what it had achieved in the past, it could now be measured more concretely against the policy toward the CEECs. As we shall see, this frame was to be useful in cementing a deal on the financial underpinnings of the EMP at a crucial meeting in Cannes in June 1995. The comparison with the aid package for the CEECs helped set the terms of the deal for the Mediterranean nonmembers.

Therefore, the process culminating in the 2004 EU enlargement paradoxically contributed in a positive way to the formulation of a policy initiative toward the Mediterranean (Barbé 1996). This consensus across the EC/EU on a link between the East and the South is all the more surprising because of the opposite situation the two regions found themselves in at the time. While the East was opening up and its economies taking off, the South remained engulfed in all sorts of political, economic, and social problems. In spite of the different conditions on the ground, part of the political momentum in the EU for CEECs "infected" also the debate about Euro-Mediterranean relations.

The Entrepreneurial Pattern

I began this chapter by suggesting that the end of the cold war triggered a new period of activism toward the Mediterranean. I then explored how cognitive uncertainty created a passive availability on the part of policy makers to discuss the Mediterranean at the European level. Differences with the United States about the Middle East, and new relations with the CEECs also contributed to this policy window. "The time was ripe" to discuss ideas about what to do toward the Mediterranean. However, all this would have amounted to little in the absence of a policy entrepreneur to capitalize on this set of favorable conditions and turn member states' passive availability into an active process of interaction.

The entrepreneurial pattern was more cooperative (and more complex) in the 1990s than in the 1970s. In the early 1970s, France was the main entrepreneur, while Italy and the Commission pursued parallel initiatives. There was very little cooperation between actors, and at times even open competition, as in the case of France and Italy. In the early 1990s, the pattern of entrepreneurial actions in contrast was coordinated among the participants. Initiatives still went on in parallel, but there was a more conscious effort to build on them, rather than sap each other's efforts. Spain, in particular, tightly linked its entrepreneurship to the support of France, while also benefiting from and elaborating on efforts from the Commission too.

Examples of entrepreneurship from both periods displayed "broker" qualities, leaving a lot of leeway for changing the content of proposals. Also, Spain, like France in the 1970s, was motivated more by ideational goals than by the prospect of material gains. The foreign policy of democratic Spain had undergone a profound change in the preceding 20 years and it needed this change to be acknowledged by its European partners in order to achieve a "middle power status" both within the EU and on the world stage.

The Foreign Policy of Democratic Spain

Similar to that of France in the 1970s, Spain's entrepreneurship began at the national level. Between 1982 and 1989, Spain reinvented its bilateral ties with the Mediterranean countries. This reorientation was part and parcel of Spain's transition to democracy. It was also an attempt to locate itself among Western democracies and be acknowledged as a middle power and a democratic state by the other Western European democracies. By refocusing its foreign policy toward the Mediterranean, Spain hoped to achieve added status among its European partners. While in this section we are going to examine the relaunch of Spanish national foreign policy toward the Mediterranean, in the next I will address Spanish entrepreneurial activities within the EC/EU.

The change in Spain's foreign policy, which resulted from the country's transition to democracy, questioned allegiances that prevailed during Franco's years, as Spain pursued a new international profile worldwide. One of the thorniest issues in this process of revision was the Spanish relationship with the Arab countries and with Israel.

Under Franco, the Arab countries had ranked high in Spain's foreign policy, thanks to several common traits that they shared (Powell 1995, 20). However, the "special relationship" between Spain and the Arab countries did not really amount to a coherent strategic design, and never developed beyond limited instrumental considerations. As Fernando Morán, minister of Foreign Affairs between 1982–1985, put it, Spanish policy toward the Maghreb and more generally the Arab world at the time of Franco lacked three things: vision, a clear perception of national interests, and a strategy to attain them.[52] In political terms, "Spain was a nonentity at the beginning of the 1980s in the Mediterranean."[53]

At the beginning of the 1980s, the new socialist government set out to fix exactly those points (Gillespie 1999, 34–35; Tovias 1998, 217; Marquina and Echeverria 1992, 43). The new prime minister, Felipe González, together with his ministers of Foreign Affairs,[54] contributed to the development of new relations with the Mediterranean and with the Maghreb in particular. Spanish foreign policy's new phase was also helped by EC and NATO accession.[55] The strategy was two-pronged, and had a negative and a positive aspect to it.[56] The first goal was to mobilize resources *against* potential challenges. The second was to reinforce relations *with* the Mediterranean (especially Maghreb) countries, in order to create a "web of common interests."[57] The second goal was the most important component, though, and it prevailed not only in socioeconomic and political relations, but also in military reforms.

The National Defense Directive of 1984 redirected the military apparatus from domestic sources of turmoil to intervention in Spain's immediate periphery (Santos 1985, 590ff.). Spain was territorially vulnerable by definition, as its territory included offshore possession such as the Canaries, Ceuta, and Melilla. Moreover, its economy relied heavily on Algerian gas (Gillespie 1999, 162–163).[58] Within this defensive strategy, Spain found room for cooperation with the southern Mediterranean countries on three main fronts: the fight against terrorism, arms sales, and military agreements. Cooperation in the fight against terrorism was widespread (Story 1995, 40). As Islamic fundamentalism grew in importance, cooperation between Ministries of Interior was expanded and institutionalized.[59] Arms sales, aimed at boosting Spanish national productive autonomy, cemented the friendship with Morocco and continued well into the decade, in spite of U.S. competition.[60] Sales were also agreed with Machrek countries such as Egypt, Jordan, and Turkey.[61] Finally, Spain signed agreements of military cooperation with Tunisia (November 1987), Algeria (December 1987), Mauritania (February 1989), and Morocco (September 1989).[62]

Parallel to the military component of its foreign policy, Spain put into place a much more relevant framework of socioeconomic cooperation with all Mediterranean countries, in the belief that from cooperation and common interests would come interdependence and stability (Moratinos 1996, 23). Consistent with this view, Spanish leaders were ready to pay over the odds in order to foster new economic and development relations. This led in February 1985 to a tough resolution of the dispute over Algerian gas, the terms of which were very negative for Spain (Marquina and Echeverria 1992, 51).[63] Subsequently, Spain and Algeria launched a flurry of cooperation agreements in other areas.[64] Trade and economic cooperation agreement, with different nuances, were signed also with Tunisia (November 1983), Jordan (April 1984), Egypt (November 1985), and Israel (June 1986).[65]

In all respects, Morocco remained Spain's best, if at times troublesome, partner. With Morocco, Spain signed several conventions ranging from prevention of drug trafficking, to financial support, health programs, and fishing rules, thus institutionalizing cooperation across the board. An agreement on good neighborhood and friendship, signed in 1991, wrapped up these several forms of cooperation.[66] Development aid, in the form of soft loans, aid and risk capital, allocated to Algeria, Morocco, and Tunisia, increased in the 1980s, to reach, respectively, 239, 324, and 224 million pesetas in 1989 (Moratinos 1996, 27). Though still a fraction of what France devoted to the area, it signaled Spain's increasing profile in the region.

While increasing political contacts with all Mediterranean countries, Spain was particularly successful in finding a balanced position on the Arab-Israeli question. In January 1986, following pressure from

EC fellow partners, Spain formally recognized the state of Israel and established the basis for cooperation in various fields. Shortly afterward, in August 1986, it also upgraded PLO offices in Madrid. As a result, the traditional friendship of Arab countries was not disrupted (Gillespie 1999, 119ff.) and Spain's position was valued sufficiently to make it the host of the Madrid conference that launched the peace process between Israel and its neighbors.

Why did Spain give such a boost to its Mediterranean policy? What motivated Spanish commitment to the Mediterranean? How are we to understand the strengthening of relations and the attention given to tightening political, economic, and military links? Several interpretations have been put forward. Some have stressed the genuine concern for the potential risks emanating from instability in a neighboring country or region (e.g., Santos 1985, 590) and for the economic opportunities of the area. Others have emphasized Spain's ambitions to become a middle power and the need to carve out an international role which would back up its status (Labatut 1995, 317ff.; Barbé 1995, 121).

Although there is some truth in all these perspectives, the most convincing point of view highlights the logics of the democratization process in Spain. The political élites in power, especially after the Spanish Socialist Party (PSOE) won the elections in 1982, wanted to anchor Spain solidly in the concert of Western European liberal democracies, and acted accordingly. Spain reinvented itself and its network of external relations according to new domestic and international conditions and assumed an identity which, in many ways, contradicted its previous self. From being a backward country receiving external aid, it became an industrialized, donor country. From an emigration country, it turned into an immigration destination.[67] From a marginal player, it set its sights on being an active member of the inner European circle, ready to contribute to the stability of Europe. What really changed in the 1980s was the role Spain perceived for itself. It joined the regional organizations of Western European democracies, such as the EC, NATO, and the WEU. In the Mediterranean, the transition to democracy and its European policy, Spain saw the means to reinventing itself as a European power. The Mediterranean and the European components of the political attitude of "new" Spain were often indicated as two sides of the same coin (e.g., Ortega 1995, 193).[68]

In the period 1989–1992, Spain's activism shifted from the national to the international level, eventually succeeding in setting the European foreign policy agenda.

Entrepreneurial Commission?

Before Spain started to act as a policy entrepreneur in the EC/EU, it was the Commission which took up the role. Unlike cases in the 1970s and in the 1980s, this was an instance where the Commission displayed clear entrepreneurial capacities as the policy window for an EFP initiative toward the Mediterranean was beginning to open. The result was not politically very powerful, although it proves that the Commission can prod member states into action. In 1989, the Commission, and in particular Commissioner Abel Matutes, invested material and ideational resources to push the Mediterranean issue up the agenda.[69] Its action followed the typical supranational/neofunctional explanation, with the Commission in active pursuit of policy change, in the absence of any action by member states. The Commission was to be active again later on in support of Spanish entrepreneurship, but more as part of the overall cognitive interaction process. In this section, I will explore this first case of entrepreneurship, while I will analyze the contribution of the Commission to the general debate in the following section.

Matutes began to raise the issue of the Mediterranean at a time when the Commission was asked to coordinate the PHARE program that in a few months had established generous aid for CEECs (Pierros et al. 1999, 128). Stressing the need to balance Eastern and southern relations and as part of efforts to establish a parallel between the two, Matutes called for a similar commitment for southern Mediterranean countries.[70] As a result, the Commission prepared a Communication to the Council for a "Renovated Mediterranean Policy,"[71] based on the analysis of the (few) achievements and (several) failures of the Global Mediterranean Policy (Marks 1996, 10–11). Having drafted the proposal, Matutes then consulted with all the European institutions and actors, and toured the Mediterranean, visiting almost all nonmember countries.[72] The Commission then negotiated Financial Protocols with Mediterranean nonmembers. This constituted the core of the RMP.

In several respects, the RMP made little change to the traditional pattern of Euro-Mediterranean relations, and therefore it does not squarely fall in the scope of my analysis in this volume. Nonetheless, it embodied several new conceptual developments, which later converged into the EMP. First, it increased the funds for the Mediterranean, thus beginning the process of updating the amount of resources devoted to the area. Second, it suggested a new way of spending money, by promoting multilateral networks, decentralized cooperation and a public/private partnership. It was thus a step toward the promotion of regionalism, as well as a more neoliberal approach to development.[73] At the same time, the RMP did not address the trade agreements negotiated 15 years before, nor did it provide new political momentum. Scope for change was there, but it was limited.

In spite of the RMP limitations, the activism of Matutes proves an important point: entrepreneurship for EFP making can be exerted by actors other than member states. The Commission can behave in such a way as to introduce foreign policy innovations by interpreting a changing environment. The RMP was the Commission's baby. Member states contributed to the initiative, but only indirectly and they never took the lead in it. Spain undertook a number of general initiatives but was not yet ready to change its pattern of foreign policy relationships. In the first half of 1989, Spain contributed to the revival of Cooperation Councils with the Maghreb countries, Under the French presidency which followed, it prepared the document "Europe and the Integration in the Maghreb," outlining the benefits of the Union which had been recently founded by Arab Maghreb countries (Marquina 1998, 237). At the same time, Spain and southern European countries opposed any introduction of trade concessions, thus preventing any innovation in this crucial aspect of relations (Constas 1995, 133).[74] In the year 1989–1991, while Spain was acting in favor of the Mediterranean, it was mainly doing so outside the EC framework and on a national basis. Therefore the Commission was on a "solo" mission. The RMP, which has at times been described as a "success" of the southern European countries vis-à-vis northern European ones (e.g., Tovias 1996, 14; 1998, 223), was mainly the Commission's success.[75] It was the Commission that managed to push the Mediterranean up the agenda, in the face of resistance from both northern and southern Europeans.

Was Matutes' nationality a factor contributing to the Commission's activism? While it might have played a role, it was not crucial. Abel Matutes, a Spaniard from Ibiza, was a member of the Spanish Conservative Party and he was in charge of Mediterranean policy in Delors' Second Commission (1989–1993). While relations with Gonzalez's government improved at the beginning of 1992, the period between 1989 and 1990 was characterized by a persistent tension, which partly reflected the fact that Spain was not convinced of the RMP's benefits.

The RMP thus offers an interesting though limited case for evaluating the Commission's autonomous entrepreneurship. The Commission was able to make an impact on the EC/EU agenda basically on its own. Its initiative, however, did not have the political clout to make much dent in the existing pattern of Euro-Mediterranean relationships. Had it remained in place, it might have had more of an impact (Gillespie 1999, 148) and led to further policy innovation. But more ambitious initiatives came to the fore and discussions about the RMP converged into a more general debate about the EMP. The conclusion to be drawn from this case, then, is that while it proves the Commission's potential as a foreign policy entrepreneur, it questions the political relevance of its actions in EFP making.

Framing the Mediterranean: Spanish Entrepreneurship, European Interactions

Two other initiatives were organized around this time, both arising from political and security concerns and both supported by member states. In 1988, France initiated regular meetings with Western European and Western Mediterranean countries, with a political agenda. In February 1990, Spain, together with Italy, launched the idea of a Conference on Security and Cooperation in the Mediterranean (CSCM) along the lines of the CSCE. The first initiative has continued up to the present day albeit with a low profile, while the latter did not take off the ground. However the political rationale behind the two initiatives was not lost, and resurfaced shortly afterward in the form of a proposal for a Euro-Maghreb Partnership, which was meant to merge political *and* economic concerns, with a regional overtone. The debate that accompanied the proposal however revealed the need to expand it to the whole Mediterranean in order to involve northern European countries in it. Having settled the geographical scope, member states thus launched the Euro-Mediterranean Partnership (EMP).

Therefore, the EMP was the result of several converging conceptual streams. The Commission made an early contribution to it with the RMP, focusing on regionalism and bringing a neoliberal touch to development. Spain, with the support of France and Italy, built on these themes, adding a political and security related component in the form of the Euro-Maghreb Partnership. Southern European countries and northern European member states then devised a geographical scope to the initiative, and strongly connected it to the Middle East, under the all-encompassing label of EMP.

The following section will describe the development of entrepreneurial activities, showing how Spain, in coordination with France, the Commission, and at times Italy, stirred the debate and tried to shape the EU agenda. On another level the story will explore how the principles and the key ideas of the EMP were elaborated in the cognitive interaction among member states and in the dialogue between them and the EC/EU institutions. In the debate, the collective puzzlement caused by new sociopolitical challenges thus turned into common ideational frames and eventually into an EU initiative toward the Mediterranean.

From the CSCM to the Euro-Maghreb Partnership

Spain's first attempt to upgrade Euro-Mediterranean relations in the post–cold war world occurred outside the EC/EU framework and was the idea, put forward jointly with Italy, of a Conference on Security and Cooperation in the Mediterranean (CSCM). Apart from the European countries, the CSCM intended to bring together a broad set of participants, ranging from the United States and the Soviet Union, to Gulf countries and the Black Sea. It would have been organized along the same lines as the CSCE, determining rules and principles for conflict-resolution, and operating around three "baskets" (security, cooperation and human affairs), of which cooperation would have been as important as security in the CSCE, as the Spanish minister of Foreign Affairs, Ordóñez, emphasized (1990, 7–11).[76]

However, the CSCM did not manage to convince key participants, thus dooming the initiative to failure. Germany, the United Kingdom and the Netherlands were lukewarm or opposed to it (Gillespie 1996, 35). The United States was totally against it. Not having been consulted beforehand, it saw the CSCM as an attempt to water down its primacy in the Mediterranean and possibly a way to discuss the role of the Sixth Fleet in it (Badini 1995, 113; Khader 1994, 273). France responded with a "non-negative" attitude (Gillespie 1996, 35), which in practice constituted a major obstacle. The inclusion of the United States in the CSCM project did not please the French (Chérigui 1997, 195, 206–207), which preferred their smaller scale project in the Western Mediterranean (Chérigui 1997, 118–211). Since 1988, Mitterrand had organized a series of meetings, first under the label of "Mediterranean Forum," then 4 + 5 and later 5 + 5 (France, Italy, Portugal, Spain, Malta + Algeria, Libya, Mauritania, Morocco, Tunisia). Moreover, the objective of the French initiative was the opposite of CSCM: while the latter aimed at elaborating general principles for international coexistence in the Mediterranean, the former wanted to tackle specific problems without interference from the United States.

The CSCM was soon off the agenda, but from that experience Spain retained several lessons.[77] First, U.S. involvement raised more problems than it solved.[78] Therefore, the geographical scope of action had to be rethought. At the same time the initiative received a broad consent for its general objectives, as it added a political-security dimension missing from European relations with the southern shore. The Gulf War in 1991 had shown how important that was. Therefore, the initial CSCM structure in baskets was retained, as many different interests could be accommodated therein. In fact one of the most important successes of Spanish diplomacy was to be the establishment of a link between on the one hand the CSCE perspective, with its global approach, and on the other European foreign policy, traditionally based on economic relations. The final lesson learned by Spain was that intra-European cooperation had to be increased, to reach concrete results. Accordingly, even when the CSCM proposal was abandoned, Spanish diplomats organized a flurry of bilateral seminars, meetings and summits to spread ideas and generate debate on the Mediterranean (Marquina 1998, 237). Spanish diplomats addressed not only representatives from southern European countries, but also universities and think tanks, both in Spain and abroad.[79]

The task of retuning the debate about the Mediterranean was facilitated by the people in charge of it. By 1989, Spain had in place a team of well connected Spanish diplomats, in the Spanish Ministry of Foreign Affairs and in the European Commission, who were to remain in place until the Euro-Mediterranean Partnership was launched (see table 5.5). They rotated posts, but they tended to remain within the area of competence of the Mediterranean, thus creating a solid group sharing a likeminded approach to Spain's entrepreneurship. The Commission's side of the team was at times isolated from the Spanish government, as Matutes and later Marín experienced. The presence of Juan Prat, who had excellent personal contacts in Madrid, helped to smoothen relationships. The diplomats acting as Spain's representatives were very close to each other and to the government. Simplifying to the extreme, we can identify three key pilots of the Spanish activism within the EC/EU.[80] The first was Miguel Angel Moratinos, who was Deputy Director and later Director of Africa and the Middle East within the Ministry of Foreign Affairs.[81] Under the supervision and with the support of Jorge Dezcallar, Moratinos' work was assisted by Alvaro Iranzo, who became one of his Deputies at the Directorate for Africa and the Middle East, and later by Gabriel Busquets, representing the Spanish Presidency. The second key person in the process was Alberto Navarro, who supported Moratinos' work from the State Secretariat for European Affairs. The third was Javier Elorza, who acted as a liaison with Brussels through his post as Spain's Permanent Representative to the EC/EU.

Table 5.5 Spanish Diplomats Covering Key Posts on the Mediterranean, 1989–1995

	1989 1990 1991	1992 1993 1994	1995
Gabriel Busquets Aparicio	Spanish Deputy Ambassador in Germany	Spanish Deputy Ambassador in Morocco	Special Ambassador for Euro-Med. Conference
Jorge Dezcallar de Mazarredo	Dir. Gen. for Africa and the Middle East, MFA[a]	Dir. Gen. of Political Affairs, MFA	
Javier Elorza Cavengt	Deputy Permanent Representative of Spain to the EC	Secretary General for European Community, MFA, with responsibility for Maastricht negotiations, K4, and Schengen	Permanent Representative of Spain to the EU
Alvaro Iranzo Gutierrez	Spanish Ambassador in Algeria	Deputy Dir. Gen. for North Africa, MFA	
Manuel Marín Gonzalez	Commissioner with responsibility for development, cooperation (Mediterranean,[b] Latin America, Asia) and fisheries, European Commission	Commissioner with responsibility for external relations with Latin America, ACP countries and the Mediterranean, European Commission	
Miguel Angel Moratinos Cuyaubé	Deputy Dir. Gen. for North Africa, MFA	Dir. Gen. Institute of Cooperation with Arab World, MFA	Dir. Gen. for Africa and the Middle East, MFA
Francisco Fernández Ordoñez	Minister of Foreign Affairs, MFA[c]		
Alberto Navarro González	Deputy Dir. Gen. for EC Programs of Dev. Cooperation, Sec. of State for International Cooperation	Dir. Gen. for Coordination of Legal and Institutional Affairs, Secretary of State for the European Union	
Juan Prat y Coll	Chef de Cabinet of Matutes, European Commission	Dir. Gen. of North/South relations, Mediterranean Policy, Latin America, and Asia, European Commission	
Javier Solana Madariaga	Minister of Education and Science	Minister of Foreign Affairs, MFA	

[a] Ministry of Foreign Affairs.
[b] In the same period, Abel Matutes was Commissioner with responsibility for Mediterranean policy (external economic relations).
[c] He died in June 1992.

Since 1991, Spanish diplomats had acted in close cooperation with their French counterparts, with the Italians (whenever possible), and with the Commission.[82] The opportunities to exchange ideas with Italy arose at meetings in early 1991 to define the CSCM proposal.[83] Since then, Italy behaved as a "loyal partner,"[84] though not always an active one. The discussions with the French took a broader approach and were particularly important, as they led France to consider Spain's activism in the Mediterranean as legitimate and useful. At the French-Hispanic summit, in October 1991, Mitterrand declared that "tout ne peut pas se faire de Paris"[85] (Chérigui 1997, 179). Moreover, Spanish and French diplomats came to see eye to eye on several issues, and increasingly coordinated their outings. The agenda on which they worked also continued to expand, as for instance at the bilateral meeting in Salamanca on 28–29 September, 1992, when the ministers of Foreign Affairs and of the Interiors of both countries met with their ambassadors in the Maghreb to assess instability sources in the area.[86] Certain key people within the Commission also became involved. In particular, Eberhardt Rhein, Marc Pierini and Eric Van Der Linden, all belonging to the DG with responsibility for the Mediterranean, helped refine ideas and build on them. They were the first to recognize that the main responsibility for furthering the debate and crafting new proposals fell to Spain.[87]

Even as the attempt to promote the CSCM ground to a halt, this Spanish team together with its close allies tackled the subject of a European policy for its southern neighbours with a renewed sense of urgency. Because of the Gulf War and the cancellation of Algerian elections, perceptions of Mediterranean challenges, as we have seen earlier, were more often related to security. In the face of these challenges, the RMP looked simply inadequate. The European policy for the Mediterranean in 1991 lacked a political vision—which was what the Spaniards possessed.[88]

The trigger for change came with the EP's decision to block the renewal of Morocco's Financial Protocol along the lines of the RMP, in January 1992, which caused a rift between the EP and Morocco. Morocco threatened to cancel the fishing agreement with the EC, which was up for renewal, and rejected European aid. Member states and the Commission faced having to find a way out of this impasse created by the EP.[89]

At this point, the EC/EU began to emerge as the main forum for discussion on Euro-Mediterranean relations, and the idea of a free trade area with nonmember countries plus a political dialogue helped catalyze the debate. In the wake of the diplomatic incident with Morocco, Spain publicly suggested the creation of a free trade area with the Maghreb countries, including a reduction of their public debts with European countries, increased financial aid and the creation of a political dialogue, later adding the plan for a Conference of ministers of Foreign Affairs.[90] At the EPC Council meeting on February 17, 1992, France's minister of

Foreign Affairs also proposed a free trade area as the basis for renewed relations with Morocco. This proposal, which had the benefit of bypassing reestablishing cooperation with Morocco, was approved by the other member states, and a dialogue to explore this possibility with Moroccan representatives followed suit. At the same meeting, France suggested—and fellow members approved—to prepare two documents considering, respectively, the political situation in the Maghreb and the economic problems of the region. At the suggestion of France, the first document was commissioned to Spain, while the second to the Commission, and more specifically to Matutes.[91]

In the following months, member states reached an agreement about the Maghreb, around several key ideas that were later to characterize the Euro-Mediterranean Partnership.

The first report, prepared by Spain,[92] was a very clear example of framing, setting out the issue of Mediterranean security challenges and the need for European intervention to defuse them. The report began by defining the Mediterranean as a "vulnerable frontier,"[93] separating two culturally different worlds. North Africa represented the closest contact point. Its problems ranged from the humiliation of the Arab people after the Gulf War to chronic underdevelopment. According to Spain, Europe's main concerns were the potential consequences of social unrest, Islamic fundamentalism and migration. Migration in particular was the unbreakable link between the two worlds. The EC had to promote the economic development of Maghrebi economies, but at the same time it had to establish a political dialogue, grant generous development cooperation, and take into account the social dimension of Euro-Maghrebi relations. The conclusion was blunt and played heavily the security card: "Without unnecessary alarmism and with sound realism, we have to conclude that the Maghreb is today a time bomb, which Europe can deactivate, as long as it establishes the means to do so."[94] Spain's report was presented at the beginning of March and was well received. Given the positive feedback, Spain raised the stakes further and suggested the creation of a Euro-Maghreb Conference, later specifying it as a Euro-Maghreb Partnership.

The Commission's report was drafted in March,[95] and, at the Council's request, it came to embody several ideas floating around at the time. The Commission spelled out how the Euro-Maghreb Partnership would work in practice. It centered the project on three Maghreb countries, namely Morocco, Tunisia, and Algeria, with which the EC would negotiate new agreements with a view to creating a free trade area. Several new instruments would complement the agreements. First, they would be accompanied by a strong political dialogue. Second, the EC would offer financial, as well as economic and technical cooperation. Other possible areas for cooperation were culture and the social sector.

Negotiations with Morocco on a possible free trade agreement started in February 1992, and had as a first positive side effect the conclusion of a fishing agreement in May, which was considered as a first step in the multifaceted project of a partnership (Marquina 1998, 238). Contacts with Tunisia followed suit, in May 1992.

Member states expressed their formal commitment to this idea of a strategy aiming at a free trade Maghreb region cum political and maybe social components at the European Summit in Lisbon, on June 27, 1992. The declaration on EU-Maghreb relations, which had been drafted by Spain (Marquina 1998, 239), covered all the key fields mentioned in the reports by Spain and the Commission, thus establishing a broad agenda for Euro-Maghrebi relations. In their final declaration, member states stated that "the southern and eastern shores of the Mediterranean, as well as the Middle East, are geographical areas in relation to which the Union has strong interests in terms of security and social stability".[96] A frame comprised of a free trade area, financial cooperation, political dialogue, and region building was thus consolidated as a response to the challenges of migration, political instability, security, and development.

The proposal did not gather enough momentum, though. A Euro-Maghreb Partnership was too limited an initiative to really involve northern European countries, whose attention was increasingly distracted by the Middle East rather than attracted to the Maghreb. As soon as the next step required formal negotiations, the northern European passive agreement turned into a passive disinterest. Although it looked like the Maghreb was firmly en route for an EFP initiative, rapid progress on the issue came to a similarly rapid halt. By October 1992, Solana, the Spanish minister of Foreign Affairs, stated that the Euro-Maghreb Partnership was "a possibility," hinting at the fact that other options could also be explored.[97]

Framing the Euro-Mediterranean Partnership

Dynamic changes in the Arab-Israeli peace process were stealing the Maghreb's limelight and the impasse was not resolved until the two sets of concerns merged into an encompassing Mediterranean initiative. In 1993–1994, EU[98] efforts centered on the peace process. The Commission issued two Communications in September 1993[99] and the European Council announced in October 1993 a Joint Action for the Middle East, according to the new CFSP rules.[100] As Palestinian-Israeli relations improved, member states were more than willing to contribute to the development of the Middle East. It soon became clear, however, that the road to a European contribution was blocked. The United States and Israel were, in different ways and for different reasons, constraining the scope for European participation, as analyzed earlier.

Given U.S. and Israeli opposition to Europe's involvement in the peace process, member states redirected their desire to "do something for the Middle East" toward a Mediterranean initiative, which thus acquired the meaning of a "Middle East policy in disguise." Three principles underpinned the shift in thinking on the part of the Europeans. First, the concept of region building was extended to the whole Mediterranean. This was an easy move, as it had been part of both the GMP and the RMP. In the context of the peace process, though, region building became the means by which the EU would contribute to peace and stability in the Middle East, that is, by putting Arab and Israeli representatives around the same table.[101] Second, the political dialogue with a security undertone that was envisaged with Maghreb countries also became a route to address Middle East politics. Finally, the idea of a free trade area among all Mediterranean countries opened the way to a "neofunctionalist" approach to peace making for the Middle East. Therefore, by reinterpreting these concepts in the light of the goals of the peace process and in a Mediterranean perspective, member states were able to make sense of their relations with all of their southern neighbors.

Determined to involve northern European countries, capitalizing on their desire to act in the Middle East, and supported by the external action of Egypt,[102] Spain and France strengthened their cooperation. From 1994, France behaved in fact as a co-entrepreneur with Spain (Gillespie 1997, 38), to the point that a lot of the thinking about the possible Mediterranean initiative was done by the French.[103] The close cooperation occurred at all levels of the political hierarchy,[104] and it led to an efficient division of roles and labor. Spain, for instance, wanted a conference to launch the European policy, whatever it turned out to be, and was prepared to leave it to the French to organize it. France, however, was wary of the conference turning into a "firework," with little consequences, and preferred that the Spaniards took the lead on it.[105] The joint entrepreneurship of Spain and France was again demonstrated by the joint letter of the two ministers of Foreign Affairs, Juppé and Solana, addressed in October 1994 to Delors, for the Commission, and Kinkel, for the German EU Presidency, in which they asked for more time on the EU agenda for the Mediterranean in the last months of 1994.[106] Although constrained by elections during its Presidency semester at the beginning of 1995 (Barbé 1996, 28), France threw its weight behind a European initiative for the Mediterranean and strove to engage northern European partners on the subject.

In June 1994 the debate was revived, this time centered on the whole Mediterranean. At the Corfu summit in June 1994, the European Council's conclusions for the first time in a while included a title on "Relations with the Mediterranean Countries." It mentioned the goal of transforming the area into a region of cooperation, peace, stability, security and well-being. It also stressed the importance of "the development of regional cooperation involving Israel and the Palestinian side," as well as the intention to encourage cooperation with the Machrek countries. The mention of a possible Euro-Mediterranean conference was also a first. Yet another indicator of intra-southern European coordination was Greece suggesting Spain as the venue for such a conference, and the proposal being accepted. The European Council also gave the Council a mandate to evaluate, together with the Commission, a "global policy" for the Mediterranean region.

Following the mandate from the European Council, the Commission prepared a report, which was mainly the work of Marín, and presented it in October.[107] The report listed the usual reasons for launching a Mediterranean initiative. Promoting stability and security in the region would require economic and social reform, which could contribute to "stemming violence and easing migratory pressure."[108] At the same time, the report mentioned the EU's contributions to the peace process. It went on to specify two fields in which to strengthen cooperation: political stability and security, and an economic area. In October, the Commission also submitted to the Council and the EP a communiqué proposing a global aid program toward the Mediterranean of ECU 6.300 million for the period 1995–1999. Member states were not yet ready to discuss the issue of aid, though, and the proposal created dissensions (Marquina 1998, 240). At the Essen summit meeting in December 1994, the European Council went on to define the Mediterranean as a priority area of strategic importance for the EU.[109]

Encouraged by a first round of exploratory talks with the potential Mediterranean "partners" in which they showed their interest in the idea of a Euro-Mediterranean Partnership,[110] the Commission produced a new document, in which it set out how the concept of a Euro-Mediterranean Partnership would work[111] and defined a list of priorities for financial cooperation for the period 1995–1999. The need for action was justified by mass migration, terrorism, fundamentalist extremism, drug trafficking, and organized crime. The Presidency Conclusions of the European Council in Cannes, in June 1995, reflected the same spirit. They listed a range of potential actions to be taken by the partnership, from the reintroduction of undocumented immigration to targeted programs to limit brain-drain in Mediterranean countries.

It is at this point, in 1995, that, having definitely set the frame for action, negotiations came to resemble "traditional" bargaining techniques and a set of two level games. Within the cognitive frame composed of "free trade region cum political dialogue cum some aid and some social component" which the Europeans saw as an answer to security and political challenges, the debate moved to the issue of who would pay for what. On the one hand, there was a strong coalition of southern European policy makers, cemented by years of cooperation on the subject and reinforced by the back to back presidencies of France, Spain, and Italy during 1995 and early 1996. On the other hand, there were actors who although giving their agreement in principle, were reluctant to pay the price for an ambitious EFP initiative for the Mediterranean.

Opposition came for instance from Spain's domestic front. Gonzalez had to defend the work done by the Ministry of Foreign Affairs from the opposition of the Ministries of Agriculture and Industry (Tovias 1998, 227). The Commission, which had continued negotiations with Morocco and Tunisia in parallel with the development of the Euro-Mediterranean ideas, went beyond its negotiating mandate, thus presenting Spain with a particularly bad deal on agriculture. In the end the Ministry of Agriculture had to give way to Spain's foreign policy ambitions.[112] It helped that negotiations on fisheries with Morocco progressed, thanks also to the fact that the EU tended to be represented by Spaniards in the Commission and in the Presidency in the second semester of 1995.[113]

Tensions arose also across the EU, on the one hand between Spain and France, and, on the other, between the northern European countries and Germany in particular, which would have borne the financial brunt of the initiative. At the European Summit in Cannes in June 1995, with financial allocations on the agenda, the Commission's proposal met with resistance from northern European countries.[114] The United Kingdom, Denmark, the Netherlands, and especially Germany were particularly staunch in their opposition, insisting on trade instead of aid. Spain "adopted tough negotiating tactics" (Barbé 1996, 32), playing the economic card, and stressing the relevance of a Euro-Mediterranean Partnership for European exports. It reminded the Europeans of their energy dependence. It used threats by hinting at the possibility that Spain might block further moves toward Eastern enlargement (Tovias 1998, 228). It accepted concessions, requiring more EU involvement in transport networks and a higher contribution by Spain to the fund aid for ACP countries (Gillespie 1997, 40). It compromised so as to reach an agreement, accepting a 10 percent reduction in the original proposal of the budget to be committed (Gillespie 1997, 40). It also helped that Gonzalez had excellent relations with Kohl. France also committed itself to the success of the endeavor. Having done much of the conceptual work on the draft Declaration to be adopted at the Euro-Mediterranean summit, France lobbied the other southern European countries into supporting it and then the northern Europeans as well.[115] This complex mix of negotiations paid off and the Summit in Cannes ended with a formal commitment of funds for the Mediterranean and a Declaration, which was in fact the draft of the Barcelona Declaration adopted at the Euro-Mediterranean summit on November 27–28, 1995. It included not only a political and security chapter and an economic one, but also a social, cultural and human affairs domain. The way was thus open to a successful Conference, in which the EU officially launched the Euro-Mediterranean Partnership together with its Mediterranean partners. It was the beginning of what soon came to be known as "the Barcelona process."

The launching of the Barcelona process was a major change in EFP, as well as a major success for Spain. The EMP was a radical departure from the previous pattern of the RMP and aimed to overcome the partition of the Mediterranean provoked by the southern enlargement. In contrast to the indifference prevailing in the 1980s, the EMP demonstrated the EU's willingness to become actively involved in the area. It marked a turnaround in Euro-Mediterranean relations. As such, it was also a success for Spanish diplomacy. At the end of the Spanish Presidency, Westendorp, who replaced Solana as minister of Foreign Affairs, declared that Spain had risen into Europe's diplomatic "first division."[116] Barcelona helped Spain to emerge as a democratic, southern European middle power, comparable to Italy. Its actions elicited praise from its EU partners and from the Arab world (Gillespie 1999, 156). Its symbolic goal of international recognition was indeed achieved, while the final outcome was in several ways shaped by the interaction among member states' representatives and EC/EU institutions. From the Commission's initial idea of a more neoliberal approach to development in a regional context, the CSCM proposal added a political (and social) dimension, the discussion about Morocco introduced the idea of a free trade area, and the debate about the peace process strengthened the significance and the scope of the regional dimension. If the Euro-Mediterranean Partnership was the child of Spain, it also had many godfathers.

Mediterranean Policies from Renewal to Innovation

While the RMP had begun to raise a set of new issues in Euro-Mediterranean relations, the EMP was on a different scale completely. It represented a true revolution in EFP toward the Mediterranean, for the network of institutions it created, for the number of topics on the agenda, and for the approach to economic development.

In essence, the RMP was a policy for allocating funds to Mediterranean countries. Trade agreements were left untouched. The institutional setting remained the same light instrument for managing agreements that were originally conceived for the GMP. There were a few innovations. The first was in the amount of funding devoted to the Mediterranean. The grand total of funds for the fourth financial protocols was about three times higher than for the previous generation of financial protocols.[117] Although this was an obvious increase, the final result was still poor: EC aid represented 3 percent of all Overseas Development Assistance received by Mediterranean nonmember countries (Tovias 1996, 14). More tellingly, aid per capita was ECU 2.4 per year, compared to Eastern European's ECU 6.8 and ACP countries' ECU 4.7 (Tovias 1996, 14).

The most interesting innovation consisted in the manner in which these funds were spent. A large part was devoted to traditional bilateral relations. A component was, however, earmarked for multilateral and decentralized cooperation. Under the label of "Med programs," the EC launched several multilateral schemes of cooperation, devoted to specific issue areas (environment, media, municipalities, small and medium enterprises, and so on) (Pierros et al. 1999, 133–134; Rahmani and Bekkouche 1995). They were meant to create regional networks of actors across the Mediterranean, thus breaking away from the established pattern of bilateral relations. Moreover, for the first time representatives of "civil society" could apply for funding from the EC. Local authorities, universities, business and the media were mentioned in this respect, while NGOs did not at first attract much attention. The seeds were planted for a revision of the doctrine which saw the state is at the center of development and economic activities. The EMP was to further expand on this trend.

The EMP has been on a different scale than the RMP and all previous initiatives. It was launched at the Barcelona Conference on November 27–28, 1995, with the adoption of the so-called Barcelona Declaration. The text was a masterpiece of diplomacy, hinting at thorny issues such as UN resolutions, the Non-Proliferation Treaty, self-determination of peoples, and the fight against terrorism.[118] The Barcelona Declaration has since acted as a "founding charter" of new Euro-Mediterranean relations.

The EMP introduced three main novelties: (1) the multilayered institutional structure of dialogue; (2) the number of topics on the agenda; (3) the new approach to economic questions and to development. The EMP has thus put in place a structure with the potential to transform geographical closeness into actual collaboration and partnership, thus "constructing" a Euro-Mediterranean region.[119]

The multilayered institutional structure proposed in Barcelona comprises three parallel levels.[120] The traditional channel is bilateral Association Councils and Association Committees, composed of member states, the Commission and Mediterranean nonmember representatives, which regularly meet to discuss and review topics in connection with the Association Agreement. In comparison to the Cooperation Councils of the GMP, the work of Association Councils tends to be more politically relevant and visible, thanks to the wide range of topics included in the agreements.

There is a unilateral channel which is formally not new, as it deals with the financial contribution of the EU to the Mediterranean countries, for the implementation of the Association Agreements and for jointly agreed priorities. The structure of five year financial plans has also been largely retained. What has changed is the degree of planning that the Commission puts into the endeavor and the transparency that publicly available Country Strategy Papers (covering four years) and National Indicative Programs (covering two years) have brought to it. The documents do not fully reflect EU goals nor do they express a clear list of priorities, for obvious diplomatic reasons. Still, they represent an unprecedented effort on the part of the EU to plan ahead and articulate a policy for a specific country.

The multilateral channel is a complete novelty, and has grown into a substantial forum for multilateral political dialogue. Questions dealt with bilaterally are first developed as general themes. By blunting differences among the parties the EMP's multilateral component serves to redraw previous maps of strategic alliances and of identities and aims at replacing them with a single economic, political, and social bloc.

Through its post-Barcelona evolution, the multilateral framework of the EMP has developed at all possible levels of the diplomatic hierarchy.

At the very top, the Barcelona Summit marking 10 years of the EMP on November 27–28, 2005, aimed at bringing together the heads of state and government of EMP partners.[121] Below that, ministers have met regularly, and at an increasing pace, over a variety of issues ranging from water to trade to health.[122] Below the ministerial level, it was decided in 2002 to hold ad hoc meetings among General Directors of Ministries of Foreign Affairs, with the participation of the Commission, whenever there is a substantial agenda but no meeting of ministers of Foreign Affairs scheduled. Occasional meetings of senior officials with other competences have also taken place. More routinely, matters are addressed by the Euro-Mediterranean Committee, made up of one ambassador from each country. Whereas the Work Program annexed to the Barcelona Conference sketched out a committee composed of the EU troika, flanked by the Commission and the Council Secretariat, and one representative from each Mediterranean partner country, the practice has instead developed of admitting "as observers" all EU member states, de facto re-creating a Euro-Mediterranean conference at a lower hierarchical level. Several working groups have also been created.

The second important revolution decided at Barcelona was the range of themes listed as possible topics for Euro-Mediterranean dialogue. Following the CSCE pattern (and also the "pillars" of the Maastricht Treaty), the Barcelona Declaration was divided into three parts (named *volets*). Alongside the economic and financial *volet* were a political and security *volet*, and another encompassing the social, cultural, and human dimension. This wide range of topics represented a real departure in practice. The GMP and the RMP were confined to purely economic matters, whereas the EAD hinted at but never carried out a political dialogue. The social dimension had only been touched upon in passing in Agreements with Morocco, Algeria, Tunisia, and Turkey, in relation to the treatment of workers. The EMP instead has given rise to plenty of discussion on a very broad range of topics. The dialogue on the first *volet* has ranged from respect for sovereignty and territorial integrity, to good governance, to security and confidence building measures.[123] The development of a dialogue on democracy and human rights is particularly noteworthy in breaking previous patterns of interaction, both in bilateral and in multilateral relations. While it has not had a huge impact on intra- and inter-national relations of southern Mediterranean partners, the debate on democracy and human rights has acquired a legitimacy that it did not have prior to the Barcelona Declaration. In 2001 and especially after 9/11, however, the gist of the dialogue has shifted to questions of terrorism and cooperation in the area of justice and migration.

The debate has shown the two sides converging on some points, as for instance in the aftermath of 9/11 or on some aspects of migration, but also and more recently there have been areas of dissent, as emphasized by the lacklustre Code of Conduct on Terrorism adopted at the summit in Barcelona in November 2005.[124]

How has the agenda developed since 1995? For a long time the economic aspects of the EMP topped the agenda, but since 2000 the discussion about security, in its various forms, has come to the fore. At first, this led to the unsuccessful path of drafting a Euro-Mediterranean Charter for Peace and Stability, along the lines of the Stability Pact within OSCE (Aliboni 1999, 137–138). The second Intifada and the strong reluctance of several partners have prevented any progress since 2000 however. After an attempt at tackling democracy and human rights directly, the agenda has shifted toward a "justice and home affairs" approach to security. At first this shift mirrored developments within the EU instigated by the Helsinki summit in December 1999. The Common Strategy for the Mediterranean[125] thus listed specific initiatives such as the promotion of transparency and correspondences of legal systems, migration (both from the point of view of just treatment and social integration of legal migrants, the fight against human trafficking and illegal immigration) and the fight against organized crime, terrorism, and drug trafficking. 9/11 gave further impetus to developments in this field, with cooperation on the issue of migration and the fight against terrorism emerging as the two leading issues on the agenda at the Barcelona +10 Summit in November 2005.[126] Whereas the former has been partly successful albeit behind closed doors, the latter has led to some very public disagreements, such as the negotiations which produced a toothless Code of Conduct on Countering Terrorism adopted at the Summit.

Together with this broad agenda and the institutional setting that underpins it, the last main novelty brought about by the EMP is the new approach it offers to economic issues, in the form of the creation of a free trade area between the EU and the Mediterranean nonmember countries. The idea was not new. The GMP originally addressed it but it was dropped at the implementation stage. The EMP has instead tackled the matter in a very direct manner, including an (indicative) deadline for its introduction in 2010. Whereas the aim of the GMP was to introduce Mediterranean industrial goods to the Common Market, with the EMP it is up to the Mediterranean countries to dismantle their national tariff and nontariff barriers to European industrial exports. The essence of the economic aspect of the EMP thus concerns the opening of Mediterranean markets—for long protected by high tariff barriers—to European competition.[127] With regard to agricultural products the position is more nuanced, since the EU, sheltered by the Common Agricultural Policy, de facto in the Association Agreements postpones the liberalization of access to the Single Market until a later round of negotiation, although it does commit to the "gradual implementation of greater liberalization" in the agricultural sphere. Taking into account the EU 2004 enlargement, what has happened is the creation of a major commercial bloc within which there will be free movement of goods, and in the future of services and capital too. The ideal shared prosperity invoked by the Barcelona Declaration rests on this ambitious economic program.[128]

The scale of the economic project has justified the negotiation of a new generation of agreements and it has transformed the quantity and type of aid provided by the EU to the Mediterranean countries.

The new agreements, collectively named Euro-Mediterranean Association Agreements[129] have been negotiated on a single pattern, with amendments made according to the specificities of each case (see table 5.6). Art. 2 of all agreements mentions the respect of human rights and democratic principles as an "essential part of the agreement."[130] All the agreements[131] explicitly provide for political dialogue, which also includes discussion of respect for human rights and the main rules of democracy. In the economic domain, they provide for the gradual implementation of a planned free trade area over a transition period of around 12 years, in which participants (mainly Mediterranean countries) undertake to reduce barriers to trade. A series of rule-related issues have also been placed on the agenda (intellectual property, services, competition and so on) in conformity with the current trend in WTO negotiations, although they are not currently part of the Agreements.[132]

The transformation all this is intended to deliver to the Mediterranean partners is accompanied by a substantial increase in the amount of funds devoted to the area under a program called MEDA,[133] with an eye to smoothening the economic and social transition. Estimates of the impact of economic liberalization in Mediterranean economies have suggested a very high rate of failure of industries that will not survive competition with Europe (Pierros et al. 1999, 193), with costly social consequences. MEDA is intended to soften the transition. It was approved for the period 1995–1999 with a budget of ECU 3,424.5 million[134] and renewed for the period 2000–2006 for an amount of €5,350 million.[135]

The way in which funds can be spent has also changed (Philippart 2001; Holden 2003), though much of the change was already foreseen

Table 5.6 Agreements between the EC and the Mediterranean Partners

	Legal Basis	Type of Agreement	Official Publication Date
Turkey *Since 1999, it has acquired the status of candidate country*	Art. 238	Association Agreement (mixed)	L217 (29.XI1.1964) Extended in 1995 (Customs Union) and in 1998 (Agricultural products)
Cyprus	Accessed to the EU in May 2004		
Malta	Accessed to the EU in May 2004		
Algeria	Art. 238	Euro-Mediterranean Association Agreement (mixed)	L265 (10.X.2005)
Egypt	Art. 238	Euro-Mediterranean Association Agreement (mixed)	L304 (30.IX.2004)
Jordan	Art. 238	Euro-Mediterranean Association Agreement (mixed)	L129 (15.V.02)
Israel	Art. 238	Euro-Mediterranean Association Agreement (mixed)	L147 (21.VI.00)
Lebanon	Art. 238	Euro-Mediterranean Association Agreement (mixed)	L143 (30.V.2006)
Morocco	Art. 238	Euro-Mediterranean Association Agreement (mixed)	L70 (18.III.00)
Palestinian Authority	Art. 113 and Art. 130y	Euro-Mediterranean Interim Association Agreement	L187 (16.VII.97)
Syria	Art. 238	Euro-Mediterranean Association Agreement (mixed)	Initialled 19.X.2004. Council to decide on signature
Tunisia	Art. 238	Euro-Mediterranean Association Agreement (mixed)	L97 (30.III.98)

Source: OJEU, various Issues.

under the RMP. At bilateral level, MEDA is not just for classical development cooperation projects (41 percent of the total for the period 1995–1999), but also and especially to deal with problems of economic transition and its social consequences (45 percent). Part of the funding is directed toward regional projects (14 percent).[136] Moreover, a special emphasis is put on the involvement of civil society: the participating countries and, where appropriate, economic and civil actors are called on to present projects. There has thus been a clear attempt to maximize MEDA's utility and flexibility. At the insistence of the European Parliament, a budget line (MEDA democracy) was devoted to funding projects relating to democracy, civil and socioeconomic rights (freedom of expression, association and so on) and protection of vulnerable groups (women, children, minorities, refugees and so on).[137]

There is thus no doubt that the EMP has introduced very important innovations in the way the Europeans address their southern neighbors. New institutional venues, a renewed emphasis on regionalism, new issues on the agenda, innovative thinking about economic development, new aid and novel ways in which to spend it, all these aspects highlight the EMP as a landmark in Euro-Mediterranean relations.

I would like to conclude on the EMP with two remarks about its content. First, while it might seem like a strong case for neoliberal explanations based on the market access for Europeans to the Mediterranean market, the rationale behind the EMP and the way its agenda has evolved emphasize its importance in noneconomic terms, particularly security. Indeed, the construction of a free trade area places the burden almost exclusively on the Mediterranean partners, whose markets are to be open to European competition. Thus, while it would seem that liberal intergovernmentalism has a point in suggesting that European foreign policy is about securing market access, the EFP embodied by the EMP is more cooperative than that, and is more focused on security than economic concerns. As we have seen, it was security perceptions which prompted initial European interest in the Mediterranean. Economic exchanges are thus instrumental to improve development in the area and are a means to realize improved security through promoting stabilization and interdependence (Niblock 1996).

Second, and very much like the GMP, the content of the dialogue shows that it is shaped by European concepts. The neoliberal approach to the Mediterranean, while difficult to avoid in the 1990s, was not really tailored to the needs of Mediterranean nonmember countries.[138] Paradoxically, the Mediterranean partners did have not only several economic concerns, ranging from the issue of their external debt to agricultural exports, but also security ones, such as the marginalization of Libya[139] and the stalled peace process in the Middle East. These however are not EMP priorities. The EMP instead addresses issues that reflect quite closely the main security concerns of the Europeans in the post–cold war period and embodies the typical recipe of economic liberalization as an instrument for development and stabilization of the area.[140] Thus, the content of the EMP suggests that the European model is being exported to the Mediterranean without major adaptations (see Bicchi 2006).

The European Neighbourhood Policy: Yet another Initiative?

The EU is currently[141] in the process of defining yet another foreign policy instrument, under the name of European Neighbourhood Policy. From the point of view of this volume, however, the ENP is not, strictly speaking, an innovation in Mediterranean relations. It has come to include the Mediterranean, but it was originally conceived to address the enlarged EU's Eastern neighbors. Its capacity to innovate on Euro-Mediterranean relations is yet to be proved and at the moment seems limited. While the ENP does contain a few novel points, most of them are vaguely defined or yet to be implemented. Therefore, it does not fall squarely in the focus of this book. In spite of that, the ENP is relevant not only because it has the Mediterranean in its remit. The entrepreneurship behind the initiative in fact has come to resemble the pattern exhibited by the RMP, where the Commission played a leading role with little support from member states.

The limited scope of the original ENP frame is reflected in the way it has changed name and geographical remit. A small-scale project was originally presented at the General Affairs Council meeting on the April 15, 2002, in the form of an initiative addressed to Ukraine, Belarus and Moldova (in this order).[142] At this stage, the project went under the name of "Wider Europe" and dealt mainly with how the EU could make its relations with the EU's postenlargement Eastern neighbors more effective. When the Commission and the High Representative for CFSP came forward with some proposals, interest was however low (Wallace 2003, 9). The idea was taken up again at the Council meeting at the end of September 2002, as the decision to enlarge was put on the agenda of the European Council of the following December. The emphasis was still very much on "new" Eastern neighbors, "given" the existence of the Barcelona process with Mediterranean countries and the Stabilization and Association Process with the Western Balkans.[143]

The Mediterranean was tagged on at a later stage. The European Council meeting in Copenhagen, on December 12–13, 2002, mentioned "enhancing relations" with the Mediterranean nonmembers, in parallel to Ukraine, Moldova and Belarus (in this new order) and

Russia.[144] The initiative remained under the cumbersome name of "Wider Europe-New Neighbours" though. It took the whole of 2003 to get rid of the "new-ness" of the initiative, the final blow dealt apparently by Greece, which stressed that Mediterranean neighbors were certainly not "new." The initiative thus acquired by January 2004 the final name of European Neighbourhood Policy.[145] The idea also started to circulate of enlarging the ENP to Armenia, Azerbaijan and Georgia.[146] It became a concrete commitment following the "rose revolution" in Georgia (Smith 2005, 759).[147] Russia for its part lost interest in the initiative along the way. In the first three years since its inception, ENP thus has come to group together three distinct (and quite different) sets of nonmembers: the "original" Eastern European ones, the "old" Barcelona partners, and the Caucasus latecomers.

It is unclear how innovative the ENP is and will be. There is a tension in its content and method between, on the one hand, a differentiated approach for every country, and, on the other, the attempt to offer equal opportunities to all partners. Prodi summarized the initial approach in the formula "all except institutions,"[148] to be understood as "everything apart from membership." It soon became customary to refer to the "four freedoms" and to "a stake in the Internal Market" on which the EU is based and which could be expanded to nonmembers too, according to their degree of preparedness. The EU would approach each country "within a differentiated framework [responding] to progress made by the partner countries in political and economic reform."[149] This "regatta approach" is different from well established tenets of EFP, such as a region-making effort built into the EMP (cf. Adler et al. 2006). It also sounds very much as though the EU is insisting on a greater degree of conditionality from neighbors (Del Sarto and Schumacher 2005, 22), which would represent a break from the previous EMP emphasis on consensus.

The ENP inner tensions are currently being solved by watering down concrete offers and it is difficult to predict where the process will eventually end up. So far, the main concrete achievements of the ENP are the drafting of Action Plans and the extension of some internal policies to external countries, while reference to the "stake in the Internal Market" has become increasingly rare. In December 2004, the Commission issued Action Plans with Israel, Jordan, Moldova, Morocco, the Palestinian Authority, Tunisia and Ukraine. These Action Plans were adopted throughout 2005, while in November 2006, it was the turn of Armenia, Azerbaijan, and Georgia. Discussions are still going on with Egypt and Lebanon. Action Plans under the ENP differ from the Country Strategy

Papers and the National Indicative Programs adopted under MEDA because of the sheer breadth of topics covered. Action Plans present an inclusive list of political, economic and social reforms which neighboring countries are expected to undertake at some stage in order to approximate EU standards. These lists are however very long and often generic, lacking clear priorities and at times resembling an exercise in "token diplomacy" (Emerson and Noutcheva 2005, 21). The potential for change seems so far to have got lost in the attempt to be inclusive. The EU has extended some internal policies, such as INTERREG or mobility for students and researchers, to include ENP countries or cross-border regions, although the way it has done so is not particularly targeted to ENP countries.[150]

The entrepreneurship behind the ENP reveals that the Commission is the main actor promoting the initiative, but it has encountered some limitations in doing so. No member state has committed itself to the ENP success. The original proposal for Ukraine, Belarus and Moldova, in April 2002, was put forward by the United Kingdom,[151] which tried to steer the debate about postenlargement but lost most of its interest along the way. The inclusion of the Mediterranean countries was supported by southern European countries, but none of them held out actively for a new type of Euro-Mediterranean relationship. The burden has been left to the Commission, which has been happy to carry it further with some help from the High Representative for CFSP. In fact, Prodi started calling for an "inclusive" approach leading to a "wider European area," in his investiture speech as President of the Commission at the EP in Strasbourg in 1999. He stressed the need for a comprehensive strategy stretching from Russia to the Mediterranean countries again in November 2002[152] and it was apparently him that took the front of the stage in spearheading the inclusion of Mediterranean countries at the European Council in Copenhagen shortly afterward.[153] In particular, the set of people within the Commission that have worked on enlargement have also taken responsibility for the ENP. In July 2003, Verheugen, who was in charge of enlargement, was given responsibility for the ENP as well. With the new Barroso Commission, inaugurated in November 2004, responsibility has shifted to the DG External Relations, but most of the people employed on the ENP have past experience in the DG Enlargement, even if it is something of a paradox that these officials work on an initiative in which enlargement is explicitly excluded.[154] The enlargement background of officials in charge of the ENP makes them ill-equipped to solve the underlying tensions of the ENP mentioned earlier, while at the same time it represents one of the main sources of potential innovation in Euro-Mediterranean relations.

The ENP, therefore, resembles the RMP in the sense that seeds of change are planted by the Commission in a terrain made rough by the absence of member states' political commitment to the endeavor. If no other policy window/policy entrepreneurship/policy initiative for the Mediterranean occurs, it could be interesting to see whether the ENP, unlike the RMP, eventually does deliver change in spite of a weak entrepreneur and weak background conditions.

Conclusions

The end of the cold war led to a broad effort to rethink Europe's role in the world. Part of this effort was devoted to the Mediterranean. The crumbling of well-established cold war concepts lifted the veil on previous Euro-Mediterranean relations. European policy makers focused on old and new developments with a sense of urgency that in several instances bordered on panic. The developments in the Mediterranean in the 1980s, which Europeans had failed to spot at the time had turned into red warning lights for European public authorities in the early 1990s. Miserable rates of economic development, mixed with the radicalization of political opposition in the form of Islamic fundamentalism, appeared to plant a "time bomb" on Europe's doorstep. More specifically, this period witnessed the (low) securitization of migration from the Mediterranean, the politicization and at times (low) securitization of Islamic fundamentalism, and the partial resecuritization of terrorism. European policy makers struggled to come to terms with these challenges and to frame both the political problems and the policy alternatives. At the same time, the marginalization of Europe in the Middle East peace process and the opening of the EU toward Eastern Europe helped to underline the importance of adopting a policy stance toward the Mediterranean.

In this context, policy entrepreneurship was provided by a number of different sources. The Commission succeeded in pushing through an initiative toward the Mediterranean, the RMP. Though not particularly innovative, it signaled that the Commission understood that Euro-Mediterranean relations were in need of improvement. The initiative also showed that the Commission could act as a policy entrepreneur and suggest innovative changes, although it also revealed how limited its action could be. It was soon overtaken by a more political effort by Spain, in conjunction with France and partly Italy. Spanish interest in the Mediterranean had grown out of the sea change in its foreign policy in the democratic post-Franco era, and its decision to combine its European and Mediterranean policy to enhance its international status as a middle power. Spain acted on several fronts, promoting the interaction of the other member states as well as of EC institutions. It contributed to the framing of Mediterranean challenges and lobbied in favor of a European initiative for the region. Its action developed on various levels, ranging from bilateral relations to multilateral fora. Its cooperation with France was particularly close, up to the point that France became a second policy entrepreneur in favor of the Mediterranean. Their activism sparked a process by which member states debated several strands of ideas about the Mediterranean and they were actively engaged in a process of EFP making.

As a consequence of the simultaneous presence of a policy window and of these policy entrepreneurs, the EU finally launched a new and innovative initiative to frame Euro-Mediterranean relations for the new millennium. It remains to be seen whether the ENP will add anything substantial to that.

This analysis sheds light on several points. While supranational/ neofunctional hypotheses are more valid than they appeared in the case of the early 1970s, their explanatory appeal is still limited. The activism of the Commission partly suggests supranational/neofunctional explanations, as the RMP was the first instance of policy entrepreneurship by the Commission, a role later repeated with the ENP. This point is crucial, as it shows that in principle actors other than member states can play this role. The Commission had tried once before at the time of the southern enlargement to push for change in relations between the "ins" and the "outs." However the lack of a policy window had prevented any real change. As the conditions for an EFP initiative ripened, the Commission's activism bore some results. On the other hand, the innovations promoted by the Commission in the RMP and in the ENP have not amounted to a paradigmatic change. Both initiatives lacked political momentum. The RMP might have led to more substantial developments, and the ENP still could. Therefore, the jury for the Commission's role (and for supranational/neofunctional hypotheses about it) is still out, waiting for a case in which an EC institution would make the difference in EFP making toward the Mediterranean at a time when there is no other concurrent initiative.

Intergovernmentalism can be said, as in the case of the early 1970s, to be right but for the wrong reasons. In the early 1970s, the status of economic relations did contribute to the formulation of the GMP and the EAD. Similarly, in the 1990s, the EMP did promote the opening of Mediterranean markets. However, it was the cognitive uncertainty generated by perceived security threats that prodded economic multilateral cooperation. Most important has been the call for an overall political and social change in the region. Rather than the final goal, economic reform and economic liberalization have been the means to an end in terms of the bigger project. Moreover, while security threats mattered, and more so than economics they were more in the minds of policy makers in the realm of perceptions and ideas than realists would have it. There was a lot of power politics, but the way it was defined depended heavily on the context, on the dynamics among actors and their reading of what was going on at the time. Both Spain's motivations and member states' security concerns were inspired by the way they chose to read facts on the ground, rather than to material changes that occurred.

More generally, the analysis of this period shows the importance of a different approach to analyzing EFP making. In this period, the formulation of a common EFP initiative toward the Mediterranean is particularly complex. Politicians "puzzled" over what to do with challenges originating from the area. National solutions were adopted and changed at an increasing speed, as for instance in the case of migration. National interests were deconstructed as national agendas changed. While several aspects were taken care of at the national level, it was the stickiness of cognitive uncertainty about the big picture that created the ground for defining a common understanding and a common initiative at the European level. The definition of a European approach to the Mediterranean occurred also because of specific actions by policy entrepreneurs. Several focused on a slowly evolving political project and involved the other member states in a debate. By interacting and negotiating, as well as framing, the components of a new understanding of Euro-Mediterranean relations and the EU's role in them were slowly crafted. The European debate about systematizing relations with the Mediterranean nonmembers found its anchor in the EMP.

This complex process has produced the most ambitious initiative the EC/EU has ever addressed to the Mediterranean. While potent in symbolism, the substance of what was agreed in the EMP signals a real change in the actual commitment of the EU multilateral cooperation. Contrary to the 1970s, very negative developments such as the deterioration of the peace process and the Second Intifada have not derailed the process. Regional dialogue thus continues, testifying to the strength of the EMP in bringing all the partners together. The ENP might add to that, in the near future. And this outcome, in a deeply fragmented region, is already an achievement.

Conclusions

In this research, I have analyzed how, when, and why the EC/EU has launched an EFP initiative toward the Mediterranean. Two periods of activism by the EC/EU have certain characteristics in common. I have shown that the dynamics between a background of cognitive uncertainty, an entrepreneurial member state, and the ensuing interaction within the EC/EU are conditions which explain how and when the Mediterranean has moved up the EC/EU agenda, and why a policy initiative has been adopted. During periods of neglect, these key conditions were not in place.

There were four periods in Euro-Mediterranean relations. First, between 1957 and 1972, the EEC did not have an EFP for the Mediterranean. Countries with a Mediterranean shore were addressed through bilateral agreements, which varied greatly in content and format. Second, in 1972 and then again in 1974, member states adopted a regional approach. They expressed it through the GMP, launched in 1972, and in the EAD, agreed in 1974. The former was addressed to the EEC's southern neighbors grouped together as Mediterranean countries, while the latter put together Arab states, most of which were Mediterranean. The third period was marked by disinterest toward the Mediterranean and no new initiative. The end of the cold war opened a fourth period, marked once again by activism on the European side. It peaked with the adoption of the Euro-Mediterranean Partnership.

The first of the common features in the two periods of activism was a shift in domestic agendas, leading policy makers to experience cognitive uncertainty. By this, I mean that they were unsure how to interpret a given phenomenon. Both periods opened with a relaxation of international tensions between superpowers, which in 1989 led to the end of the cold war. As military threats receded, European countries came to perceive fresh challenges originating from the Mediterranean, and new topics were politicized/securitized. In the early 1970s, two issues attracted attention, terrorism and economic relations. In the early 1990s, the issues which dominated European perceptions of the Mediterranean were migration, Islamic fundamentalism, and a new form of terrorism. Similarly, in both periods, the relevance of approaching these challenges through a common European discussion was reinforced by diverging transatlantic perspectives on the Middle East and by potentially conflicting European agendas between northern and southern European member states. In the two periods of inactivity a well established cold war pattern dominated the European agenda, leaving no room for other issues.

In all the initiatives adopted, member states were the most effective policy entrepreneurs. In the early 1970s, it was France that took the lead. In the 1990s, Spain was in the front. In both cases, what prompted them into action and the process they set in motion were very similar. Both wanted international recognition. France was after a role as a "big power," while Spain's aspiration was membership in the club of Western democracies. The manner in which their entrepreneurial efforts unfolded was also analogous across time. They behaved as "brokers," rather than "believers," as their input consisted of maintaining the momentum of the process rather than attempting to convey a specific policy proposal. Both countries started in one direction (France by proposing a parallel between Spain and Israel, Spain with a joint initiative together with Italy in the CSCE), but ended up promoting more complex propositions (France suggested a free trade area with all Mediterranean countries, Spain pushed the idea of a partnership with a strong economic core). Moreover, they acted in conjunction with other actors, including the European Commission. This was particularly clear in the case of Spain, which worked together with France, the Commission, and at times Italy. The Commission has displayed only a limited capacity for independent action, although its capacity evolved through time. While in the 1970s the Commission was not a front runner, in the 1980s and early 1990s it displayed a certain degree of activism, which is still evident within the ENP. It continues to lack, however, the capacity to force political momentum in EFP making.

Entrepreneurial activism triggered a process of cognitive interaction among member states and EC/EU institutions, which framed new understandings of Euro-Mediterranean relations. During the process, ideas about the nature of the problems (deemed to be linked to security) combined with possible policy solutions (generally linked to economic cooperation and regionalism) to reflect the economic doctrine of the time. The geographical scope of the potential EC/EU initiative was always a key issue, expressing the politics of proximity. Discussions between member states and EC/EU institutions led to the "piecing together" of these conceptual elements, which developed partly in connection with one another and partly in parallel. The empirical analysis has also shown the complexity of the division of labor and of the venues involved in the process, which have exceeded the boundaries of Council meetings. This development has been particularly evident since the early 1990s.

What does this empirical evidence amount to and what is its theoretical relevance? The first conclusion is that an approach based on Policy Analysis pays off. I framed the analysis of EFP making in terms of policy windows and policy entrepreneurship, along the lines of Kingdon (1984/95) and this contributed to systematize and prioritize the history of European approaches to the Mediterranean. It also helped to disentangle (but not separate) the interacting structural and agency elements. Thus, this research supports the adoption of a Policy Analysis perspective when focusing on EC/EU policies and their context. While there is an increasing trend in this direction in European studies devoted to internal policies (e.g., Heritier 1999), this volume suggests that EFP analysis might benefit from following the suit.

A second conclusion from the Mediterranean case relates to the role of cognitive uncertainty and shifting national interests for the definition of a European interest and a European initiative. National policies toward the domestic aspects of more global issues entered a period of turbulence shortly before the process of EFP formulation began. I have taken these changes in national attitudes as the best available proxy to detect a break in national preferences and, in particular, the presence of a sense of uncertainty about how to address a new phenomenon. National preferences "in flux" are a precondition for the definition of a new foreign policy initiative at the European level. More specifically, the increase in public importance of one or more issues (from private to public sphere, from "ordinary politics" to security, from low security to high security, or a sum of these possibilities), paralleled by the decrease in importance of some others, contributes to create the background conditions for EFP making. The reason for this lies in the fact that national policy makers are more likely to discuss understandings of an issue and alternative policy options, including multilateral ones, when cognitively motivated to do so by domestic politics. National preferences in flux create a passive availability to debate common problems and solutions at the European level. To cast this in a broader perspective, uncertainty at the national level offers the opportunity to pursue cooperation at the multilateral level.

This conclusion opens up new research questions. First of all, the microfoundations of this point need to be explored. It would be interesting to focus in more detail on where and when perceptions change, and which changes are most relevant to create cognitive uncertainty. In spite of widespread references to crises and "critical junctures," the process of deconstruction of national preferences remains an underresearched topic. In other terms, we need to know more about cognitive uncertainty as a *dependent* variable. This would make it possible to see how and why perceptions change, and what makes it difficult or impossible to redefine policy options in a solely national settings and what in contrast makes the European option an attractive one. This exploration would, in my opinion, represent the most interesting way forward for the literature on socialization and on the indirect effects of Europeanization.

As my focus was on cognitive uncertainty as a necessary condition for EFP, my aim was on grasping its main indicators and understanding the conditions under which the EC/EU arena becomes connected with the national setting. In this light, this research has also shown the importance of competing views of world events in EFP making. Cognitive uncertainty is first and foremost ideational in nature. The importance of cognitive uncertainty for policy windows thus supports the argument of constructivism about ideational conditions over the reductive material approach taken by intergovernmentalism and much of (but not all) traditional realism. The analysis of sheer material aspects obscured more than it enlightened the Mediterranean case. Sometimes there was no material change on the ground *and* yet there was EFP formulation, as in the case of economic exchanges in the early 1970s. Sometimes the opposite case occurred, such as the lack of consequences during the 1980s to rising Islamic fundamentalism in the Arab world. Sometimes the change was limited to a period prior to the EFP formulation, as in the case of migration flows. The examination of European understandings of what was going on was much more to the point. It suggested why an issue was deemed to be a problem and why it required a policy response. It stressed how interpretations of the same issue can differ. Most importantly, the ideational analysis highlights the connection between, on the one hand, the deconstruction of established policy positions and, on the other, the attempt to reconstitute them through a collective process. If the ideational side is not taken into account, it becomes impossible to explain how, when, and why the EC/EU adopts an initiative.

The juxtaposition between material and ideational conditions raises several points, some of which would also require further research. A first point is the relationship between the two. To be fair, changes in perceptions were at times preceded by changes in material conditions.

When this was the case, an interesting pattern worthy of further exploration seemed to develop, especially when security issues were at stake. The initial reaction by member states occurred at the national level, and it was expressed by domestic changes and in bilateral relations with the Mediterranean countries involved. This tended to be a very effective step which was generally able to redress the situation. In parallel to it, a European "internal" process might be launched, focusing on the issue at stake, which could also produce tangible results. Only as a third channel would a more general EFP initiative be considered. However, by the time this third possibility was envisaged, the other two channels were likely to already have delivered the tangible and material results hoped for. This was the case, for instance, with the oil shock. Bilateral relations quickly reestablished disrupted supplies before any multilateral initiative was formulated. Similarly, the increase in migrant numbers coming from Mediterranean nonmembers in the early 1990s was effectively curbed by 1993 through national policies and in part by means of European cooperation within Schengen. By the time the debate about EMP entered its decisive stage, the issue in material terms had lost much of its relevance. But despite a turnaround in material conditions, the ideational process continued. The tentative conclusion that we can draw from this trend is that cognitive uncertainty tends to be "sticky," that is, it continues to affect behavior of policy makers even after policy decisions have been effectively implemented.

A second issue refers to what exactly happens when issues become politicized/securitized and they move up the political agenda. Do member states and policy entrepreneurs deliberately *construct* the reality to which they then respond? Is their behavior instrumental, even cynical, that is constructing the reality as cognitively uncertain *in order to* justify their response? Given the symbolic nature of most of the EFP initiatives, an approach à la Edelman (1988), for instance, would support this argument. I am not entirely convinced how compelling it would be, however. Policy makers act according to a vision they have and it is that vision which is interesting in this argument regardless of how it came about. This research did show, however, that often other concomitant factors tended to magnify the relevance of an issue on the agenda of European policy makers. For instance, when Arab terrorism appeared in Europe, it was accompanied by a huge variety of other types of terrorism, mainly from within member states (RAF, Red Brigades, and so on). The same applied to migrations in the early 1990s. Therefore, issues were "constructed," but in this research there was little evidence of them being constructed only in order to respond to them.

A third objection would question my exclusive focus on political and security issues. This is partly a limitation of the research. In order to test the independence of discourse over material factors, it would have been necessary to show that there were competing interpretations of the Mediterranean, which emphasized the economic opportunities or a humanitarian dimension. It would also have been important to analyze how the securitization discourse prevailed over the others and came to dominate the process of EFP making. While I showed the predominance of discourses about political and security challenges, I addressed the alternatives only in an indirect way, and I did not focus on how that predominance emerged, rather accepting it from changes in public authorities' policy agenda. That is also why I generally refrained from speaking about "discourses" and "discourse analysis," as the terms would be more appropriate for research that compares various discourses and how they come to establish themselves as the dominant interpretation of a given subject.

While all these points would need further research, the findings presented here make it clear how intriguing the addition of uncertainty could be for analyses of European integration. It suggests that member states' cooperation is a collective journey in the dark, in which they share their "puzzlement" as much as their preferences. European integration would thus be more of a contingent and underdetermined process than some literature suggests, and rationality would be a socially contingent phenomenon.

A third conclusion, together with the relevance of Policy Analysis and cognitive uncertainty, refers to the actions of member states and to the processes taking place among them. The link between national arenas and the EC/EU is founded on the activism of a policy entrepreneur and on the specific type of process its activism triggers among fellow member states and EC/EU institutions. The empirical evidence has shown that the most effective entrepreneur is a member state, while the case in favor of the Commission is at best mixed. What takes place then is a "thick" process of cognitive interaction, among trusted partners.

There are a few aspects that intermingle here. First, this research has shown that there is room for expanding the range of entrepreneurial states' motivations. A member state that acts as a policy entrepreneur can both try to push a well defined national interest (and this is the way liberal intergovernmentalism would see its action) or if its own national interest is defined in broad and vague terms, stimulate the debate at the European level in order to determine the nature of the problem and the possible common solutions. In this second case, the rationale of a state's entrepreneurialism springs from the intention to "do something" rather than promoting a specific policy proposal. This distinction between a specific and a generic interest in a European action is different from an emphasis on material or ideational aspects of national preferences. It helps to pinpoint the type of entrepreneurship as a consequence of different types of motivations. I have thus suggested distinguishing between different types of entrepreneurs, by putting forward the idea of "brokerage" entrepreneurship. In this case, the entrepreneurial state differs from others only in its more intense focus on reaching a positive conclusion, rather than seeing the difference in terms of it having a ready-made solution that it wants to push through. The debate on entrepreneurship is obviously far from exhausted.

The case for Commission entrepreneurship is mixed. As we have seen, the Commission could, in principle, act as a policy entrepreneur. Moreover, the historical trend seems to indicate an increasing Commission willingness to do so, from early hesitations to later activism. The impact of the policy initiative promoted by the Commission might be more substantial, if allowed time to unfold. The ENP might still provide that opportunity. As a consequence, there could be part of the supranational/neofunctional argument that is supported by these findings. There are a few major limitations, though. It is clear that, in comparison with the case of Eastern Europe, the Commission never played an active role in relation to the Mediterranean "to a unique extent." It would thus be important to address two further points in order to pass judgment on the Commission's entrepreneurship. First, it should be analyzed whether the Commission has been able to impinge upon member states' preferences. On matters related to the Mediterranean, this does not seem to have been the case, but it could be a matter of focusing on conditions under which the Commission does exert an influence. Second, it should be examined whether the Commission can add political momentum to the process of EFP making. For the Mediterranean case the answer is negative, but again, the question is worth examining.

The process that follows from this type of entrepreneurship and from these actors is framing and cognitive (socially "thick") interaction. My main concern here is to stress the importance of cognitive aspects of policy making and of EFP making in particular. The most intriguing element of the findings reported in this volume is the way in which fellow member states and EC/EU institutions represent not only valuable sources of information, but also and most importantly trusted partners in a process of knowledge creation. This suggests that at times of uncertainty member states turn to each other (even if prodded by an entrepreneur and after having explored national solutions). The implication of this could potentially lead to reimagining European Integration theory in social terms, along the lines of group theory à la Merton (1957). When, how and to what extent did fellow partners in EC/EU institutions become a reference group for each other on matters of foreign policy? While EFP analysis has tried to demonstrate this point for a long time, grounding it in sociology and social theory might represent the best way to approach the issue.

I thus suggest that there is an alternative way to look at European cooperation on EFP initiatives toward the Mediterranean to those put forward by other approaches. It starts from the simultaneous existence of two conditions. First, there are states, defined as uncertainty minimizers, which are forced to tackle new international challenges. Second, there is an entrepreneurial member state with national, ideational and underspecified motives to champion a European initiative for the Mediterranean (though this role could potentially be covered by the Commission or other actors as well). Based on the existence of these two conditions, member states and EC/EU institutions are then involved in a process of interaction, which rather than truth-finding or bargaining, is directed at piecing together new understandings and new policy solutions. Such a process constitutes the basis for a common EFP initiative and, potentially, for at least a part of the European integration process.

This conclusion suggests some theoretical considerations about intergovernmentalism and rational choice, as well as supranationalism/neofunctionalism and constructivism. The importance of member states in formulating an EFP toward the Mediterranean does not really support intergovernmentalism beyond a generic focus on member states because the type of states' motivations and the type of ensuing interaction I have emphasized are not what intergovernmentalists would expect. A tenet of intergovernmentalism is that states enter negotiations with well defined preferences. Liberal intergovernmentalists specify this argument further, emphasizing that preferences are defined at the domestic level. My research has shown, on the contrary, a case of negotiations beginning under conditions of cognitive uncertainty and prompted by it. In other terms, the issue at stake in this research is a setting not contemplated by intergovernmentalists, namely a case in which member states do not have a clear idea of what is going on or what is their role. This could suggest that my conclusions and intergovernmentalist arguments are in fact focusing on two parallel sets of cases, the former applying to cases with cognitive uncertainty, the latter to cases with specified preferences.

My argument here does, however, differ from the intergovernmentalist understanding of what is the crucial moment in negotiations and how preferences are defined (on top of the different emphasis on material/ideational conditions). This research suggests that the key moment in negotiations is not the final bargaining process, but the process that leads to it. It could be that preferences are formed at the domestic level and cooperation occurs because of partial overlapping of preferences combined with side payments. However, I question the border-tight process that liberal intergovernmentalists propose and that rational choice has made so famous. The evidence shown here suggests that when member states are simultaneously redefining their policy stance (and thus their national preferences) on given issues, the possibility opens up for interaction at the multilateral level. In an apparent paradox, interaction among uncertain member states can lead to common action. This point is important because it suggests, once again, a new understanding of intergovernmental cooperation. While the term intergovernmental cooperation has become synonymous with cooperation among self-interested, instrumental sovereign states, the perspective I propose understands cooperation among governments as a form of redefinition of interests, which can in fact foster European integration and create limits to member states' independent freedom of action.

Similarly, I have suggested that it is possible to reinterpret traditional themes of realism, intergovernmentalism and of the rational choice agenda, but in a constructivist perspective. The case of EFP toward the Mediterranean has shown several examples of power politics and of behavior aimed at achieving a balance of power in Europe. Here again, my understanding is that especially intergovernmentalism and rationalist approaches are often right, but for the wrong reasons. In other terms, they argue as if it was possible to predict specific behavior and as if behavioral patterns would indefinitely apply. On the contrary, my understanding is that not only "anarchy is what states make out of it," as Wendt has argued, but also competition for power is contextually and socially constructed. These considerations are particularly relevant for the analysis of entrepreneurship. Whereas some readers might be tempted to conclude that France's and Spain's quest for power has dominated the story of EFP toward the Mediterranean, I would emphasize once again that, yes, there has been this element, but we need to contextualize it and to look at the broader picture of cognitive uncertainty, at the specific definition of national interests and at the contingent social dynamics unleashed by cognitive interaction.

Does this mean these findings corroborate a constructivist perspective? The socialization version of European integration does focus on interaction among member states as the cause for changing national preferences. This point is indeed supported by the evidence gathered in this research. From the socialization perspective within a supranational/neofunctional approach, interaction works because it leads to the learning of cooperation rules and to a habit of coordination. Cooperative interaction and changes in national attitudes derive from a coordination reflex that develops among national representatives. Therefore, this approach emphasizes passive aspects, as well as the unconscious and unintended consequences of interaction, to the point that entrepreneurship is apparently not needed.

The evidence presented here does not confirm the microfoundations of the socialization process as usually described. It suggests instead that the passive availability of member states to discuss a multilateral initiative is turned into an active process of interaction by the spur of an entrepreneurial member state. In other words, while there might have been aspects of unintended coordination, there was in this research also a lot of *in*tended coordination aimed at exchanging ideas about the situation member states were in and what had to be done about it. It was neither a process that was effortless nor an interaction that sprang from low levels of the hierarchy. It was a process that required assiduous commitment by the entrepreneurial member state at all levels involved, within and also outside the EC/EU, as well as a conscious, active participation on the part of other parties involved. Therefore, while the argument of the socialization approach in the supranational/neofunctional vein could represent a background condition that reinforces interaction, the two processes do not necessarily follow each other but may, however, be seen in a complementary perspective.

More to the point of constructivist approaches, cognitive interaction suggests that knowledge definition is a key component of policy making and that it is a "thick" process. The focus of empirical constructivist analyses has centered on cases of arguing, as an alternative or complementary mode of negotiation. Much of it has been interpreted as a process of "truth finding," by which members converge on the "best" argument. Framing and cognitive interaction, as defined in this volume, are instead rather contingent processes, by which cognitive elements are pieced together because of proximity (in temporal and spatial terms), rather than because of their validity per se. Once again, cognitive interaction would require a research (and a book) of its own.

Much of the debate about European integration has moved from the intergovernmental-supranational/neofunctional juxtaposition to the rationalist-constructivist debate. In this perspective, the analysis offered here highlights the limitations of both rational choice and constructivism in their accounts of European integration. These findings address many points on the rational choice agenda from a constructivist perspective. They acknowledge that rationality and power politics among states matter, but they are socially contingent and socially constructed. Therefore, the findings of this book could be taken as complementing constructivism but not rational choice, unless rational choice evolves to the point of adding a social dimension to preference formation. The findings offered by this research are that policy making within the EC/EU occurs by addressing the conceptual and cognitive foundations of prospective initiative and, more generally, that an incentive to European cooperation is information exchange and knowledge creation. In terms of rational choice as it currently stands, this does not make sense, as knowledge cannot be shared nor it can be created in common. Interaction can pass on information, but such processes are "thin." This case showed instead that policy was founded on the sharing of information with a view to knowledge creation.

It remains an empirical question whether these conclusions can be generalized to other geographical areas toward which the EC/EU has developed EFP initiatives or if they apply to other negotiation contexts as well. Be that as it may, I believe the findings of this research bear some relevance for several ongoing theoretical and empirical debates. In particular, they highlight that there is more to ideas and to states' action than intergovernamentalism would concede. There is material to suggest that traditional supranational/neofunctional analyses have been too limited in their focus on the supranational effects of actions on the part of supranational actors. There is a possibility that, at times of uncertainty and ultimately indeterminacy, member states choose to stand together, rather than follow parallel or divergent paths.

It remains to be seen whether this is good news for the Mediterranean countries. The conclusions put forward here hint at a grim possibility: namely that European activism springs out of European perceptions of Mediterranean problems, which might take quite a while to emerge and are not always precise in their understanding of Mediterranean societies. EFP making toward the Mediterranean has been so far a process of "much ado about Europe." Hopefully, the EU will one day be able to offer a less Europe-centered contribution to Mediterranean politics.

Notes

Unless otherwise noted, all translations are my own.

Introduction

1. While I am aware of the various feedback loops, my starting point is different from that of researchers such as Ginsberg (2001), who focus on the impact of European foreign policy, thus analyzing the implementation of an initiative and its effects.
2. In the period before the EEC southern enlargement of the 1980s, the Mediterranean nonmember countries were Algeria, Cyprus, Egypt, Greece, Israel, Lebanon, Malta, Morocco, Spain, Syria, Tunisia, and Turkey. In spite of not having a shore on the Mediterranean, Jordan was also included because of its links with the Arab-Israeli conflict. After the southern enlargement (1981–1986), Greece, Spain, and Portugal became members, since then the expression Mediterranean nonmembers does not include them any longer. Since the Madrid Conference (1991), moreover, the EC/EU has allowed an increasing presence to the Palestinian Authority. With the 2004 enlargement, Cyprus and Malta have become member states, while since 1999 Turkey has acquired candidate status. Libya never manifested an interest in the EC/EU. The Balkans have generally been considered as Central and Eastern European countries.
3. For a discussion of definitions of EFP, see Carlsnaes, Sjursen, and White (2004).
4. For analyses that take EPC/CFSP as their central focus, see for instance authors in Pijpers et al. (1988); Regelsberger et al. (1997); as well as Holland (1997); and Zielonka (1998).
5. For analyses that include member states' foreign policy in the picture, see Hill (1993, 322–323; 1998, 18) and White (1999, 44).
6. Cf. Kingdon (1984/95) and Checkel (1997).
7. On policy makers' "puzzlement," see Heclo (1974).
8. See Fischer and Forester (1993), Braun and Busch (1999); and Surel (2000).
9. Contributors to this debate include Finnemore (1996); Weldes (1996); Legro (1996); Pollack (1997); Moravcsik (1999); Checkel (2001); and Hug (2003).

10. The concept of *long durée* was articulated by Braudel, who forcefully applied it to the study of the Mediterranean. See Braudel (1949).
11. As contraposed to the European rescue of nation states articulated by Milward (1992).

Chapter 1 European Foreign Policy Making in Search of a Theory

1. See also contributors to the special issue of the *Journal of European Public Policy*, December 1999, vol. 6, n.4.
2. This is a long standing argument about market failures and informational transaction costs that has been examined by economic and rational choice institutionalism (Williamson 1975; Milgrom and Roberts 1992; Dixit 1996; Epstein and O'Halloran 1999; see also Krasner 1982, Haggard, and Simmons 1987; Rittberger 1995). An intense debate has also followed the argument presented by Fearon that lack of reliable information is one of the main causes of war (1995).
3. Notice two interesting issues. First, foreign policy sits uncomfortably in this literature. According to Pollack, it is an issue area characterized by informational intensity (2003, 63), but he then dismisses the role of uncertainty in the common commercial policy as the latter is instead a domain in which member states are said to aim for credible commitments (2003, 102). Similarly, Franchino attributes a 55/45 ratio to credible commitments and informational intensity in common commercial policy (2002, 683), while Moravcsik claims a notable exception to his theory for European political cooperation as long as there is "no immediate economic impact" (2003, 478).

    Second, credibility is here presented as a rational strategy, while other authors offer a different perspective. Meseguer, for instance, suggests that learning and emulation deriving from the need of credible commitments belong to a model of bounded rationality, as the sole purely rational attitude is problem solving (2005).
4. Morrow 1999, Meseguer 2003.
5. For a recent strand in economics, labeled knowledge management, which tries to address the link between knowledge and socialization, see Nonaka and Reinmoeller (2000) and Abou-Zeid and Cheng (2004).
6. Rational choice accounts *not* focusing on the EU have been paradoxically less rigid than liberal intergovernmentalism in the way they have encompassed unintended consequences to agential behavior. See most notably Olson (1965/71). I thank an anonymous reviewer for pointing this out to me.
7. As opposed to the "European rescue" put forward by Milward (1992).
8. On the agency-structure debate, see Wendt (1987). See also Giddens (1993) and Archer (1996).
9. National Commission on Terrorist Attacks upon the United States (2004, 344), quoting from W. Heinrichs, *Threshold of War*, Oxford: Oxford University Press, 1988, 215.

10. Haas has even suggested that uncertainty is increasing in the present times, due to the more complex and technical nature of issues at stake in contemporary politics (1992, 12–14). See also Giddens (1991, 28).
11. On the Copenhagen school, see among others Huysmans (1998); McSweeney (1999); Hansen (2000); Balzacq (2005); as well as Buzan and Wæver (2003). One key aspect of this literature is whether the security arena is in fact part of the broader arena of politics or constitutes a separate context, in which political debates are suspended.
12. On the distinction between public/political and private, see Bobbio (1989) and Weintraub (1997).
13. Other authors who suggest that security threats create a crisis that is in turn conducive to preference change include for instance Brecher (1980) and Moltz (1993).
14. Authors supporting this point include the contributors to the special issue of *Confluences Méditerranée*, n.7, 1993; contributors in Aliboni et al. (1996); Pierros et al. (1999).
15. For a similar problem, see Baumgartner and Jones: "One major reason for the limited number of studies of agenda-setting has been its intractability. The lack of general, as opposed to case-specific, indicators of agenda status has operated against theoretical progress." (1993, 39).
16. For a review, see among others Guzzini (1998).
17. For an early analysis of entrepreneurship, see Schumpeter (1939).
18. Young goes on however to specify that "brokers" are able to play such a role because they are not part of the bargain itself, an assertion that I do not share.
19. It is fair to note that in this research I stick to a macroapproach and I do not delve into the personal qualities of the entrepreneurs. There is a literature on the qualities that policy entrepreneurs should posses in order to be successful. According to Kingdon, the two key characteristics of successful entrepreneurship are technical expertise and political skills. The person acting as a policy entrepreneur must have "some claim to a hearing" (1984/95, 180), be it based on expertise, representation or position of authority. The entrepreneur should also possess impressive political connections and negotiating skills, as well as persistency (1984/95, 181). This thread has led to contributions about the relevance of reputation for expertise and "honest brokerage," on which the Commission can capitalize (e.g., Young 1999), and to counter-arguments that deny the relevance of this type of argument in the case of the Commission (e.g., Moravcsik 1999).

This type of considerations belongs to a different level of analysis than the one I have adopted in this volume. Whereas I have set the focus of this research on macroconditions, assessing the reputation of entrepreneurs and potential entrepreneurs would open up a different type of research avenue, based on the analysis of microconditions, which would be the subject of a different research.
20. Other authors shift the emphasis to one or the other aspects. According to Checkel, policy entrepreneurs are in fact spurred into action by the existence

of a policy window (1997, 124), while Finnemore and Sikkink emphasize the fact that that norm entrepreneurs create their own windows (1998, 897).
21. For a first stab at the issue, see Bicchi (2006).
22. On this, see Adler et al. (2006) and Pace (2006).

Chapter 2 The Euro-Mediterranean Relations from 1957 to 1972: When No Tailored European Foreign Policy Existed

1. At the time, the "Mediterranean area," in EEC jargon, extended from Spain to Greece through the Southern rim.
2. The expression is adopted from Grilli (1993), who applies it to the whole of EC/EU external relations. It is appropriate also for the early times of EEC relations with the Mediterranean.
3. The literature is unanimous in underlining the desire (Hager 1974, 239), the support (Weil 1970, 88; Tovias 1977, 28), and even the pressure (Papa and Petit-Laurent 1976, 278; Henig 1976, 312) of the United States to consolidate the Western bloc through intra-allies links.
4. Moreover, once the agreement with Greece was in process, the push toward negotiating a similar agreement with Turkey became even stronger than before. The situation in Cyprus was looming over relations with both countries, and influenced a relatively even behavior toward them (Tovias 1977, 48 fn.).
5. What remains unexplained is the timing of the agreement with Lebanon, which seemingly was prompted by the technical assistance program set up by single member states toward the country (Weil 1970, 191).
6. On "mixed" agreements, see Rosas (2000).
7. I did not find a single voice suggesting this hypothesis.
8. As Couve de Murville, minister of Foreign Affairs at the Quai d'Orsay from 1958 to 1968, avowed: "L'idée d'une politique méditerranéenne d'ensemble m'a toujours paru manquer de contenu, car une multitude d'Etats bien divers bordent cette mer, et chacun pose son problème particulier" (Couve de Murville 1971, 467). [I have always thought that the idea of a joint Mediterranean policy seems to lack substance, as a multitude of very different states border that sea and each of them poses a specific problem.]
9. On the parallelism between Spain and Israel, see Greilsammer (1981, 79). See also chapter 3.
10. Interestingly, the link between treatment accorded to Israel, Spain, and the Arab countries occurred again in the early 1970s, contributing to the formulation of a common policy for the whole region, as we will see in next chapter.
11. After the coup d'état in the spring of 1967, the agreement was partially frozen until the conditions for democracy were restored and the agreement fully revived in 1974.
12. Already in September 1960, Israel sent a note to the EEC Commission asking for an association agreement. In the words of a later Israeli foreign

minister: "the ink of the signatures on the Treaty of Rome was not yet dry when Israel tried to establish contact with the Community." Negotiations did not take off until late 1962. See Minerbi (1976, 243).
13. The first negotiating mandate was granted in June 1965, while the second was passed in 1967.
14. See Everts (1972, 119).
15. In this sense, Algeria was a true legal anomaly. For more details, see Aliboni 1976; Weil 1970, 178–179.
16. See COREPER, Project de compte rendu, meeting of March 8–10, 1972 (Archives nationales de France, Centre des archives contemporaines, 19771473, Art. 92)
17. Portugal, which could have been considered a Mediterranean country, at least on a par with Jordan, had since become a member of EFTA, thus regulating its relations with the EEC as part of the EFTA group.
18. Rossi Report to the European Parliament, Doc. de Seance, Doc.246/70.
19. For comprehensive reviews of the agreements, see especially Weil (1970); Shlaim and Yannopoulos (1976); Tovias (1977).
20. For a detailed description of the agreement, see Pierros et al. (1999, 59–62).
21. See Pierros et al. (1999, 62–65) and Rosenthal (1982, 11–15).
22. The issue ended up in front of the European Court of Justice. See chapter 4.
23. In the Greek agreement, a clause specified that in case of clash with the possibility to use the U.S. aid (partially earmarked for the purchase of U.S. goods) the agreement would recede, thus according priority to the U.S. aid program. See Protocol n.9 of the agreement.
24. These agreements, basically rooted on the principles of balance in the agricultural sector and expansion in the industrial sector, hinge on the principle of reciprocity in concessions.
25. "The net result of these trade concessions was so slight that the agreement became best known for the reductions given on bathing suit imports," as 3 of the 21 goods included in the agreements were actually bathing suits (Weil 1970, 182).

Chapter 3   Inventing the Mediterranean: From the Global Mediterranean Policy to the Euro-Arab Dialogue

1. The following data is taken from *The Military Balance* (1972–1973 and 1974–1975) and a survey of *Le Monde Diplomatique* (March 1973).
2. For the negative reaction in the French ministry of Foreign affairs, see Note, Ministère des Affaires Etrangère de France, Sous-Direction d'Europe Orientale, 29.IX.69 (Archives du Ministère, Dépot de Paris, vol. Europe, 1966–1970, Art. 2728).
3. For an analysis, see for example, Glassman (1977, 65ff.).

4. Scholars suggesting that the Mediterranean was the place where détente was tested include Halliday (1997, 10) and Bell (1977, 81).
5. For a periodization of détente, see, in a vast literature, Young and Kent (2003, parts III and IV).
6. See Note, Ministère des Affaires Etrangère de France, Sous-Direction d'Europe Orientale, 7.XI.1968 (Archives du Min., Dépot de Paris, vol. Eur. 1966–1970, Art 2728).
7. See Communiqué, from the French Embassy in Ankara, Ministère des Affaires Etrangère de France, Sous-Direction d'Europe Orientale, 26.II.1969; and Adresse, from the French Embassy in Athens, Ministère des Affaires Etrangère de France, Sous-Direction d'Europe Orientale, 14.II.1969 and 21.II.1969 (idem).
8. For both positions, see Note de l'Ambassade de France à Rome, 25.V.71 Sous-Direction Europe, Communautés Européennes, c.3801 Archives du Min., Dépot de Paris.
9. See for instance the attempt to raise the issue at the UN General Assembly, in November 1972.
10. See the document prepared by Italy on security in the Mediterranean in May 1971 (Note de la Direction Affaires Politiques Européennes, Ministère des Affaires Etrangère de France, 12.V.71 in Archives du Min., Dépot de Paris, Sous-Direction Europe, Communautés Européennes, c.3801).
11. The withdrawal was made public in the famous speech of January 16, 1968 by Wilson, in which he announced a dramatic cut in British defense commitments worldwide (Northedge 1974, 298–299). Moreover, in 1970, the new Libyan government unilaterally terminated the 1953 Anglo-Libyan Defense Agreement and requested a withdrawal of British troops. The Maltese government made a similar request in 1972 (Sanders 1990, 228–229).
12. The USSR military means in the Mediterranean as of today are not yet an urgent threat.
13. There is a substantial unbalance in favor of the United States in terms of fire capabilities, means of intervention, and independent action. Quotations from Note, Ministère des Affaires Etrangère de France, Sous-Direction d'Europe Orientale, 7.X.68 (Archives du Ministère, Dépot de Paris vol. Europe, 1966–1970, Art. 2728).
14. I have recorded the public debate by making use principally of *Le Monde*, and *Le Monde Diplomatique*, with occasional reference to German and Italian newspapers. Parliamentary debates in member states and documentation from the French archives were also used, where available.
15. The table has been constructed by using the ITERATE database (as in Mickolus 1980), which is incomplete before 1968. The table includes all incidents that the database indicates as responsibility of Arab terrorists or Arab-Palestinian organizations and that are recorded in ITERATE as *taking place* on EEC territory (distinguishing between EEC–6 and EEC–new members). No attacks occurred in Luxembourg and Ireland. Only violent attacks have been recorded, while threats of attacks, release of prisoners as a consequence of threats/attacks, and arrests have not been recorded. As a result, the data included here offers a conservative estimate.

The table does not reflect the magnitude of attacks but simply the number of occurrences.
16. Hostages came mainly from these countries.
17. *Le Monde*, 9.IX.70.
18. Quoted in *Le Monde*, 9.IX.1970.
19. Atti parlamentari, Senato della Repubblica, VI Legislatura, 38 seduta, 8.X.1972, 1858ff.
20. The most important changes were however introduced in 1978–1979, in reaction to the kidnapping of Aldo Moro.
21. *Le Monde*, 19.IX.1972.
22. See Circulaire n.403, Ministère des Affaires Etrangères, Direction des Affaires Politiques, Paris, 13.IX.73 (Archives du Min., Dépot de Paris, Vol. NUOI, c.1409).
23. See Circulaire n.426, Ministère des Affaires Etrangères, Direction des Affaires Politiques, Paris, 13.IX.73 (Archives du Min., Dépot de Paris, Vol. NUOI, c.1409).
24. See Note, Ministère des Affaires Etrangères, Direction des Affaires Politiques, Paris, 3.X.73 (Archives du Min., Dépot de Paris, Vol. NUOI, c.1409).
25. *Le Monde*, 13.IX.1972. See also UN Doc.A/C.6/SR.1369.
26. See Explication de vote sur la question du terrorism international, prononcée le 18 décembre 1972 par l'Ambassadeur de France en séance pléniére (in Archives du min., Dépot de Paris, Vol. NUOI, 1970–1973, c.1409).
27. The main sources for this indicator are in this section official documents and French diplomatic archives, as well as secondary material.
28. For a description of measure and a chronology of oil negotiations see also Kolodziej (1974a, 529–540) and *Le Monde* (29.IX.70, 26.II.71, 1–3).
29. See for instance the exchange of letters among French diplomats about the opportunity (eventually rejected) to link negotiations between the EEC and Algeria in July 1972 to the issue of indemnization of French possessions (in Archives du Min., Dépot de Paris, Direction des Affaires Economiques et Financieres, Service de la Cooperation Economique, c.1077 serie CEE, cote VI 6600, Dossier Association et adhesion: Pays du Maghreb 1972–1975).
30. For an analysis of trade relations between France and the Arab world, see Balta and Rulleau (1973, Annex 1).
31. OECD (1973, 35).
32. On the issue, see Luciani (1976).
33. The report was completed in mid-1972 and it commented the OECD oil statistics.
34. European Commission, "First Guidelines for a Community Energy Policy" (December 18, 1968), Supplement to *Bulletin of the European Communities*, n.12: European Commission, "Necessary Progress in Community Energy Policy" (Communication to the Council, October 13, 1972), Supplement to *Bulletin of the European Communities*, n.11; European Commission, "Guidelines and Priority Actions Under the Community Energy Policy" (Communication to the Council, April 27, 1973), Supplement to *Bulletin of the European Communities*, n.6.
35. The actual implementation of the measures was left to single OPEC members, which interpreted it in their own way. Some included Portugal

and South Africa in the embargo, others further increased their prices. See Szyliowicz (1975, 185).
36. The data includes articles, books, reports, and working papers quoted in the *Bibliographie der Wirtschaftswissenschaften*, compiled by the Bibliothek des Instituts für Weltwirtschaft an der Universität Kiel, under the classification number XVII.510 and XVII.511. Only the general texts and those, of the general texts, referring to Western Germany, Western Europe, and the Middle East, have been included. Publications have been included according to the year of publication, rather than to the year of inclusion in the *Bibliographie*. I thank Michiel Tegelaars for pointing the *Bibliographie* to me.
37. Arm deals with Israel are revealing in this period. The enormous extent of arms deals struck in 1971–1973 by the United States (Howard 1974, 135; Quandt 1977, chapter 5) was paralleled by a de facto boycott from the British and the French (Soetendorp 1999, 96–97).
38. Interview n.52, London, 28/4/99.
39. See the speech of Schumann, French minister of Foreign Affairs to the UN General Assembly (September 28, 1971). Quoted in Aruri and Hevener (1974, 87).
40. Jarring was appointed by UN Res. 242 of the role of mediator with the parties (Quandt 1977, 65).
41. The only exception was Portugal, under strong U.S. pressure.
42. While the other European countries for sure did not know about the alert, it is controversial whether the United Kingdom was informed. On this issue, see Ovendale (1998, 141–142).
43. I thank Piers Ludlow for first emphasizing the link between the status of the Commonwealth at the time of the enlargement and the debate about the status of the Mediterranean partners.
44. On the political meaning of relations with the Commonwealth, see Robins (1979, 21) and Wilkes (1997, 25).
45. The decision to curtail the military presence of the United Kingdom abroad was taken in 1968 and carried out by 1971 (see fn.11). The financial component of the Commonwealth, which was the Overseas Sterling Area, came to an end with the devaluation of the pound, at the end of 1967 (Sanders 1990, 200–204).
46. With some notable exceptions, the Commonwealth was constituted of African, Asian, Caribbean, and Pacific countries which were part of the Third (and Fourth) World.
47. See chapter 2.
48. For a complete account of Ostpolitik and Western Germany's foreign policy in this period, see Garton Ash (1993), Kreile (1980), Pfetsch (1988, 218 ff.), Hanrieder (1989, 190ff.), Morgan (1978).
49. An independent international role.
50. It should be stressed here that according to the Constitution of the Fifth Republic it is the President of the Republic who is in charge of the direction of French foreign policy. On the constitutional basis and the institutional

organization of foreign affairs in France, see *Les Affaires étrangères et le corps diplomatique français. Tome II 1870–1980*, 1984, CNRS, 600.

51. Relations with Israel did not deteriorate substantially, however, as French arms continued to reach Israel through Belgium, the Netherlands, and South Africa (Chérigui 1997, 51).
52. Relations with Tunisia were then defined as "exemplaires" by both parties. Quoted in *Le Monde* (23–24.XI.69, 1).
53. Relations had been severed because of the "affaire Ben Barka," as Ben Barka, founding father of the main Moroccan opposition party, was kidnapped in Paris in October 1969.
54. The decision marked a split between the president and his minister of Foreign Affairs, Maurice Schumann, who was completely against it. But Pompidou was so in favor of it that he stated that de Gaulle would have done the same, as Schumann later recollected (in Messmer 1990, 270–271). The decision sparked a substantial international controversy, especially as the embargo toward Israel was mainly centered on not supplying 50 Mirages Israel had already paid for. Michel Debré, minister of Defense, was accused of being "a merchand de canons" and Pompidou had to face an aggressive crowd in Chicago, which ruined his tour in the United States. See Diallo (1992, 177–184), Roussel (1994, 342–346), Fontaine (1970, 13–14), *Le Monde* (23, 24.I.70, and especially "Par-delà les Mirages" of André Fontaine, 4.II.70).
55. See Kolodziej (1974b, 520–522), *Le Monde* (10, 13.II.70).
56. Strengthening of the French presence in the Mediterranean, and especially in the Western Mediterranean, marked by the visit of Maurice Schumann to Algiers and Tunis, the reestablishment in the near future of all our traditional relations with North Africa, and the maintenance of cordial relations with the Libyan government. Quoted in *Le Monde* 17.XII.69, 2.
57. For the width of the cultural cooperation, see the thorough summary made in "La coopération culturelle française avec l'Afrique du Nord" in *Le Monde* (3.VI.70, 6) and the chapter on the subject in the book by Balta and Rulleau (1973, 107–141).
58. In every respect, France has a role to play in the Mediterranean.
59. Quoted in *Le Monde* (20–21.VI.71, 1).
60. Quoted in Balta and Rulleau (1973, 55).
61. Quoted in de Saint Robert (1970, 17).
62. Quoted in de Saint Robert (1970, 121).
63. Quoted in de Saint Robert (1970, 300).
64. For an in-depth analysis of the ideological aspects ("méditerranéisme"), see Chérigui (1997).
65. The expression, allegedly first used by Boumedienne, was often employed by the press (see for instance *Le Monde diplomatique*, III.73, 6ff.; *Le Monde* 3.II.70) and it became a catch phrase (Kolodziej 1974a, 514).
66. As Jobert put it: "sur les affaires du Proche-Orient, malgré l'obstination méritoire de Maurice Schumann à pròner la concertation des Quatre—U.S.A.,

U.R.S.S., France et Grande-Bretagne—comme seule issue possible, nous savions que l'Amérique n'adhérerait jamais à cette idée lancée par le général de Gaulle" (Jobert 1976, 140). [In relation to the Middle East, we knew that the United States would never embrace the idea, launched by General de Gaulle, of the Quartet—United States, USSR, France, and the United Kingdom—despite the praiseworthy obstinacy with which Maurice Schumann promoted it.]
67. See also the analysis of Jacques Fauvet, in *Le Monde* (24.I.70, 1).
68. Find a balance in this Europe, by emphasizing the Mediterranean and latin influence. Quoted in "Un pacte méditerranéen?" in *Problèmes Politiques et Sociaux* (28.II.71, 20).
69. Pointless and argument-ridden EEC activities.
70. Note de l'Ambassade de France à Rome 25.V.71 Sous-Direction Europe, Communautés Européennes, c.3801, Archives du Min., Dépôt de Paris.
71. Télégramme diplomatique de la Direction Affaires Politique à l'Ambassade de France à Rome, 28.V.71 Sous-Direction Europe, Communautés Européennes, c.3801, Archives du Min., Dépôt de Paris.
72. Télégramme diplomatique de Maurice Schumann à l'Ambassade de France à Rome, 8.VI.71 Sous-Direction Europe, Communautés Européennes, c.3801, Archives du Min., Dépôt de Paris.
73. Considerations sur les relations economiques de la CEE et le Maghreb, 13.07.72, Association et adhesion Maghreb, Ministere du Developpement industriel et scientifique, Diréction des études et programmes, Service des relations extérieurs, Sous-diréction échanges internationales et coopération, (Archives du min., Dépôt de Paris, Direction des Affaires Economiques et Financieres, Service de la Cooperation Economique, carton 1077 serie CEE, cote VI 6600, Dossier Association et adhesion: Pays du Maghreb, 1972–1975).
74. Summary of the interministerial meeting at the Sécretariat Général, Comité Interministériel pour les Questions de Coopération Economique Européenne, on the EEC Council to be held on 20.VII.1972, 17.VII.1972 (idem).
75. See chapter 1.
76. There were other actors promoting the Mediterranean, beyond EEC members. I have already mentioned the attempts by Mediterranean nonmembers and countries such as Yugoslavia to create a nonaligned block of countries. They were not successful. Moreover, the focus of this section (and of this book) is on initiatives pursued by European actors. See p. 67 under cold war.
77. Doc. de Seance 246/70, Rapport de André Rossi sur la Politique Commerciale de la Communauté dans le bassin méditerranéen (PE 25 843/déf).
78. European Parliament, Session of February 9, 1971, 27–52.
79. See for instance the *Memorandum on a Community Policy on Development Cooperation*, in Supplement to the EC Bull. 5/1971.

80. See Telegramme de Bonn à Paris, 7.IV.71 and Note de l'Ambassade de France en Italie, 25.V.71 Sous-Direction Europe, Communautés Européennes, c.3801, Archives du Min., Dépot de Paris.
81. See Document in annex to the Note de la Direction Affaires Politiques Européennes, 12.V.71 Sous-Direction Europe, Communautés Européennes, c.3801, Archives du Min., Dépot de Paris.
82. See Circulaire n.189, 22.V.71 Sous-Direction Europe, Communautés Européennes, c.3801, Archives du Min., Dépot de Paris.
83. On the workings of the group, see also Nuttall (1992, 69–70).
84. See Lettre de l'Ambassade Italienne à Paris, 22.XI.71 Sous-Direction Europe, Communautés Européennes, c.3801, Archives du Min., Dépot de Paris.
85. See p. 78.
86. This was at a time when the two countries were under a de facto embargo, due to their authoritarian regimes. The report was leaked and Germany went through an embarrassing moment. See *Rapport de la delegation allemande au groupe de travail Mediterranee, La Peninsule Iberique*, D(72)1/II, 2.V.72 Sous-Direction Europe, Communautés Européennes, c.3801, Archives du Min., Dépot de Paris.
87. It was however leaked to the press (Greilsammer, 1982, 87–89).
88. See Comité Politique, Rapport du Groupe de travail sur la Méditerranée, Med (72)11 P, 8.II.72 Sous-Direction Europe, Communautés Européennes, c.3801, Archives du Min., Dépot de Paris. Writing on the original.
89. See Télégramme 61/62 by Jurgensen, 4.II.72 Sous-Direction Europe, Communautés Européennes, c.3801, Archives du Min., Dépot de Paris.
90. See Télégramme de l'Ambassade de France au Luxembourg n.204–207, 12.V.72 (Archives du Min., Dépot de Paris, Sous-Direction Europe, Communautés Européennes, c.3801).
91. The three candidate countries were associated to the Working Group once enlargement negotiations finished.
92. See Note à l'attention du Directeur Adjoint des Affaires Politiques, 25.X.72 Sous-Direction Europe, Communautés Européennes, c.3801, Archives du Min., Dépot de Paris.
93. The limits of Italy's entrepreneurship became dramatically evident when the country tried, after the approval of the GMP, to organize a conference of Central Mediterranean countries in November 1972 with Malta, Tunisia and Libya. But instead of hammering out a common political stance, the participants exposed their divergences on the subject and Italy was unable to forge a compromise (Silvestri 1974, 109).
94. See European Commission, *Community Policy on Development Cooperation: Programme for Initial Actions*. Memorandum from the Commission to the Council. In Supplement to the EC Bulletin 5/71.
95. In September and then again in December 1971.

96. See Note by the French Permanent Representation in Brussels to Paris-d'Orsay, 17.III.72 Sous-Direction Europe, Communautés Européennes, c.3801, Archives du Min., Dépot de Paris.
97. The substance and the structure of existing agreements.
98. Specific and concrete difficulties. See quotes in Adresse de la Délégation Français à Bruxelles à Diplomatie Paris, 17.III.72 Sous-Direction Europe, Communautés Européennes, c.3801, Archives du Min., Dépot de Paris.
99. See Annex III to "Project de Rapport sur les Conséquences économiques de l'éargissement des Communautés européennes pour leurs relations avec les pays co-contractants du bassin méditerranéen" Rapporteur: M.Rossi, Parlement Européenne, Commission des Relations Economiques Exterieures, PE 29.993/rév, 19.VI.1972.
100. Council document "Examen de la communication de la Commission au Conseil sur les relations de la Communaute avec les pays du Maghreb", VI6600, 18.VII.72 (Archives du min., Dépot de Paris, Dossier Association et adhesion Maghreb, S/660/72 Direction des Affaires Economiques et Financieres, Service de la Cooperation Economique, carton 1077 serie CEE, cote VI 6600, Dossier Association et adhesion: Pays du Maghreb, 1972–1975).
101. See *Agence Europe*, 1.VI.72.
102. Schumann might have referred to the parallel between Spain and Israel already on May 8, 1972. See *Agence Europe*, 1.VI.72.
103. Spain and Israel had already been addressed together in 1970, when the first agreement with Spain and the second with Israel were signed. On the parallel between Israel and Spain in 1970, see p. 54–55.
104. *Agence Europe*, 1.VI.72. Having negotiated within the framework of the EFTA agreements, Portugal and the EC signed a preferential trade agreement based on free trade of industrial goods.
105. More generally, the Netherlands and Germany favored the "communitarisation" of cooperation and developmental aid. See for instance *Mémorandum du Gouvernément néerlandais concernant le rôle de la Communauté dans le domaine de la coopération au développement* in Document Preparatoires au Sommet de Paris, 1972 (Archives nationales de France Centre des archives contemporaines 900568, Art. 390). In it, the Dutch government also specified that "les relations de la Communauté avec un certain nombre de pays du bassin méditerranéen devront évoluer progressivement." In van *Aide Mémoire* prepared by the German government in the same occasion, it is also clearly stated that the EEC "devrait se donner pour objectiv de communautariser progressivement la politique en matière de coopération."
106. *Agence Europe* (7.VI.72), *Le Monde* (9.VI.72, 36).
107. See Annex IV to "Project de Rapport sur les Conséquences économiques de l'éargissement des Communautés européennes pour leurs relations avec les pays co-contractants du bassin méditerranéen" Rapporteur: M.Rossi,

Parlement Européenne, Commission des Relations Economiques Exterieures, PE 29.993/rév, 19.VI.1972.
108. See "Project de Rapport sur les Conséquences économiques de l'éargissement des Communautés européennes pour leurs relations avec les pays co-contractants du bassin méditerranéen" Rapporteur: M.Rossi, Parlement Européenne, Commission des Relations Economiques Exterieures, PE 29.993/rév, 19.VI.1972.
109. Note that the free trade clause was then dropped. More than forty years later, the clause is one of the main issues in Euro-Mediterranean relations, time having shown its crucial importance in the actual construction of the Mediterranean region.
110. European Commission, *Community's Relations with the Magrab Countries*, S. 569/72, presented to the Council on June 26–27, 1972. See EC Bulletin 8/72, 97. See also *Agence Europe*, 17.VI.72.
111. A global approach, with a common framework.
112. *Agence Europe* (19–20.VI.72).
113. A global and balanced approach. See EC Bulletin, vol. 5, n.10–1972, 20.
114. European Commission, *The Relations between the Community and the Countries of the Mediterranean Basin*. Brussels, SEC(72) 3111def. See also *Agence Europe*, 5.X.72, Tovias (1977, 71) and Faber (1982, 41).
115. Since the end October 1972, representatives of the United Kingdom, Denmark, and Ireland participated to discussions about the GMP in the COREPER. See *Agence Europe*, 25.X.72. For a review of the controversy between the United States and the EC on the Mediterranean policy, see Kreinin (1976).
116. See for instance Memorandum From the Deputy Secretary of State (Irwin) to President Nixon, Washington, 7.X.72, doc. n.102 (FRUS, 1969–1976, Volume III, Foreign Economic Policy, 1969–1972; International Monetary Policy, 1969–1972). See also Memorandum From the President's Assistant for International Economic Affairs (Flanigan) to President Nixon, Washington, 11.X.72, doc. n. 103 (FRUS, 1969–1976, Volume III, Foreign Economic Policy, 1969–1972; International Monetary Policy, 1969–1972).
117. FRUS, Foreign Economic Policy, 1972, Doc. 100. Memorandum of Conversation, 11.IX.1972.
118. See Secrétariat Général de la Commission des Communautés Européennes, Note sur les critiques adressées par les Etats-Unis à l'égard de la politique de la Communauté en matière d'accords préférentiels, Séc(72)4767, 27.XII.72 (Archives des Communautés Européennes, Villa il Poggiolo, Florence).
119. See Télégramme de la Délégation Français à Bruxelles, n.3461–3482, 7.XI.72 Sous-Direction Europe, Communautés Européennes, c.3801, Archives du Min., Dépôt de Paris. On the meeting, see also *Agence Europe*, 1.XI.72, 6–7.XI.72, 8.XI.72, 9.XI.72, 10.XI.72.

120. For an in-depth analysis of the following period, see Pierros et al. (1999, 85–88) and Grech (1974). The end product of negotiations is analyzed in p. 104–108.
121. See the intervention of Moro, Italian minister of Foreign Affairs at the Council of General Affairs on June 6, 1972 (*Agence Europe*, 7.VI.72).
122. *Agence Europe* (11.X.72, 8.XI.72, 7, 14–15, 16.III.73); *Europolitique* (7.III.73); *Le Monde Diplomatique* (VII.1973).
123. *Agence Europe* (1.XI.72).
124. See for instance the summary of the meeting on June 18, 1973, in *Agence Europe* (18–19.VI.73).
125. On the consequences of this decision for Mediterranean imports, see Marsh (1976). The only sector which was exempted from this treatment was citrus fruit, on which Italy obtained to receive compensations for its producers, thus overcoming the staunch opposition of Germany. See Grech (1974, 57).
126. See *Le Monde*, 4.XII.73, quoted in de La Serre (1979, 82).
127. A prospective framework for a Euro-Arab conference, its main stages and its timetable.
128. On the choice of "dialogue" to express the desire of cooperation, see Brahimi and Dekker (1986, 15) and also Waterbury (1979, 24).
129. Do these scattered mentions of a potential dialogue point to an orchestration of the arrival of the Arab representatives at the above mentioned European summit? Was this a stint orchestrated by France, with the help of the United Kingdom, to push reluctant partners into a dialogue? More archival evidence will be needed to square the issue, although several authors have hinted to such an explanation. See Wallace and Allen (1977, 238); Allen (1982, 70); Al-Mani' (1983); see also Kissinger (1979, 729). According to Lieber (1976, 18), France had the active support of the United Kingdom and the irritated acquiescence of West Germany.
130. See Kissinger (1979, 875, passim).
131. Their coordination was such that Ortoli, President of the Commission, stressed the fact that European unity on oil had been achieved in two hours thanks to the United States. Quoted in Lieber (1976, 21) from *New York Times*, 11.II.74.
132. For a full description of the Agreements and of the additional protocols, see *The European Community and the Mediterranean Basin* (1984, 41–49), as well as Cova (n.d.), Richard (1980) and Bouchard (1982).
133. Greece, Turkey, Portugal (with whom a free trade area was on the making anyway), and Spain. But the definition of this group was very vague, as Israel, which had often been equaled to Spain, should have granted reverse preferences too.
134. *Agence Europe* (28.VI.73).
135. This was the case with Morocco, Algeria, Tunisia, and Turkey.
136. See instances in Shlaim and Yannopoulos (1976).
137. For a description of meetings of their composition and, see Al-Mani (1983, 53 ff.).

Chapter 4 The Partition of the Mediterranean

1. On the issue of the construction of the Soviet gas pipeline to Western Europe, see Garthoff (1985, 1034ff.).
2. Gary Sick, (1985) *All Fall Down: America's Tragic Encounter with Iran*. New York: Random House, 106. Quoted in Kuniholm (1987, 25).
3. Commission of the European Communities. (1984). *The European Community and the Mediterranean Basin*. Brussels.
4. For instance, in Morocco the debt-service ratio in 1983 was over 45 percent, while in Algeria, by 1988, it was 77 percent (Payne 1993).
5. Economic and Social Committee (Doc. (89)386 final, 16.VI.89) *Report on the Mediterranean Policy of the EC*. This report, reproduced in Comunità europee/Comitato Economico e Sociale (1993) *La politica mediterranea della Comunità europea*, specified (4, fn. 5) that the drop in GDP per person was mainly due to the drop in the GDP and not in the demographic growth of the countries. Only in the case of Tunisia was the demographic trend the principal reason for the loss of revenues.
6. See the perception of southern Mediterranean countries in Commission of the European Communities, *Report on the Exploratory Talks with the Mediterranean Countries and the Applicant Countries*, COM(84)107 final.
7. Iran being a Shi'a country, it did not manage to directly orchestrate similar political changes in the other Sunni states (Kepel 2000, passim).
8. For a thorough analysis of the impact of southern enlargement on Turkey, Morocco and Tunisia, see Rosenthal (1982).
9. Data from Buysse (1984, 25).
10. Commission (1984). The study was prepared by François Duchêne, Jacques Bourrinet, Stefan Musto, and Antonio Tizzano.
11. See Commission of the European Communities, *A Mediterranean Policy for the Enlarged Community*. COM(82)353 final. Brussels: June 24, 1982.
12. Commission of the European Communities, *Report to the Council on the Exploratory Talks with the Mediterranean Countries and the Applicant Countries and Proposals concerning the Implementation of a Mediterranean Policy for the Enlarged Community*. COM(84)107 final. Brussels: May 11, 1984.
13. European Parliament (Committee on External Economic Relations), *Report on economic and trade relations between the EEC and the Mediterranean countries pending the development of the plans to enlarge the European Community to include Spain and Portugal*. Rapporteur: C.Galluzzi. Document A2-24/85, 30 April 1985. European Parliament (Committee on Development and Cooperation), *Report on the cooperation agreements with the developing countries of the Mediterranean region in the context of a global Mediterranean policy of the Community*. Rapporteur: M.L. Cassanmagnago Cerretti. Document A2-27/85. April 30, 1985.
14. Commission of the European Communities, *The European Community and the Mediterranean Basin*. Brussels: 1984, 102–143. See also Grilli (1993, 200–201) and Pierros et al. (1999, 102–103).

15. For the Additional Protocols with Algeria, Egypt, Jordan, Lebanon and Tunisia, see OJEC, L 297, October 21, 1987. The others, more problematic, followed within the span of two years. See Pierros et al. (1999, 314 ff.).
16. For the Protocols on financial and technical cooperation with Algeria, Egypt, Jordan, Lebanon, and Tunisia, see Official Journal of the European Communities, L 22, January 27, 1988. The other countries soon followed.
17. Commission of the European Communities, *The Community and the Mediterranean Countries: Guidelines for Economic Cooperation.* COM(85)517 final. Brussels: September 26, 1985.

Chapter 5   The New Post–Cold War Activism

1. Several labels, all beginning with the re- suffix, have been used: renovated, redirected, revamped, refurbished. On terminology, see Pierros et al. (1999, 126 ff. and 165 fn.3) and Gomez (1998).
2. The Conference brought together the 15 EU member states of the time, plus Morocco, Algeria, Tunisia, Egypt, Jordan, Israel, the Palestinian Authority, Lebanon, Syria, Cyprus, Malta, and Turkey. Libya was kept at the margins because of sanctions, while the Balkans were never considered for participation. Jordan was included because of its involvement in the Israeli-Palestinian issue.
3. On this, see below, p. 142.
4. Data from *The Military Balance*, various years.
5. The previous one had been published in 1972. See Lacoste (1993).
6. *The Military Balance 1992–1993*, 39.
7. The disappearance of all main [military] threats on the continent.
8. Economic and social crises, with their ethnic and religious spin-offs.
9. See also the other articles by military experts in the special issue of *Défense Nationale*, vol. 49, December 1993.
10. See for instance the roundtable in *Limes* (1994, n.2) among people from the Italian Army or very close to it.
11. See for instance Trebous (1970).
12. It is important to mention the fact that SOPEMI, on which the following data is based, records only the most important foreign groups per country.
13. While in 1990 the stock of foreign population in Italy was 1.37 percent in proportion to total population and in Spain 1.06 percent, in Germany it was 8.2 percent and in Belgium 9.1 percent (Venturini 1994, 28).
14. The issue was magnified by illegal immigration. Estimates vary greatly. Part of the phenomenon can be examined through the number of immigrants regularized. In three waves of regularizations between 1987 and 1996, Italy regularized approx. 515,000 persons. With two programs in 1992 and 1996, Portugal regularized approx. 75,000, while Spain, between 1985 and 1996 regularized 172,000. Greece did not conduct a regularization program until

1998, when around 200,000 were regularized. However, at least an equal number of immigrants remained undocumented during the period under examination (Poulain 1994, 693).
15. SOPEMI, various years. A similar trend occurred in Belgium, Denmark, and the Netherlands.
16. The statement was soon qualified in "zero illegal immigration," but the original intention is revealing (SOPEMI, various years).
17. See for instance CeSPI (2000) and the repeated denunciations by Caritas, the biggest catholic NGO in Italy.
18. A Report presented to the Assembly on November 4, 1996 (Doc.1543), stated: "It is no secret that many Europeans regard the problem of migration from the south not only as a social and economic challenge and a problem of organization but also as a threat to the cultural identity of the northern countries, and the unease felt in those countries has reached such a point as to precipitate protests that migration is a danger to the internal security and stability of some European countries" (16).
19. In OJEC, C158, 17.VI.91.
20. Commission of the European Communities, *Immigration*. Communication from the Commission to the Council and the European Parliament. SEC(91)915 final. Brussels, 11.X.91.
21. *From the Single Act to Maastricht and Beyond*, COM(92)2000, 11.II.92, 15.
22. Economic and Social Committee (92)1041.
23. On this, see Kepel (1991, 56 ff.)
24. As Halliday underlines, "if there are myths about 'Islam,' they are ones invented and propagated not just in the supposed hegemonic world of Europe and the USA, but also within the supposedly dominated and oppressed arena of 'Islam' itself" (1996, 111).
25. For a broad and passionate discussion about perceptions, misperceptions, and intentional misperceptions between Islam and "the West," see the contributions in Martín Muñoz (1999).
26. As quoted in Belguendouz (1992).
27. *Europe*, 9.II.95.
28. See also NATO Review December 1994–January 1995; *The Independent* (8.II.95); *International Herald Tribune* (9.II.95).
29. See chapter 2, p. 68–73.
30. Originally created to counter Arab-Palestinian terrorism, in 1974. See chapter 2, p. 62.
31. Interview n.66, Florence, 11/95.
32. On the transformation of the Middle East in this period, see Rodman (1991); Indyk (1992); Quandt (1993, 383–414); Rubin (1994, 184–208); Bregman and el-Tahri (1998, 177 255); Sela (1998, 332ff.).
33. The incisiveness of the European presence was not increased by the quarrels between the Commission and the Presidency over which of them should speak on Europe's behalf (Hollis 1997, 21). The Presidency prevailed (Salamé 1994, 230).

34. According to Tovias (1996, 14), Israel accepted the European presence only after the EC had accepted to renegotiate the 1975 agreement.
35. These activities were going to be financed from the EU budget, MEDA line, starting from 1995. For the period 1995–1998, around $32 million were allocated to these projects.
36. Richard Haass was the Head of the Middle East Office on the National Security Council staff during the Bush presidency. For his role in policy making, see Quandt (1993, 386).
37. Commission of the European Communities, *Future Relations and Cooperation between the Community and the Middle East*, COM(93) 375 final. Brussels: September 8, 1993. Commission of the European Communities, *EC support to the Middle East Peace Process*, COM(93) 458 final. Brussels: September 29, 1993.
38. Joint Action n.94/276/CFSP.
39. As an interviewee said, "the EMP is not a Middle East policy in disguise. It is much more than that." Interview n.46, Brussels, 20/7/99.
40. Interview n.12, Florence, 17/5/00.
41. Interview n.1, Brussels, 20/7/99.
42. This cooperation was going to lead to the EU-U.S. Declaration on the Wye Memorandum, issued in December 1998.
43. See, for instance, the acknowledgement made right at the start of the *Rapport d'Information*, Assemblée Nationale. Paris, November 15, 1995, 5.
44. Quoted in Rodrigo (1992, 112).
45. On the Spanish leadership in the formulation and adoption of a new initiative directed to the Mediterranean countries, see next section.
46. Francisco Granell was at the time the Director of the Task Force Enlargement of the European Commission. He later became Director of the DG Development of the EC.
47. See Conclusions of the Presidency, Annex I in Bulletin of the European Communities, 6–1992, 18–22.
48. Commission of the European Communities, *From the Single Act to Maastricht and Beyond*, COM(92) 2000, 11.II.92, 15.
49. Commission of the European Communities, *The Future of Relations between the Community and the Maghreb*, SEC(92) 401final, 30.IV.92, 5.
50. Commission of the European Communities, *Strengthening the Mediterranean policy of the European Union: Establishing a Euro-Mediterranean Partnership*, COM(94) 427final, 19.X.94, 4.
51. *Resolution on the Mediterranean policy of the European Union*, Parliamentary Resolutions B4–0164, 0165 and 0166, 29.X.94 in OJEC, C305, 82.
52. Morán, Ferdinando (1980) *Una política exterior para España*. Barcelona: Planeta. Chapter 9. Quoted in Gillespie (1995, 160).
53. Interview n.55, Florence, 9/7/99.
54. The first minister appointed by González was Fernando Morán López (December 1982–June 1985). The second was Francisco Fernández

Ordoñez (July 1985–June 1993). While the former was an expert politician, the latter had no background in foreign affairs, thus allowing a broader role to be played by González himself (Tovias 1998, 217). However, Ordoñez was also a pragmatist, with a clear view of Mediterranean problems, which became his sector of expertise.
55. Spain's partial participation in NATO was confirmed after a referendum in March 1986, while Spain joined WEU in 1988. Full integration into the NATO Military Command Structure came in January 1999.
56. Not everything was new, though. On the continuities between the socialist and presocialist period, see Story (1995, 37) and Gillespie (1996, 194–197).
57. Suárez, who was prime minister at the time, already announced this idea in the late 1970s. However, domestic politics completely absorbed politicians of the time. Quoted in Gillespie (1995, 162).
58. Reliance on gas instead of nuclear energy was decided in 1983.
59. See for instance the meeting of ministers of Mediterranean countries in Paris (7.XII.94) and Tunis (20–21.I.95) (*Actividades, Textos y Documentos de la Politica Exterior Española, Año 1995*, 899).
60. The United States also used aid deal earmarked for arm acquisition. Gómez Gil (1995, 8–9), quoted in Gillespie (1999, 57).
61. In the period 1980–1987, Spain's arm sales increased by 22.3 percent, in comparison with a mere 4 percent by other big exporters. Sources: Gillespie (1999, 198 n.14) and *Actividades, Textos y Documentos de la Politica Exterior Española, Año 1985*.
62. On the basis of these agreements, joint exercises and training were often held (*Actividades, Textos y Documentos de la Politica Exterior Española, Año 1987*; Labatut 1995, 326).
63. Interestingly, France had to pay the same penalty for its Mediterranean ambitions, when in 1971–1972 it was forced to renegotiate relations after Algeria's nationalization of French oil.
64. See *Actividades, Textos y Documentos de la Politica Exterior Española, Año 1985, 1986, 1987*.
65. See *Actividades, Textos y Documentos de la Politica Exterior Española*, relevant years.
66. It entered into force on February 1993, *Actividades, Textos y Documentos de la Politica Exterior Española*, 1991, 1992, 1993.
67. See above, p. 139.
68. As Gillespie specifies, it was by no means clear at the beginning of the transition period that the Maghreb and Mediterranean dimension of Spain's foreign policy would have figured so prominently in its external relations. In his view, the main determinants of such an outcome were "the political ascendancy of the Spanish Socialist party (PSOE), Spain's successful entry into the European Community, the country's strong economic performance in the second half of the 1980s, and a growing domestic realization that the

problems of the Maghreb would be ignored at Spain's own peril" (Gillespie 1995, 161). A post hoc confirmation of Spain's success in "selling an image of being a serious and stable country" came with the confidence it inspired to investors (Tovias 1995, 104–105).
69. With a similar view, Gillespie (1996, 210 fn.14).
70. *Agence Europe*, 20.X.89, 7; 24.V.90. On the importance of demography to explain Commission's behavior, see also Rhein (1993).
71. Commission of the European Communities (1990). *Vers une politique méditerranéenne rénovée. Propositions pour la périod 1992–1996.* SEC(90)812 final.
72. *Agence Europe*, 20.IV.90. The only country Matutes did not visit was Israel, with which the EP had imposed a semi-freeze of relations because of Palestinians' conditions (Khader 1997, 157).
73. For details on the RMP, see below, p. 168.
74. A partial exception was Italy, which called for a compromise formula, but to no avail (Constas 1995, 134; *Agence Europe*, 13.VII.90).
75. It was a southern European success only in the sense that southern European countries managed to bloc trade concessions and they contributed to pass a financial update of Protocols.
76. The project was mentioned in 1990 often and in various contexts, by either Italy or Spain. See *Agence Europe*, (29.III.90; 18.V.90; 28.VI.90; 17-18.IX.90). The paternity of the idea remains contested, with both Italians and Spaniards claiming the copyright of the initiative. If they were not fully original in their suggestions, the Spaniards were primarily responsible for drafting it (Gillespie 1996, 205; contra Badini—an Italian diplomat—1995, 112).
77. The proposal, formalized on March 4, 1991 (Marquina 1995, 42), was officially rejected on May 11, 1991.
78. Interview n.55, Florence, 9/7/99.
79. Interview n.55, Florence, 9/7/99. See also, for a fraction of what took place at the time, the collection of discourses by Miguel Angel Moratinos and Jorge Dezcallar in Moratinos, Dezcallar, Arbos (1996).
80. Interview n.13, Brussels, 26/7/99; interview n.31, Brussels, 27/7/99, interview 29 bis, Florence 15/9/05.
81. He later became Special EU Envoy for the Middle East and then went on to become minister of Foreign Affairs.
82. Interview n.13, Brussels, 26/7/99.
83. A first Italian-Spanish seminar, which included academics, was held on February 4–5, 1991. See Chérigui (1997, 196).
84. Interview n.29 bis, Florence, 15/9/05.
85. Not everything can be done in Paris.
86. *Annuaire de l'Afrique du Nord, 1992.* See also Gillespie (1997, 39).
87. Interview n.23, Florence, 5/97, interview n.12, Florence, 17/5/00.
88. Interview n.44, Florence, 9/7/99.
89. The EP had started to criticize Morocco's record on human rights in April 1991. Morocco had answered by releasing some political prisoners,

thus clearing the way to the visit of Spain's king in July 1991 and the visit of Morocco's king to the United States in September 1991. When the renewal of the Financial Protocol came up for EP approval, MEPs began to leave the room thus making it impossible for the Protocol to pass. However, in the same occasions, the Protocol for Israel was approved, thus singling out Morocco for apparent disapproval from the EP. The whole issue, often represented as the EP vetoing Morocco's Protocol on the basis of human rights' abuses, was in fact a big diplomatic gaffe (interview n.12, Florence, 17/5/00). See also Vaquer (2003, 63 and 80 fn.14).

90. February 16, and February 29, 1992. *Annuaire de l'Afrique du Nord, 1992*.
91. *Annuaire de l'Afrique du Nord, 1992*, 502; see also Marquina (1998, 238).
92. It was essentially the work of Dezcallar (Gillespie 1999, 199).
93. *Actividades, Textos y Documentos de la Politica Exterior Española 1992*, 877.
94. *Actividades, Textos y Documentos de la Politica Exterior Española 1992*, 881. My translation.
95. The report was written by Matutes and it was adopted in April, under the title "The future of relations between the Community and the Maghreb," SEC(92)401 final, 30.IV.92.
96. Member states also adopted a regulation for the application of the Financial Protocols signed the previous year, fixing modalities and management rules for financial cooperation (EEC Reg. n.1762/92, June 29, 1992, in OJEC L(181), July 1, 1992). Another regulation (EEC Reg. n.1763/92, June 29, 1992, in OJEC L(181), July 1, 1992) specified cooperation in the environment sector, promotion of risk capitals, and horizontal cooperation. A third regulation focused on the regime for imports of agricultural products (EEC Reg. n.1763/92, June 29, 1992, in OJEC L(181), July 1, 1992).
97. *Annuaire de l'Afrique du Nord, 1992*.
98. The Maastricht Treaty came into force on November 1, 1993, together with the new acronyms.
99. COM(93)375 final, and COM(93)458 final.
100. It was approved in April 1994 and it called for an increased role of the EC in the region, together with an offer to support the Palestinians especially in the creation of a police force (94/276/CFSP).
101. On this, Adler and Crawford (2006). See also Pace (2006).
102. Concerned about possible developments that would have excluded it, Egypt began in late 1991 to push Spain and France for the creation of a Mediterranean Forum, including all the Mediterranean bordering countries. The ten countries were Algeria, Egypt, France, Greece, Italy, Morocco, Portugal, Spain, Tunisia, and Turkey. For a sample of the discussions, see the intervention of Solana, Spanish minister of Foreign Affairs, in *Actividades, Textos y Documentos de la Politica Exterior Española 1994*, 712.
103. Interview n.46, Brussels, 20/7/99.
104. Interview n.44, Florence, 9/7/99; interview n.13, Brussels, 16/7/99.
105. Interview n.46, Brussels, 20/7/99.

214 • Notes

106. A similar joint letter had been sent to the Belgian EU Presidency in December 1993, pleading for an improvement in relations with Morocco (Gillespie 1997, 39).
107. *Strengthening the Mediterranean policy of the European Union: Establishing a Euro-Mediterranean partnership* COM(94)427 final, 19.X.94. The European Council endorsed it at its meeting in Essen, in December 1994.
108. Idem, 2.
109. On the Essen European Council, see Barbé and Izquierdo (1997, 120).
110. Consultations took place in February, March, and May 1995 (Barbé 1996, 33).
111. *Strengthening the Mediterranean policy of the European Union: Proposals for implementing a Euro-Mediterranean partnership.* COM(95)72 final, 8.III.95.
112. Interview n.31, Brussels, 27/7/99.
113. Interview n.29bis, Florence, 14/9/05. On the more general aspects of the Morocco's Fisheries Agreement, see Damis (1998).
114. Interview n.46, Brussels, 20/7/99.
115. Interview n.46, Brussels, 20/7/99.
116. *El País*, international edition, 25.XII.95. Quoted in Gillespie (1996, 208).
117. The grand total was set at ECU 4,400 million. ECU 2,375 million was for bilateral aid (an increase of 47 percent on the previous provision), of which ECU 1,075 million in the form of grants and ECU 1,300 million in the form of loans from the EIB. The rest was earmarked for multilateral and decentralized projects (Tovias 1996, 13, 23 n.4). Further funds were later provided also for this aim (Assemblée Nationale, Document n.2367, 15.XI.95, 15).
118. For a detailed analysis of the drafting of the Declaration, see Barbé (1995, 34–36).
119. On the Barcelona Declaration and more generally on the EMP, there is a broad literature, which justifies the relatively short description I will offer here. For a more detailed analysis, see among others Pierros et al. (1999); Xenakis and Chryssochoou (2001, 74–84).
120. See Edwards and Philippart (1997).
121. The event was marred by the informal boycott that most Arab countries, as well as Israel, carried out, by sending lower level delegations.
122. Syria and Lebanon abstained from ministerial meetings at the height of the second Intifada.
123. The debate on this aspect has attempted to formalize a "Charter for Peace and Stability," including a list of confidence-building measures. The deterioration in Arab-Israeli relations put this project on the backburner. See Tanner (1996) and Bojji (1999).
124. See Jünemann (2004) and Bicchi and Martin (2006).
125. Common Strategy of the European Council of June 19, 2000 on the Mediterranean Region, 2000/458/CFSP.
126. At this meeting, the ten EU applicant members also participated.

127. On this point, see Hoekman and Djankov (1996), Aghrout and Alexander (1997), Michalet (1997).
128. For an interim evaluation, see Handoussa and Reiffers (2002) and Radwan and Reiffers (2005).
129. The term "Euro-Mediterranean" was introduced at a second stage, in a desire to stress, once the expression "Association Agreement" had become established, that the agreements were not comparable with the Association Agreements with candidate countries from Central and Eastern Europe and thus they were not in any way to be understood as a first step toward entry to the EU.
130. In theory, such a formula lends ground to a suspension of the agreement in case of gross violations. In practice and in spite of some attempts on the part of the EP, it has never happened. On Art. 2 provisions of trade agreements, see Bartels (2005).
131. With the notable exception of the "interim" agreement with the Palestinian Authority.
132. See Geradin (2003) and Tovias and Ugur (2004).
133. An acronym of "MEsures D'Accompagnement financières et techniques à la réforme des structures économiques et sociales dans le cadre du partenariat euro-méditerranéen."
134. Council Regulation (EC) No. 1488/96, of 23 July 1996, OJEU L 189, 30 July 1996. MEDA covers the costs of reforms in Mediterranean Partner Countries as indicated by the European Council in Cannes in June 1995. At the time, the European Council had indicated an amount equal to 4,685 Million ECU. The difference between that amount and MEDA was allocated to specific protocols for each country, and thematic initiatives. See note 1, annexed to the Council Decision of December 6, 1996, OJEU L 325, December 14, 1996.
135. Council Regulation (EC) No. 2698/2000 of 27 November 2000, OJEU L 311, 12 December 2000. The total funds available (MEDA plus EIB loans) accordingly amount to €13,000 Million.
136. Cyprus and Malta (while they were nonmembers), Turkey and Israel have received funds only from the regional MEDA programmes because of their level of development.
137. This line (B7–705) was part of the budget for the European Democracy and Human Rights Initiative (EIDHR, budget line B7–7). In 2001, the EIDHR was reorganized according to thematic, instead of geographic, lines and "target countries." On democracy promotion in the Mediterranean, see Youngs (2001); Gillespie and Youngs (2002); and Holden (2005).
138. Witness the practice that took hold soon after Barcelona to use the criteria of the World Bank and the IMF to measure the performance of Mediterranean economies. Interview n.15, Florence, 10/5/02.
139. Interview n.54, Rabat, 30/10/97.
140. On the perverse effects of this strategy, see Kienle (1998) and more generally Williams (2001).

141. As of November 2006.
142. Written Answers, Question by Mr. Hoon, House of Commons, 19.IV.2002, vol. 383, part 132.
143. See Danish Presidency, Background Note to the meeting of the General Affairs and External Relations Council, 30.IX.2002.
144. Presidency Conclusions, Copenhagen European Council, 12-13.XII.2002.
145. See for instance Presidency Conclusions, General Affairs and External Relations Council, doc. 5519/04, 26.I.2004.
146. See Presidency Conclusions, General Affairs and External Relations Council, doc. 10369/03, 16.VI.2003.
147. See Presidency Conclusions, General Affairs and External Relations Council, doc. 10189/04, 14.VI.2004.
148. *Agence Europe*, 20.XI.2002.
149. European Commission, *Wider Europe—Neighbourhood: A New Framework for Relations with our Eastern and Southern Neighbours*, COM(2003)104 final, Brussels, 11.III.2003.
150. For instance: Albania has been included in a project with Italy; Israel benefits of research cooperation since a long time.
151. Written Answers, Question by Mr. Hoon, House of Commons, 19.IV.2002, vol. 383, part 132.
152. *Agence Europe*, 20.XI.2002.
153. See the speech by Ana Palacio Vallelersundi, Spanish minister of Foreign Affairs, IFRI, 4.IX.2003. *Actividades, Textos y Documentos de la Politica Exterior Española, 2003*, 458.
154. On the link between enlargement policy and the ENP, see Kelley (2005).

References

Abou-Zeid, El-Sayed and Qianzhen Cheng. 2004. The Effectiveness of Innovation: A Knowledge Management Approach. *International Journal of Innovation Management* 8 (3).

Adelman, Morris A. 1991. Oil Fallacies. *Foreign Policy* (82).

Adler, Emanuel and Steven Bernstein. 2005. Knowledge in Power: The Epistemic Construction of Global Governance. In *Power in Global Governance*, edited by M. Barnett and R. Duvall. Cambridge: Cambridge University Press.

Adler, Emanuel, Federica Bicchi, Beverly Crawford, and Raffaella Del Sarto, eds. 2006. *The Convergence of Civilizations: Constructing a Mediterranean Region*. Toronto: University of Toronto Press.

Adler, Emanuel and Beverly Crawford. 2006. Normative Power: The European Practice of Region Building and the Case of the Euro-Mediterranean Partnership (EMP). In *The Convergence of Civilizations. Constructing the Mediterranean Region*, edited by E. Adler, F. Bicchi, B. Crawford, and R. Del Sarto. Toronto: University of Toronto Press.

Aghrout, Ahmed and Martin S. Alexander. 1997. The Euro-Mediterranean New Strategy and the Maghreb Countries. *European Foreign Affairs Review* 2 (3).

Aguirrebengoa, Pedro Lopéz. 1998. Transatlantic Co-ordination and the Middle East Peace Process. In *The New Transatlantic Agenda and the Future of EU-US Relations*, edited by J. Monar. London/The Hague/Boston: Kluwer Law International.

Ahmed, Akbar S. 1992. *Postmodernism and Islam. Predicament and Promise*. London/New York: Routledge.

Aliboni, Roberto, ed. 1992. *Southern European Security in the 1990s*. London/New York: Pinter Publishers.

———. 1996. Collective Political Co-operation in the Mediterranean. In *Security Challenges in the Mediterranean Region*, edited by R. Aliboni, G. Joffé, and T. Niblock. London/Portland: Frank Cass.

———, ed. 1998. *Partenariato nel Mediterraneo. Percezioni, politiche, istituzioni*. Milano: FrancoAngeli.

———. 1999. European Union Perceptions and Policies towards the Mediterranean. In *Mediterranean Security into the Coming Millennium*, edited by Stephen J. Blank. Strategic Studies Institute: Carlisle (Pennsylvania).

Aliboni, Roberto, George Joffé, and Tim Niblock, eds. 1996. *Security Challenges in the Mediterranean Region*. London/Portland: Frank Cass.

Allen, David. 1982. Political Cooperation and the Euro-Arab Dialogue. In *European Political Cooperation*, edited by D. Allen, R. Rummel, and W. Wessels. London: Butterworth Scientific.

Allen, David and Michael Smith. 1989. Western Europe in the Atlantic System of the 1980s: Towards a New Identity? In *Atlantic Relations. Beyond the Reagan Era*, edited by S. Gill. New York: St.Martin's Press.

Al-Mani', Saleh A. 1983. *The Euro-Arab Dialogue. A Study in Associative Diplomacy*. New York: St.Martin's Press.

Andersen, Svein S. and Kjell A. Eliassen. 2001. *Making Policy in Europe*. 2nd ed. London: Sage.

Arango, Joaquín. 2000. Becoming a Country of Immigration at the End of the Twentieth Century: The Case of Spain. In *Eldorado or Fortress? Migration in Southern Europe*, edited by R. King, G. Lazaridis, and C. Tsardanidis. London/New York: Macmillan/St.Martin's Press.

Archer, Margaret S. 1995. *Realist Social Theory: The Morphogenetic Approach*. Cambridge/New York: Cambridge University Press.

———. 1996. *Culture and Agency. The Place of Culture in Social Theory*. Rev. ed. Cambridge: Cambridge University Press.

Aruri, Naseer Hasan and Natalie Hevener. 1974. France and the Middle East: 1967–68. In *The Middle East in World Politics: A Study in Contemporary International Relations*, edited by T. Y. Ismael and N. H. Aruri. Syracuse: Syracuse University Press.

Avant, Deborah. 2000. From Mercenary to Citizen Armies: Explaining Change in the Practice of War. *International Organization* 54 (1).

Badini, Antonio. 1995. Efforts at Mediterranean Cooperation. In *Maelstrom. The United States, Southern Europe, and the Challenges of the Mediterranean*, edited by J. W. Holmes. Cambridge, MA: The World Peace Foundation.

Bagge, Lausten Carsten and Ole Wæver. 2000. In Defence of Religion: Sacred Referent Objects for Securitization. *Millennium* 29 (3).

Balta, Paul and Claudine Rulleau. 1973. *La politique arabe de la France de De Gaulle à Pompidou*. Paris: Sindbad.

Balzacq, Thierry. 2005. The Three Faces of Securitization: Political Agency, Audience and Context. *European Journal of International Relations* 11 (2).

Bandura, Albert. 1977. *Social Learning Theory*. Englewood Cliffs, NJ: Prentice Hall.

Barbé, Esther. 1995. European Political Cooperation: The Upgrading of Spanish Foreign Policy. In *Democratic Spain. Reshaping External Relations in a Changing World*, edited by R. Gillespie, F. Rodrigo, and J. Story. London/New York: Routledge.

———. 1996. The Barcelona Conference: Launching Pad of a Process. *Mediterranean Politics* 1 (1).

Barbé, Esther and Ferran Izquierdo. 1997. Present and Future of Joint Actions for the Mediterranean Region. In *Common Foreign and Security Policy. The Record and Reforms*, edited by M. Holland. London/Washington: Pinter.

Barravecchia, Giuseppe. 1996. I movimenti di popolazione dal Medio Oriente e dal Nord Africa. In *Rischio da Sud. Geopolitica delle crisi nel bacino mediterraneo*, edited by C. M. Santoro. Milano: FrancoAngeli.

Bartels, Lorand. 2005. Human Rights Conditionality in the EU's International Agreements. Oxford: Oxford University Press.

Baumgartner, Frank R. and Bryan D. Jones. 1991. Agenda Dynamics and Policy Subsystems. *The Journal of Politics* 53 (4).

———. 1993. *Agendas and Instability in American Politics*. Chicago/London: The University of Chicago Press.

Belguendouz, Abdelkrim. 1992. L'Emigration, Elémente de Rupture ou Facteur de Partenariat entre le Maghreb et l'Europe des Douze? *Annales du Centre d'Etudes Stratégiques 1990–1992* (4–5).

Bell, Coral. 1977. *The Diplomacy of Detente. The Kissinger Era*. London: Martin Robertson.

Bennoune, Mahfoud. 1988. *The Making of Contemporary Algeria. 1830–1987*. Cambridge: Cambridge University Press.

Bensidoun, Isabelle and Agnès Chevalier. 1998. La diversité du développement économique et des échanges dans le Bassin méditerranéen. Paper read at Migrations, libre-échange et intégration régionale dans le Bassin méditerranéen, at Athens, Greece.

Berger, Thomas U. 1996. Norms, Identity, and National Security in Germany and Japan. In *The Culture of National Security. Norms and Identity in World Politics*, edited by P. J. Katzenstein. New York: Columbia University Press.

Berstein, Serge and Jean-Pierre Rioux. 1995. *La France de l'expansion. 2. L'apogée Pompidou 1969–1974*. Paris: Editions du Seuil.

Bicchi, Federica. 2006. "Our size fits all": Normative Power Europe and the Mediterranean. *Journal of European Public Policy* 13 (2).

Bicchi, Federica and Mary Martin. 2006. Talking Tough or Talking Together? European Security Discourses towards the Mediterranean. *Mediterranean Politics* 11 (2).

Blumer, Herbert. 1971. Social Problems as Collective Behavior. *Social Problems* 18 (3).

Bobbio, Norberto. 1989. *Democracy and Dictatorship*. Cambridge: Polity Press.

Bojji, Ali. 1999. La charte euro-méediterranéenne pour la paix et la stabilité. In *L'Annuaire de la Méditerranée 1999*, édited by Groupement d'Etudes et de Recerces sur la Méditerranée Rabat: GERM—Editions Le Fennec.

Bonifazi, Corrado. 2000. European Migration Policy: Questions from Italy. In *Eldorado or Fortress? Migration in Southern Europe*, edited by R. King, G. Lazaridis, and C. Tsardanidis. London/New York: Macmillan/St.Martin's Press.

Bouchard, Roger. 1982. *CEE 10: Les accords méditerranéens en 1982*. Brussels: Agence Europe/Prométhée.

Brahimi Lakhdar and Dekker, Wisse. 1986. *Who Is Speaking to Whom in the Euro-Arab Dialogue? States in Regional Alliances as Counterparts*. The Hague: The Lutfia Rabbani Foundation.

Braudel, Fernand. 1949. *La Méditerranée et le monde méditerranéen à l'époque de Philippe II*. Paris: Armand Colin.

Braun, Dietmar and Andreas Busch, eds. 1999. *Public Policy and Political Ideas*. Cheltenham, UK: Edward Elgar; Northampton, MA: Edward Elgar.

Brecher, Michael. 1980. *Decisions in Crisis: Israel, 1967 and 1973*. Berkeley: University of California Press.

Breen, Richard. 1999. Beliefs, Rational Choice and Bayesian Learning. *Rationality and Society* 11 (4).

Bregman, Ahron and Jihan el-Tahri. 1998. *The Fifty Years War. Israel and the Arabs*. London: Penguin Books/BBC Books.

Bressand, Albert. 1984. De la décennie pétrolière à la décennie financière. *Politique Internationale* 26.

Bridge, John N. 1976. The EEC and Turkey: An Analysis of the Association Agreement and Its Impact on Turkish Economic Development. In *The EEC and the Mediterranean Countries*, edited by A. Shlaim and G. N. Yannopoulos. Cambridge: Cambridge University Press.

Brochmann, Grete and Tomas Hammer. 1999. *Mechanisms of Immigration Control. A Comparative Analysis of European Regulation Policies*. Oxford/New York: Berg.

Brown, Carl L. 1984. *International Politics and the Middle East. Old Rules, Dangerous Game*. London: I. B.Tauris.

Brown, Leon Carl. 1991. Bâtir sur du sable? La politique américaine au Moyen-Orient. 1945–1991. *Monde Arabe/Maghreb-Machrek* (132).

Buysse, Didier. 1984. *The Effects of Enlargment* [sic] *on Other Mediterranean Countries*. Bruxelles: European News Agency.

Buzan, Berry. 1991. *People, States, and Fear*. 2nd ed. Hemel Hempstead, UK: Harvester Wheatsheaf; Boulder, CO: Lynne Rienner.

Buzan, Berry and Ole Wæver. 2003. *Regions and Powers. The Structure of International Security*. Cambridge: Cambridge University Press.

Buzan, Berry, Ole Wæver, and Jaap de Wilde. 1998. *Security. A New Framework for Analysis*. Boulder/London: Lynne Rienner.

Cagiano de Azevedo, Raimondo. 1994. *Migration and Development Cooperation*. Strasbourg: Council of Europe.

Camdessus, Michel. 1984. Dette: Sortie de crise? *Politique Internationale* 26.

Campbell, David. 1992. *Writing Security. United States Foreign Policy and the Politics of Identity*. Minneapolis: University of Minnesota Press.

Campbell, John. 1993. *Edward Heath. A Biography*. London: Jonathan Cape.

Campbell, John C. 1975. The energy crisis and U.S. policy in the Middle East. In *The Energy Crisis and U.S. Foreign Polic*, edited by J. S. Szyliowicz and B. E. O'Neill. London/Washington/New York: Praeger.

Carlsnaes, Walter. 1994. In lieu of a Conclusions: Compatibility and the Agency-Structure Issue in Foreign Policy Analysis. In *EC and Changing Perspectives in Europe*, edited by W. Carlsnaes and S. Smith. London: Sage.

Carlsnaes, Walter, Helene Sjursen, and Brian White, eds. 2004. *Contemporary European Foreign Policy*. London/Thousand Oaks/New Delhi: Sage.

Carrère, René and Pierre Valat-Morio. 1973. Mesure du terrorism de 1968 à 1972. *Etudes Polémologiques* (8).

CESPI. 2000. Il governo dei processi migratori nel quadro europeo: obiettivi, strumenti, problemi. Paper read at Migrazioni. Scenari per il XXI secolo, at Rome, Italy.

Chatelus, Michel. 1997. L'énergie en Méditerranée: espace régional ou marché mondial? *Monde Arabe/Maghreb-Machrek* Hors série.

Checkel, Jeffrey T. 1997. *Ideas and International Political Change*. New Haven: Yale University Press; London: Yale.

———. 1999. Norms, Institutions, and National Identity in Contemporary Europe. *International Studies Quarterly* 43 (1).

———. 2001. Why Comply? Social Learning and European Identity Change. *International Organization* 55 (3).

Chérigui, Hayète. 1997. *La politique méditerranéenne de la France: Entre diplomatie collective et leadership*. Paris: L'Harmattan.

Christiansen, Thomas, Knud Erik Jørgensen, and Antje Wiener, eds. 2001. *The Social Construction of Europe*, London: Sage.

Clawson, Patrick. 1992. What's So Good about Stability? In *The Politics of Economic Reform in the Middle East*, edited by H. Barkely. New York: St.Martin's Press.

Cobb, Roger W. and Charles D. Elder. 1972. *Participation in American Politics: The Dynamics of Agenda-Building*. Baltimore: Johns Hopkins University Press.

Colard, Daniel. 1996. La Conférence de Barcelone et le partenariat euroméditerranéen. *Défense nationale* 52.

Collinson, Sarah. 1996. *Shore to Shore. The Politics of Migration in Euro-Maghreb Relations*. London: RIIA.

Commission of the European Communities. 1984. *The European Community and the Mediterranean Basin*. Brussels.

Constas, Dimitri. 1995. Southern European Countries in the European Community. In *Maelstrom. The United States, Southern Europe, and the Challenges of the Mediterranean*, edited by J. W. Holmes. Cambridge, MA: The World Peace Foundation.

Cooley, John. 1997. The Beginning of International Terrorism. In *Encyclopedia of World Terrorism*, edited by M. Crenshaw and J Pimlott. New York: M. E. Sharpe.

Cortell, Andrew P. and James W. Davis. 2005. When Norms Clash: International Norms, Domestic Practices, and Japan's Internalisation of the GATT/WTO. *Review of International Studies* 31 (1).

Couve de Murville, Maurice. 1971. *Une Politique Étrangère, 1958–1969*. Paris: Plon.

Cova, Colette. n.d. *The Arab Policy of the E.C.C.* Brussels: Bureau d'Informations Européennes.

Cram, Laura. 1994. The European Commission as a Multi-organization: Social Policy and IT Policy in the EU. *Journal of European Public Policy* 1 (2).

Damis, John. 1998. Morocco's 1995 Fisheries Agreement with the European Union: A Crisis Resolved. *Mediterranean Politics* 3 (2).

de la Gorce, Paul-Marie. 1993. Contexte international et défense. *Défense nationale* 49 (December).

de la Serre, Françoise. 1979. Conflit du Proche-Orient et dialogue euro-arabe: La position de l'Europe des Neuf. In *Le Dialogue Euro-Arabe*, edited by J. Bourrinet. Paris: Economica.

de Saint Robert, Philippe. 1970. *Le jeu de la France en Méditerranée.* Paris: Julliard.

de Schoutheete, Philippe. 1980. *La coopération politique européenne.* 2nd ed. Paris: Nathan; Bruxelles: Labor.

Dehousse, Renaud and Joseph H. H. Weiler. 1991. EPC and the Single Act: From Soft Law to Hard Law? In *The Future of European Political Cooperation. Essays on Theory and Practice*, edited by M. Holland. London: Macmillan.

Dekker, Sander and Dan Hansén. 2004. Learning under Pressure: The Effects of Politicization on Organizational Learning in Public Bureaucracies. *Journal of Public Administration Research and Theory* 14 (2).

Del Fabbro, René. 1995. A Victory of the Street. In *New Xenophobia in Europe*, edited by B. Baumgartl and A. Favell. London/The Hague/Boston: Kluwer Law International.

Del Sarto, Raffaella and Tobias Schumacher. 2005. From EMP to ENP: What's at Stake with the European Neighbourhood Policy towards the Southern Mediterranean? *European Foreign Affairs Review* 10 (1).

Deutch, John. 1997. Terrorism. *Foreign Policy* (108).

Devret, Jean-François. 1986. La Méditerranée, nouvelle frontière pour l'Europe des Douze? Paris: Khartala.

Di Nolfo, Ennio. 1994. *Storia delle relazioni internazionali 1918–1992.* Roma/Bari: Laterza.

Diallo, Thierno. 1992. *La politique étrangère de Georges Pompidou.* Paris: LGDJ.

Dixit, Avinash. 1996. *The Making of Economic Policy: A Transaction-Cost Politics Perspective.* Cambridge, MA: The MIT Press; London: The MIT Press.

Dunbabin, J. P. D. 1994. *International Relations since 1945: A History in Two Volumes, the Postwar World.* London/New York: Longman.

Duwaji, Ghazi. 1967. *Economic Development in Tunisia. The Impact and Course of Government Planning.* New York: Praeger.

Ecrement, Marc. 1986. *Indépendence politique et libération économique. Un quart de siècle du développement de l'Algerie. 1962–1985.* Alger/Grenoble: Entreprise Alg. de Press/Office des Publications Universitaires/Presses Universitaire de Grenoble.

Edelman, Murray J. 1988. *Constructing the political spectacle.* Chicago: University of Chicago Press.

Edwards, Geoffrey and Eric Philippart. 1997. The Euro-Mediterranean Partnership: Fragmentation and Reconstruction. *European Foreign Affairs Review* 2 (4).

el-Malki, Habib and Jean-Claude Santucci. 1987. Introduction. L'état et le développement des économies arabes: Un modèle en question? *Annuaire de l'Afrique du Nord* 26.

El Oufi, Noureddine. 1990. *La Marocanisation*. Casablanca: Toubkal.

Elkins, Zachary and Beth Simmons. 2005. On Waves, Clusters and Diffusion: A Conceptual Framework. *Annals of the American Academy of Political and Social Science* 598 (1).

Elster, Jon. 1995. The Strategic Uses of Argument. In *Barriers to Conflict Resolution*, edited by K. E. A. Arrow. New York: W. W. Norton.

Emerson, Michael and Gergana Noutcheva. 2005. From Barcelona Process to Neighbourhood Policy. Assessments and Open Issues. In *CEPS Working Document 220*: CEPS.

Engene, Jan Oskar. 2004. *Terrorism in Western Europe: Explaining the Trends since 1950*. Cheltenham/Northhampton, MA: Edward Elgar.

Entman, Robert M. 1993. Framing: Toward Clarification of a Fractured Paradigm. *Journal of Communication* 43 (4).

Epstein, David and Sharyn O'Halloran. 1999. Asymmetric Information, Delegation and the Structure of Policy-Making. *Journal of Theoretical Politics* 11 (1).

Erikson, Erik Odvar and John Fossum, eds. 2000. *Democracy in the European Union. Integration through Deliberation*. London: Routledge.

Esposito, John L. 1999. "Clash of Civilizations?" Contemporary Images of Islam in the West. In *Islam, Modernism and the West*, edited by G. Martín Muñoz. London/New York: Tauris Publishers.

Everts, Phillip. 1972. *The European Community in the World. The External Relations of the Enlarged European Community*. Rotterdam: Rotterdam University Press.

Faber, Gerrit. 1982. *The European Community and Development Cooperation*. Assen: Van Gorcum.

Farrell, Theo. 2001. Transnational Norms and Military Development: Constructing Ireland's Professional Army. *European Journal of International Relations* 7 (1).

Fearon, James. 1995. Rationalist Explanations of War. *International Organization* 49 (3).

Fearon, James and Alexander Wendt. 2002. Rationalism v. Constructivism: A Skeptical View. In *Handbook of International Relations*, edited by W. Carlsnaes, T. Risse, and B. Simmons. London: Sage.

Featherstone, Kevin. 1989. The Mediterranean Challenge: Cohesion and External Preferences. In *The European Community and the Challenge of the Future*, edited by J. Lodge. London: Pinter Publishers.

Feld, Walter J. 1965. The Association Agreements of the European Communities: A Comparative Analysis. *International Organization* 19 (2).

Fenech, Dominic. 1997. The Relevance of European Security Structures to the Mediterranean (and Vice Versa). *Mediterranean Politics* 2 (1).

Finnemore, Martha. 1996. Norms, Culture, and World Politics: Insights from Sociology's Institutionalism. *International Organization* 50 (2).

Finnemore, Martha and Kathryn Sikkink. 1998. International Norm Dynamics and Political Change. *International Organization* 52 (4).

Fischer, Frank and John Forester, eds. 1993. *The Argumentative Turn in Policy Analysis and Planning.* London: UCL Press.

Florini, Ann. 1996. The Evolution of International Norms. *International Studies Quarterly* 40 (3).

Flory, Thiébault. 1982. Les accords CEE—pays méditerranéens. La coopération commerciale en matière de produits industriels. In *La Communauté Économique Européenne Élargie et la Méditerranée: Quelle Coopération?* edited by J. Touscoz. Paris: PUF.

Fontaine, André. 1970. Pompidou's Mediterranean Policy. *Interplay* 3 (3).

Franchino, Fabio. 2000. Control of the Commission's Executive Functions: Uncertainty, Conflict and Decision Rules. *European Union Politics* 1 (1).

———. 2002. Efficiency or Credibility? Testing the Two Logics of Delegation to the European Commission. *Journal of European Public Policy* 9 (5).

Freedman, Robert O. 1991. *Moscow and the Middle East. Soviet Policy since the Invasion of Afghanistan.* Cambridge: Cambridge University Press.

Fritsch-Bournazel, Renata. 1987. The French View. In *Germany between East and West*, edited by E. Moretona. Cambridge: Cambridge University Press/RIIA.

Fuller, Graham E. 1995. Interests in the Middle East. In *Malestrom. The United States, Southern Europe, and the Challenges of the Mediterranean*, edited by J. W. Holmes. Cambridge, MA: The World Peace Foundation.

Funk, Albrecht and Herbert Reinke. 1992. La police en République Fédérale d'Allemagne. In *Polices d'Europe*, edited by J.-M. Erbes, J. C. Monet, A. Funk, H. Reinke, P. Ponsaers, C. Janssens, Y. Cartuyvels, M. Dauge, J. J. Gleizal, C. Journes, and S. Palidda. Paris: L'Harmattan.

Gama, Jaime. 1995. Southern Europe and the United States: The Bilateral Approach. In *Malestrom. The United States, Southern Europe, and the Challenges of the Mediterranean*, edited by J. W. Homes. Cambridge, MA: The World Peace Foundation.

Garfinkle, Adam. 1981. America and Europe in the Middle East: A New Coordination? *Orbis* 25 (3).

Garrett, Geoffrey and Barry R. Weingast. 1993. Ideas, Interests, and Institutions: Constructing the European Community's Internal Market. In *Ideas and Foreign Policy: Beliefs, Institutions, and Political Change*, edited by J. Goldstein and R. O. Keohane. Ithaca, NY: Cornell University Press.

Garthoff, Raymond L. 1985. *Détente and Confrontation. American-Soviet Relations from Nixon to Reagan.* Washington, DC: The Brookings Institution.

Garton Ash, Timothy. 1993. *In Europe's Name. Germany and the Divided Continent.* London: Jonathan Cape.

Gasteyger, Curt. 1974. Changes and Challenges in the Western Mediterranean: The Political and Strategic Aspects. In *The Western Mediterranean. Its Political, Economic, and Strategic Importance*, edited by A. J. Cottrell and J. D. Theberge. New York/London: Praeger Publishers.

Geddes, Andrew. 2000. *Immigration and European Integration: Towards Fortress Europe?* Manchester: Manchester University Press.

Geradin, Damien and Nicolas Petit. 2003. Competition Policy and the Euro-Mediterranean Partnership. *European Foreign Affairs Review* 8 (2).

Giddens, Anthony. 1991. *Modernity and Self-Identity*. Cambridge: Polity Press.

———. 1993. *New Rules of Sociological Method. A Positive Critique of Interpretative Sociologies*. 2nd ed. Cambridge: Polity Press.

Gillespie, Richard. 1995. Spain and the Maghreb: Towards a Regional Policy? In *Democratic Spain. Reshaping External Relations in a Changing World*, edited by R. Gillespie, F. Rodrigo, and J. Story. London/New York: Routledge.

———. 1996. Spain and the Mediterranean: Southern Sensitivity, European Aspirations. *Mediterranean Politics* 1 (2).

———. 1997. Spanish Protagonismo and the Euro-Med Partnership Initiative. *Mediterranean Politics* 2 (1).

———. 1999. *Spain and the Mediterranean: Developing a European Policy towards the South*. London: Macmillan.

Gillespie, Richard and Richard Youngs, eds. 2002. *The European Union and Democracy Promotion: The Case of North Africa*. London/Portland, OR: Frank Cass.

Gilpin, Robert. 1987. *The Political Economy of International Relations*. Princeton: Princeton University Press.

Ginsberg, Roy H. 1983. The European Community and the Mediterranean. In *Institutions and Policies of the European Community*, edited by J. Lodge. London: Pinter.

———. 1989. *Foreign Policy Actions of the European Community. The Politics of Scale*. Boulder/London: Lynne Rienner Publishers/Adamantine Press Ltd.

———. 2001. *The European Union in International Politics. Baptism by Fire*. Lanham/Boulder/New York/Oxford: Rowman & Littlefield Publishers.

Giuliani, Marco. 1998. Sul concetto di "imprenditore di *policy*." *Rivista Italiana di Scienza Politica* 28 (2).

Glassman, Jon D. 1977. *Arms for the Arabs. The Soviet Union and War in the Middle East*. Baltimore/London: The Johns Hopkins University Press.

Golan, Galia. 1977. *Yom Kippur and after. The Soviet Union and the Middle East Crisis*. Cambridge: Cambridge University Press.

Gomez, Ricardo. 1998. The EU's Mediterranean policy: Common Foreign Policy by the Back Door? In *A Common Foreign Policy for Europe? Competing visions of the CFSP*, edited by J. Peterson and H. Sjursen. London/New York: Routledge.

Gómez Gil, Carlos. 1995. *La ayuda de España al Mediterráneo*. Madrid: Centro de Investigación para la Paz/Asociación para la Cooperacion con el Sur.

Gordon, Philip H. 1998. *The Transatlantic Allies and the Changing Middle East.* Adelphi Paper. London: International Institute for Strategic Studies.

Gowa, Joanne S. 1994. *Allies, Adversaries, and International Trade.* Princeton, NJ: Princeton University Press.

Granell, Francisco. 1994. The European Union's Enlargement Negotiations with Austria, Finland, Norway and Sweden. *Journal of Common Market Studies* (382).

Grech, John C. 1974. *Trade Relations between the European Economic Community and Mediterranean Countries.* Malta: Royal University of Malta.

Greilsammer, Ilan. 1982. *Israel et l'Europe. Une historie des relations entre la Communauté européenne et l'Etat d'Israel.* Lausanne: Fondation jean Monnet Pour l'Europe.

Grilli, Enzo. 1993. *The European Community and the Developing Countries.* Cambridge: Cambridge University Press.

Guazzone, Laura. 1991. Il Mediterraneo e l'Europa comunitaria: Gli anni '80 e le prospettive per gli anni '90. In *L'Europa degli anni novanta. La geopolitica del cambiamento*, edited by L. Guazzone. Milano: FrancoAngeli.

Guessous, Bensalem. 1970. Les Relations du Maghreb avec la Communauté Economique Européenne. In *La Communaté et le problème du developpement. La Communauté et les pays Méditerranéens.* Bruxelles: Editions de l'Institut de Sociologie.

Guzzini, Stefano. 1998. *Realism in International Relations and International Political Economy. The Continuing Story of a Death Foretold.* London/New York: Routledge.

Haas, Ernst B. 1958. *The Uniting of Europe. Political, Social, and Economic Forces: 1950–1957.* Stanford, CA: Stanford University Press.

———. 2001. Does Constructivism Subsume Neo-functionalism? In *The Social Construction of Europe*, edited by T. Christiansen, K. E. Jørgensen, and A. Wiener. London: Sage.

Haas, Peter M. 1992. Introduction: Epistemic Communities and International Policy Coordination. *International Organization* 46 (1).

———. 1993. *Saving the Mediterranean. The Politics of International Environmental Cooperation.* New York: Columbia University Press.

Haass, Richard N. 1996. The Middle East: No More Treaties. *Foreign Affairs* 75 (5).

Hager, Wolfgang. 1974. The Mediterranean: A European Mare Nostrum? *Orbis* 18 (1).

Haggard, Stephan and Beth A. Simmons. 1987. Theories of International Regimes. *International Organization* 41 (3).

Hajer, Maarten A. 1993. Discourse Coalitions and the Institutionalization of Practice: The Case of Acid Rain in Britain. In *The Argumentative Turn in Policy Analysis and Planning*, edited by F. Fischer and J. Forester. London: UCL Press.

Hall, Peter A. 1993. Policy Paradigms, Social Learning, and the State. The Case of Economic Policymaking in Britain. *Comparative Politics* 25 (3).

Halliday, Fred. 1983. *The Making of the Second Cold War.* London: Verso.

———. 1996. *Islam and the Myth of Confrontation*. London/New York: Tauris Publishers.

———. 1997. The Middle East, the Great Powers, the Cold War. In *The Cold War and the Middle East*, edited by Y. Sayigh and A. Shlaim. Oxford: Clarendon Press.

Handoussa, Heba and Jean-Louis Reiffers. 2002. *The FEMISE Report on the Evolution of the Structure of Trade and Investments between the European Union and Its Mediterranean Partners*. FEMISE Network. www.femise.org.

Hanrieder, Wolfram F. 1989. *Germany, America, Europe. Forty Years of German Foreign Policy*. New Haven/London: Yale University Press.

Hansen, Lene. 2000. The Little Mermaid's Silent Security Dilemma and the Absence of Gender in the Copenhagen School. *Millennium* 29 (2).

Hargreaves, Alec G. 1995. *Immigration, "Race" and Ethnicity in Contemporary France*. London/New York: Routledge.

Heclo, Hugh. 1974. *Modern Social Politics in Britain and Sweden: From Relief to Income Maintenance*. New Haven: Yale University Press.

Henig, Stanley. 1976. Mediterranean Policy in the Context of the External Relations of the European Community 1958–73. In *The EEC and the Mediterranean Countries*, edited by A. Shlaim and G. N. Yannopoulos. Cambridge: Cambridge University Press.

Héritier, Adrienne. 1999. *Policy-Making and Diversity in Europe. Escaping Deadlock*. Cambridge: Cambridge University Press.

Héritier, Adrienne and Christoph Knill. 2000. *Differential Responses to European Policies: A Comparison*. Bonn: Max-Planck Project Group Preprint No 2000/7.

Hermant, Daniel and Didier Bigo. 2000. Les Politiques de Lutte contre le Terrorism: Enjeux Français. In *European Democracies against Terrorism. Governmental Policies and Intergovernmental Cooperation*, edited by F. Reinares. Dartmouth: Ashgate.

Hill, Christopher. 1993. The Capability-Expectations Gap, or Conceptualizing Europe's International Role. *Journal of Common Market Studies* 31 (3).

———, ed. 1996. *The Actors in Europe's Foreign Policy*. London: Routledge.

———. 2003. *The Changing Politics of Foreign Policy*. Basingstoke/New York: Palgrave.

Hine, Robert C. 1988. Customs Union Enlargement and Adjustment: Spain's Accession to the European Community. *Journal of Common Market Studies* 28 (1).

Hix, Simon. 1994. Approaches to the Study of the European Community: The Challenge to Comparative Politics. *West European Politics* 17 (1).

Hoekman, Bernard M. 1995. *The WTO, the EU and the Arab World: Trade Policy Priorities and Pitfalls*. London: Centre for Economic Policy Research

Hoekman, Bernard M. and Simeon Djankov. 1996. The European Union's Mediterranean Free Trade Initiative. *The World Economy* 19 (4).

Hoffmann, Stanley. 2000. Towards a Common European Foreign and Security Policy? *Journal of Common Market Studis* 38 (2).

Holden, Patrick. 2003. The European Community's MEDA Aid Programme: A Strategic Instrument of Civilian Power? *European Foreign Affairs Review* 8 (3).

———. 2005. Hybrids on the Rim? The European Union's Mediterranean Aid Policy. *Democratization* 12 (4).

Holland, Martin. 1997. *Common Foreign and Security Policy. The Record and Reforms*. London/Washington: Pinter.

Hollifield, James. 1999. Ideas, Institutions and Civil Society: On the Limits of Immigration Control in France. In *Mechanisms of Immigration Control: A Comparative Analysis of European Regulation Policies*, edited by G. Brochmann and T. Hammar. Oxford: Berg.

Hollis, Rosemary. 1997. Europe and the Middle East: Power by Stealth? *International Affairs* 73 (1).

Holmes, John W., ed. 1995. *Maelstrom. The United States, Southern Europe, and the challenges of the Mediterranean*. Cambridge, MA: The World Peace Foundation.

Hooghe, Liesbet and Gary Marks. 2001. *Multi-level Governance and European Integration*. Lanham, MD: Rowman and Littlefield.

Horton, Christine. 1995. *Policing Policy in France*. London: Policy Studies Institute.

Hourani, Albert. 1991. *A History of the Arab Peoples*. London: Faber and Faber Ltd.

Howard, Harry N. 1974. The United States and the Middle East. In *The Middle East in World Politics. A Study in Contemporary International Relations*, edited by Tareq Y. Ismael. Syracuse, NY: Syracuse University Press.

Howlett, Michael and M. Ramesh. 1995. *Studying Public Policy. Policy Cycles and Policy Subsystems*. Toronto/New York/Oxford: Oxford University Press.

Huber, George P. 1991. Organizational Learning: The Contributing Processes and the Literature. *Organization Science* 2 (1).

Hug, Simon. 2003. Endogenous Preferences and Delegation in the European Union. *Comparative Political Studies* 36 (1–2).

Huntington, Samuel P. 1993. The Clash of Civilizations? *Foreign Affairs* 72 (3).

———. 1996. *The Clash of Civilizations and the Remaking of World Order*. New York: Simon & Schuster.

Huysmans, Jef. 1998. Security! What Do You Mean? From Concept to Thick Signifier. *European Journal of International Relations* 4 (2).

———. 2006. *The Politics of Insecurity: Fear, Migration, and Asylum in the EU*. Milton Park: Routledge.

Ifestos, Panayiotis. 1987. *European Political Cooperation: Towards a Framework of Supranational Diplomacy?* Aldershot: Avebury.

Indyk, Martin. 1992. Watershed in the Middle East. *Foreign Affairs/America and the World 1991/92* 71 (1).

Ismael, Tareq Y. 1986. *International Relations of the Contemporary Middle East*. New York: Syracuse University Press.

Jachtenfuchs, Markus. 2001. The Governance Approach to European Integration. *Journal of Common Market Studies* 39 (2).

Jobert, Michel. 1976. *L'autre regard*. Paris: Bernard Grasset.

Joffé, George. 1996. Low-level Violence and Terrorism. In *Security Challenges in the Mediterranean Region*, edited by R. Aliboni, G. Joffé, and T. Niblock. London: Frank Cass.

Jørgensen, Knud Erik. 1997. PoCo: The Diplomatic Republic of Europe. In *Reflective Approaches to European Governance*, edited by K. E. Jørgensen. London/New York: Macmillan/St.Martin's Press.

Jünemann, Annette, ed. 2004. *Euro-Mediterranean Relations after September 11. International, Regional and Domestic Dynamics*. London/Portland, OR: Frank Cass.

Kaplan, Thomas J. 1993. Reading Policy Narratives: Beginnings, Middles, and Ends. In *The Argumentative Turn in Policy Analysis and Planning*, edited by F. Fischer and J. Forrester. Durham/London: Duke University Press.

Kaufman, Burton I. 1996. *The Arab Middle East and the United States*. New York: Twayne Publishers/Prentice Hall.

Kelley, Judith. 2005. New Wine in Old Wineskins: Policy Learning and Adaptation in the New European Neighbourhood Policy. In *Working Paper Series, SAN05/01*. Duke: Terry Sanford Institute for Public Policy.

Kelsay, John. 1993. *Islam and War: The Gulf War and Beyond*. Louisville: John Know Press.

Kepel, Gilles. 1991. *La Revanche de Dieu. Chrétiens, juifs et musulmans à la reconquête du monde*. Paris: Seuil.

———. 2000. *Jihad: Expansion et déclin de l'islamisme*. Paris: Gallimard.

Khader, Bichara. 1994. *L'Europe et la Méditerranée. Géopolitique de la proximité*. Paris: L'Harmattan.

———. 1997. *Le Partenariat Euro-Méditerranéen après la conférence de Barcelone*. Paris: L'Harmattan.

Kienle, Eberhard. 1998. Destabilization through Partnership? Euro-Mediterranean Relations after the Barcelona Declaration. *Mediterranean Politics* 3 (2).

King, P. J. and Nancy C. Roberts. 1987. Policy Entrepreneurs: Catalysts for Policy Innovation. *Journal of State Government* (1).

King, Russell. 1998. The Mediterranean: Europe's Rio Grande. In *The Frontiers of Europe*, edited by M. Anderson, and E. Bort. London/Washington: Pinter.

———. 2000. Southern Europe in the Changing Global Map of Migration. In *Eldorado or Fortress? Migration in Southern Europe*, edited by R. King, G. Lazaridis, and C. Tsardanidis. London/New York: Macmillan/St.Martin's Press.

Kingdon, John W. 1984/1995. *Agendas, Alternatives, and Public Policies*. Boston/Toronto: Little, Brown and Company.

Kirzner, Israel M. 1997. *How Markets Work: Disequilibrium, Entrepreneurship and Discovery*. London: The Institute for Economic Affairs.

Kissinger, Henry. 1979. *White House Years*. Boston/Toronto: Little, Brown and Company.

Knodt, Michèle. 2004. International Embeddedness of European Multi-level Governance. *Journal of European Public Policy* 11 (4).

Kolodziej, Edward A. 1974(a). France and the Western Mediterranean. In *The Western Mediterranean. Its Political, Economic, and Strategic Importance*, edited by A. J. Cottrell and J. D. Theberge. London: Praeger Publishers.

———. 1974(b). *French International Policy under de Gaulle and Pompidou*. Ithaca/London: Cornell University Press.

Koremenos, Barbara, Charles Lipson, and Duncan Snidal. 2001. The Rational Design of International Institutions. *International Organization* 55 (4).

Krasner, Stephen D., ed. 1982. *International Regimes*. Vol. 36 (Spring), special issue of International Organization.

Kratochwill, Friedrich V. 1989. *Rules, Norms and Decisions: On the Conditions of Practical and Legal Reasoning in International Relations and Domestic Affairs*. Cambridge: Cambridge University Press.

Krause, Alexandra. 2003. The European Union's Africa Policy: The Commission as Policy Entrepreneur in the CFSP. *European Foreign Affairs Review* 8 (2).

Kreile, Michael. 1980. Ostpolitik Reconsidered. In *The Foreign Policy of West Germany. Formation and Contents*, edited by E. Krippendorff and V. Rittgerger. London/Beverly Hills: Sage Publications.

Kreinin, Mordechai E. 1976. US Trade Interests and the EEC Mediterranean Policy. In *The EEC and the Mediterranean Countries*, edited by A. Shlaim and G. N. Yannopoulos. Cambridge: Cambridge University Press.

Kuniholm, Bruce R. 1987. Retrospect and Prospects: Forty Years of US Middle East Policy. *The Middle East Journal* 41 (1).

Labatut, Barnard. 1995. Les politiques méditerranéennes de l'Espagne à la recherche d'un équilibre entre l'imperatif de la sécurité et l'ethique de l'interdépendance. *Etudes Internationales* 26 (2).

Lacoste, Pierre. 1993. En attendant le prochain Livre blanc. *Défense nationale* 49 (December).

Laffan, Brigid. 1997. From Policy Entrepreneur To Policy Manager: The Challenge Facing the European Commission. *Journal of European Public Policy* 4 (3).

Langlois, Alain and Gilles Blanchi. 1979. Les téchniques de la coordination inter-européenne. In *Le Dialogue Euro-Arabe*, edited by J. Bourrinet. Paris: Economica.

Lavenex, Sandra. 2004. EU External Governance in "Wider Europe." *Journal of European Public Policy* 11 (4).

Lavenex, Sandra and Emek M. Uçarer, eds. 2002. *Migration and the Externalities of European Integration*. Lanham, MD: Lexington Books.

Legro, Jeffrey. 1996. Culture and Preferences in the International Cooperation Two-Step. *American Political Science Review* 90:118–137.

———. 2000. The Transformation of Policy Ideas. *American Journal of Political Science* 44 (3).

Lesser, Ian O. 1995. Growth and Change in Southern Europe. In *Malestrom. The United States, Southern Europe, and the Challenges of the Mediterranean*, edited by J. W. Holmes. Cambridge, MA: The World Peace Foundation.

Levi, Mario. 1972. La C.E.E. et les pays de la Méditerranée. *Politique Etrangère* (6).
Levy, Jack S. 1994. Learning and Foreign Policy: Sweeping a Conceptual Minefield. *International Organization* 48 (2).
Lewis, Jeffrey. 1998. Is the "Hard Bargaining" Image of the Council Misleading? The Committee of Permanent Representatives and the Local Elections Directive. *Journal of Common Market Studies* 36 (4).
Lieber, Robert J. 1976. *Oil and the Middle East War: Europe in the Energy Crisis*. Boston: Harvard University Press.
Loeff, Joseph. 1973. La Communauté élargie et l'espace méditerranéen. In *La Politique Économique Extérieure de la Communauté Européenne Élargie*, edited by Brugmans, Hendrik. Bruges: De Tempel.
Luciani, Giacomo. 1976. *L'OPEC nella economia internazionale*. Torino: Einaudi.
———. 1994. The Oil Rent, the Fiscal Crisis of the State and Democratization. In *Democracy without Democrats? The Renewal of Politics in the Muslim World*, edited by G. Salamé. London/New York: Tauris Publishers.
Lundestad, Geir. 1998. *"Empire" by Integration. The United States and European Integration, 1945–1997*. Oxford: Oxford University Press.
Macleod, I., I. D. Hendry, and Stephen Hyett. 1996. *The External Relations of the European Communities*. Oxford: Clarendon Press.
Madelin, Henri. 1974. La guerre pétrolière. *Project. Civilisation, travail, économie* (82).
Magdi Wahba, Mourad. 1994. *The Role of the State in the Egyptian Economy: 1945–1981*. Reading: Ithaca.
Majone, Giandomenico. 2001. Two Logics of Delegation: Agency and Fiduciary Relations in EU Governance. *European Union Politics* 2 (1).
Mansfield, Peter. 1970. A Middle East Policy. In *Britain and the World of the Seventies. A Collection of Fabian Essays*, edited by G. Cunningham. London: Weidenfeld and Nicolson.
March, James G., and Johan P Olsen. 1988. The Uncertainty of the Past: Organizational Learning under Ambiguity. In *Decisions and Organization*, edited by J. G. March. Cambridge, MA: Blackwell.
Marks, Gary, Liesbet Hooghe, and Kermit Blamk. 1996. European Integration from the 1980s: State-Centric versus Multi-level Governance. *Journal of Common Market Studies* 34 (3).
Marks, Jon. 1996. High Hopes and Low Motives: The New Euro-Mediterranean Partnership Initiative. *Mediterranean Politics* 1 (1).
Marquina, Antonio. 1995. Mediterraneo e sicurezza nell'ottica spagnola. *Relazioni Internazionali* 59.
———. 1998. Spanish Foreign and Security Policy in the Mediterranean. *Spain and the Mediterranean since 1898* 13 (1–2).
Marquina, Antonio, and Carlos Echeverria. 1992. La politique de l'Espagne au Maghreb. *Monde Arabe/Maghreb-Machrek* (137).
Marsh, J. S. 1976. The Common Agricultural Policy and the Mediterranean Countries. In *The EEC and the Mediterranean Countries*, edited by A. Shlaim and G. N. Yannopoulos. Cambridge: Cambridge University Press.

Martín Muñoz, Gema, ed. 1999. *Islam, Modernism and the West*. London/New York: Tauris Publishers.
Martin, Philip L. 1994. Germany: Reluctant Land of Immigration. In *Controlling Immigration: A Global Perspective*, edited by W. A. Cornelius, P. L. Martin, and H. J. F. Stanford: Stanford University Press.
Martines, Francesca. 1994. *The Cooperation Agreements with the Maghreb Countries*. Florence: European University Institute.
Maull, H. 1980. *Europe and World Energy*. London: Butterworth.
McSweeney, Bill. 1999. *Security, Identity and Interests. A Sociology of International Relations*. Cambridge: Cambridge University Press.
Merton, Robert K. 1957. *Social Theory and Social Structure*. Glencoe: Free Press.
Meseguer, Covadonga. 2003. *Learning and Economic Policy Choices: A Bayesian Approach*. Florence: European University Institute.
———. 2005. Policy Learning, Policy Diffusion, and the Making of a New order. *Annals of the American Academy of Political and Social Science* 598 (1).
Messmer, Pierre, ed. 1990. *Georges Pompidou hier et aujourd'hui*. Actes du Colloque, 30 novembre et 1er décembre, 1989. Neuilly-sur-Seine: Éditions Breet.
———. 1997. Investissements étrangers: Les économies du sud de la Méditerranée sont-elles attractives? *Monde Arabe/Maghreb-Machrek hors série*.
Mickolus, Edward F. 1980. *Transnational Terrorism: a Chronology of Events, 1968–1979*. London: Aldwych.
Milgrom, Paul and John Roberts. 1992. *Economics, Organization, and Management*. Englewood Cliffs: Prentice Hall.
Milward, Alan S. 1992. *The European Rescue of the Nation-State*. London: Routledge.
Minerbi, Sergio. 1976. The EEC and Israel. In *The EEC and the Mediterranean Countries*, edited by A. Shlaim and G. N. Yannopoulos. Cambridge: Cambridge University Press.
Minerbi, Sergio I. 1970. Les relations d'Israël avec la Communauté économique européenne. In *La Communaté et le problème du developpement. La Communauté et les pays Méditerranéens*. Bruxelles: Editions de l'Institut de Sociologie.
Mintrom, Michael. 1997. Policy Entrepreneurs and the Diffusion of Innovation. *American Journal of Political Science* 41 (3).
Mitzen, Jennifer. 2006. Anchoring Europe's Civilizing Identity: Habits, Capabilities and Ontological Security. *Journal of European Public Policy* 13 (2).
Moe, Terry M. 1984. The New Economics of Organization. *American Journal of Political Science* 28:739–777.
Moïsi, Dominique. 1980. L'Europe et le conflit israélo-arabe. *Politique Étrangère* 45 (4).
Moltz, James Clay. 1993. Divergent Learning and the Failed Politics of Soviet Economic Reform. *World Politics* 45 (2).

Montanari, Armando and Antonio Cortese. 1993. South to North Migration in a Mediterranean Perspective. In *Mass Migration in Europe. The Legacy and the Future*, edited by R. King. London: Belhaven Press.

Moratinos, Miguel Ángel. 1996. Colaboracion española al desarrollo del Norte de Africa. In *El Mediterraneo y Oriente Medio*, edited by M. Á. Moratinos, J. Dezcallar, and F. Arbos. Madrid: Ministerio de Asuntos Exteriores. Dirección General de Política Exterior para Africa y Medio Oriente.

———. 1999. Europe and the Muslim World in International Relations. In *Islam, Modernism and the West*, edited by G. Martín Muñoz. London/New York: Tauris Publishers.

Moratinos, Miguel Ángel, Jorge Dezcallar, and Federico Arbos, eds. 1996. *El Mediterraneo y Oriente Medio*. Madrid: Ministerio de Asuntos Exteriores. Dirección General de Política Exterior para Africa y Medio Oriente.

Moravcsik, Andrew. 1997. Taking Preferences Seriously: A Liberal Theory of International Politics. *International Organization* 51 (4).

———. 1998. *The Choice for Europe. Social Purpose and State Power from Messine to Maastricht*. Ithaca/New York: Cornell University Press.

———. 1999. A New Statecraft? Supranational Entrepreneus and International Cooperation. *International Organization* 53 (2).

———. 2001. Bringing Constructivist Integration Theory out of the Clouds: Has It Landed Yet? *European Union Politics* 2 (2).

Morgan, Roger. 1978. *West Germany's Foreign Policy Agenda*. London/Beverly Hills: Sage Publication.

Morrow, James D. 1999. The Strategic Setting of Choices: Signaling, Commitment, and Negotiation in International Politics. In *Strategic Choice and International Relations*, edited by D. A. Lake and R. Powell. Princeton: Princeton University Press.

Muller, Pierre. 1995. Les politiques publiques comme construction d'un rapport au monde. In *la Construction du Sens dans les Politiques Publiques. Débats autour de la Notion de Référential*, edited by A. Faure, G. Pollet and P. Warin. Paris: OECD Publications.

Müller, Harald. 2004. Arguing, Bargaining, and All That: Communicative Action, Rationalist Theory and the Logic of Appropriateness in International Relations. *European Journal of International Relations* 10 (3).

Mureau, Anne-Marie. 1984. *L'Europe communautaire dans la negociation Nord-Sud. Ambitions, intérêts et réalités*. Paris: PUF.

National Commission on Terrorist Attacks upon the United States. 2004. *The 9/11 Commission Report*. Washington.

Niblock, Tim. 1996. North-South Socio-Economic Relations in the Mediterranean. In *Security Challenges in the Mediterranean Region*, edited by R. Aliboni, G. Joffé, and T. Niblock. London: Frank Cass.

Niemann, Arne. 2004. Between Communicative Action and Strategic Action: The Article 113 Committee and the Negotiations on the WTO Basic Telecommunications Services Agreement. *Journal of European Public Policy* 11 (3).

Nonaka, Ikujiro and Patrick Reinmoeller. 2000. Dynamic Business Systems for Knowledge Creation and Utilization. In *Knowledge Horizons: The Present and the Promise of Knowledge Management*, edited by C. Despres and D. Chauvel. Boston: Butterworth-Heinemann.
Northedge, F. S. 1974. *Descent From Power. British Foreign Policy. 1945–1973*. London: George Allen and Unwin Ltd.
Nuttall, Simon J. 1992. *European Political Co-operation*. Oxford: Clarendon Press.
OECD. 1973. *Oil. The Present Situation and Future Prospects*. Paris: Organisation for Economic Co-operation and Development.
Øhrgaard, Jakob C. 1997. "Less than Supranational, More than Intergovernmental": European Political Cooperation and the Dynamics of Intergovernmental Integration. *Millennium* 26 (1).
Olson, Mancur. 1965/1971. *The Logic of Collective Action: Public Goods and the Theory of Groups*. Harvard: Harvard University Press.
Ordóñez, Fernández F. 1990. Quelle structure de sécurité pou la Méditerranée? *Revue de l'OTAN* (5).
Ortega, Andrés. 1995. Spain in the Post-Cold War World. In *Democratic Spain. Reshaping External Relations in a Changing World*, edited by R. Gillespie, F. Rodrigo, and J. Story. London/New York: Routledge.
Ovendale, Ritchie. 1998. *Anglo-American Relations in the Twentieth Century*. London: Macmillan.
Pace, Michelle. 2006. *The Politics of Regional Identity: Meddling with the Mediterranean*. London/New York: Routledge.
Papa, Gian-Paolo and Jean Petit-Laurent. 1976. Commercial Relations between the EEC and the Mediterranean Countries: An Analysis of Recent Trends in Trade Flows. In *The EEC and the Mediterranean Countries*, edited by A. Shlaim and G. N. Yannopoulos. Cambridge: Cambridge University Press.
Papademetriou, Demetrios G. and Kimberly A. Hamilton. 1996. *Converging Paths to Restriction: French, Italian, and British Responses to Immigration*. Washington, DC: Carnegie Endowment for International Peace.
Patomäki, Heikki and Colin Wight. 2000. After Postpositivism? The Promises of Critical Realism. *International Studies Quarterly* 44 (2).
Payne, Rhys. 1993. Economic Crisis and Policy Reform in the 1980s. In *Polity and Society in Contemporary North Africa*, edited by W. I. Zartman and W. M. Habeeb. Boulder/San Francisco/Oxford: Westview Press.
Payne, Rodger. 2001. Persuasion, Frames and Norms Construction. *European Journal of International Relations* 7 (1).
Perthes, Volker. 1992. The Syrian Economy in the 1980s. *Middle East Journal* 46 (1).
Peterson, John and Elizabeth Bomberg. 1999. *Decision-Making in the European Union*. Basingstoke/London: Macmillan.
Pfetsch, Frank R. 1988. *West Germany: Internal Structures and External Relations. Foreign Policy of the Federal Republic of Germany*. New York: Prager.
Philippart, Eric. 2001. The MEDA Programme: Analysis of the New Design of EU Assistance to the Mediterranean. In *The Barcelona Process and Euro-Mediterranean*

Issues from Stuttgart to Marseille, edited by F. Attinà and S. Stavridis. Milano: Giuffrè.

Pierros, Filippos, Jacob Meunier, and Stan Abrams. 1999. *Bridges and Barriers. The European Union's Mediterranean Policy, 1961–1998*. Aldershot: Ashgate.

Pijpers, Alfred E. 1991. European Political Cooperation and the Realist Paradigm. In *The Future of European Political Cooperation. Essays on Theory and Practice*, edited by M. Holland. London: Macmillan.

Pijpers, Alfred, Elfriede Regelsberger, and Wolfgang Wessels, eds. 1988. *European Political Cooperation in the 1980s. A Common Foreign Policy for Western Europe?* Dordrecht/Boston/London: Martinus Mijhoff Publishers.

Pluchinsky, Dennis. 1982. Political Terrorism in Western Europe: Some Themes and Variations. In *Terrorism in Europe*, edited by Y. Alexander and K. A. Myers. London/Cranberra: Croom Helm.

Pollack, Mark A. 1997. Delegation, Agency, and Agenda-Setting in the European Community. *International Organization* 51 (1).

———. 2003. *The Engines of European Integration. Delegation, Agency, and Agenda Setting in the EU*. Oxford: Oxford University Press.

———. 2005. Theorizing the European Union: International Organization, Domestic Polity, or Experiment in New Governance? *Annual Review of Political Science* 8:357–398.

Pomfret, Richard. 1986. *Mediterranean Policy of the European Community. A Study of Discrimination in Trade*. London: Macmillan.

Ponsaers, Paul, Christiane Janssens, and Yves Cartuyvels. 1992. Le système policier belge. In *Polices d'Europe*, edited by J.-M. Erbes, J. C. Monet, A. Funk, H. Reinke, P. Ponsaers, C. Janssens, Y. Cartuyvels, M. Dauge, J. J. Gleizal, C. Journes, and S. Palidda. Paris: L'Harmattan.

Poulain, Michel. 1994. Les flux migratoires dans le bassin méditerranéen. *Politique Etrangère* 59 (3).

Powell, Charles T. 1995. Spain's External Relations 1898–1975. In *Democratic Spain. Reshaping External Relations in a Changing World*, edited by R. Gillespie, F. Rodrigo, and J. Story. London/New York: Routledge.

Pridham, Geoffrey. 1991. The Politics of the European Community, Transantional Networks and Democratic Transition in Southern Europe. In *Encouraging Democracy. The International Context of Regime Transition in Southern Europe*, edited by G. Pridham. Leicester/London: Leicester University Press.

Putnam, Robert, D. 1988. Diplomacy and Domestic Policy: The Logic of Two-Level Games. *International Organization* 42 (3).

Quandt, William B. 1977. *Decade of Decisions. American Policy toward the Arab-Israeli Conflict, 1967–1976*. Berkeley/Los Angeles/London: University of California Press.

———. 1993. *Peace Process. American Diplomacy and the Arab Israeli Conflict since 1967*. Washington/Berkeley/Los Angeles: The Brookings Institution/University of California Press.

Radaelli, Claudio M. 1999. *Technocracy in the European Union*. New York: Longman.

Radwan, Samir and Jean-Louis Reiffers, eds. 2005. *FEMISE Report. The Euro-Mediterranean Partnership, 10 Years after Barcelona: Achievements and Perspectives*. FEMISE Network. www.femise.org.

Rahmani, Tahar and Adda Bekkouche. 1995. *Coopération décentralisée. L'Union Européenne en Méditerranée occidentale*. Paris: Editions Continent Europe.

Regelsberger, Elfriede, Philippe de Schoutheete de Tervarent, and Wolfgang Wessels. 1997. *Foreign Policy of the European Union. From EPC to CFSP and beyond*. Boulder/London: Lynne Rienner Publishers.

Rein, Martin and Donald Schön. 1993. Reframing Policy Discourse. In *The Argumentative Turn in Policy Analysis and Planning*, edited by F. Fischer and J. Forester. London: UCL Press.

Richards, Alan. 1994. Oil Wealth in the Arab World: Whence, to Whom, and Whither? In *The Arab World Today*, edited by D. Tschirgi. Boulder/London: Lynne Rienner Publishers.

Richards, Alan and John Waterbury. 1990. *A Political Economy of the Middle East*. Boulder/San Francisco/Oxford: Westview Press.

Richard, P. 1980. *Les accords méditerranéens de la CEE en 1980*. Brussels: Prométhée.

Richardson, Jeremy, ed. 2005. *European Union. Power and Policy-Making*. 3rd ed. London: Routledge.

Risse, Thomas. 2000. "Let's Argue!" Communicative Action in World Politics. *International Organization* 54 (1).

———. 2004. Social Constructivism and European Integration. In *European Integration Theory*, edited by Antje Wiener and Thomas Diez. Oxford: Oxford University Press.

Rittberger, Volker, ed. 1995. *Regime Theory and International Relations*. Oxford: Clarendon Press.

Roach, John. 1985. The French Police. In *Police and Public Order in Europe*, edited by J. Roach and J. Thomaneck. London: Croom Helm.

Robins, L. J. 1979. *The Reluctant Party: Labour and the EEC, 1961–1975*. Ormskirk: GW & A. Hesketh.

Rodman, Peter W. 1991. Middle East Diplomacy after the Gulf War. *Foreign Affairs* 70(2).

Rodrigo, Fernando. 1992. The End of the Reluctant Partner: Spain and Western Security in the 1990s. In *Southern European Security in the 1990s*, edited by R. Aliboni. London/New York: Pinter.

Rosamond, Ben. 2005. Conceptualizing the EU Model of Governance in World Politics. *European Foreign Affairs Review* 10 (4).

Rosas, Allen. 2000. The European Union and Mixed Agreements. In *The General Law of E.C. External Relations*, edited by A. Dashwood and C. Hillion.

Rosenthal, G. 1982. *The Mediterranean Basin, Its Political Economy and Changing International Relations*. London: Butterworths Scientific.

Roussel, Eric. 1994. *Georges Pompidou, 1911–1974*. Paris: Lattes.

Rubin, Barry. 1985. *Secrets of State: The State Department and the Struggle over U.S. Foreign Policy*. New York: Oxford University Press.

———. 1994. *Revolution until Victory? The Politics and History of the PLO.* Cambridge, MA/London: Harvard University press.

Sabatier, P. A. and H. C. Jenkins-Smith 1993. *Policy Change and Learning. An Advocacy Coalition Approach.* Boulder/S.Francisco/Oxford: Westview Press.

Salamé, Ghassan. 1994. Torn between the Atlantic and the Mediterranean: Europe and the Middle East in the Post-Cold War Era. *Middle East Journal* 48 (2).

Sampson, Anthony. 1975. *The Seven Sisters. The Great Oil Companies and the World They Made.* London: Hodder and Stoughton.

Sanders, David. 1990. *Losing an Empire, Finding a Role: An Introduction to British Foreign Policy since 1945.* Basingstoke: Macmillan Education.

Sandholtz, Wayne and Alec Stone Sweet. 1998. *European Integration and Supranational Governance.* Oxford: Oxford University Press.

Santos, Alberto. 1985. Le basculement vers le sud de la politique de défense de l'Espagne. *Etudes Internationales* (3).

Sartori, G. 1970. "Concept Misinformation in Comparative Politics." *American Political Science Review* 64(4).

Sayigh, Yezid and Avi Shlaim, eds. 1997. *The Cold War and the Middle East.* Oxford: Clarendon Press.

Scharpf, Fritz W. 1988. The Joint-Decision Trap: Lessons from German Federalism and European Integration. *Public Administration* 66 (3).

Schimmelfennig, Frank. 2001. The Community Trap: Liberal Norms, Rhetorical Action, and the Eastern Enlargement of the European Union. *International Organization* 55 (1).

———. 2003. *The EU, NATO and the Integration of Europe. Rules and Rhetoric.* Cambridge: Cambridge University Press.

Schmitt, Maurice. 1993. Données spécifiques de sécurité. *Défense nationale* 49 (March).

Schneider, Gerard and Lars-Erik Cedermann. 1994. The Change of Tide in Political Cooperation: a Limited Information Model of European Integration. *International Organization* 48 (4).

Schneider, Mark and Paul Teske. 1992. Toward a Theory of the Political Entrepreneur: Evidence from Local Government. *American Political Science Review* 86 (3).

Schumpeter, Joseph A. 1939. *Business Cycles: A Theoretical, Historical and Statistical Analysis of the Capitalist Process.* New York: McGraw-Hill.

Sciortino, Giuseppe. 1999. Planning in the Dark: The Evolution of Italian Immigration Control. In *Mechanisms of Immigration Control: A Comparative Analysis of European Regulation Policies*, edited by G. Brochmann and T. Hammar. Oxford: Berg.

Searle, John R. 1995. *The Construction of Social Reality.* London: Allen Lane.

Sela, Avraham. 1998. *The Decline of the Arab-Israeli Conflict.* Albany. State University of New York Press.

Shlaim, Avi. 1976. The Community and the Mediterranean Basin. In *Europe and the World. The External Relations of the Common Market*, edited by K. J. Twitchett. London: Europa Publications.

Shlaim, Avi, and G. N. Yannopoulos, eds. 1976. *The EEC and the Mediterranean Countries*. Cambridge et al.: Cambridge University Press.
Shonfield, Andrew. *1973. Europe, Journey to an Unknown Destination: An Expanded Version of the BBC Reith Lectures 1972*, London: Allen Lane.
Shultz, Richard, Roy Godson, and Ted Greenwood, eds. 1993. *Security Studies for the 1990s*. New York: Brassey's.
Silvestri, Stefano. 1974. Italy between the Mediterranean and Europe. In *The Western Mediterranean. Its Political, Economic, and Strategic Importance*, edited by A. J. Cottrell and J. D. Theberge. New York: Praeger/Center for Strategic and International Studies of Georgetown University.
Simonian, Haig. 1985. The Priviledged Partnership. Franco-German Relations in the European Community. 1969–1984. Oxford: Clarendon Press.
Smith, Karen E. 1999. *The Making of EU Foreign Policy: The Case of Eastern Europe*. London/New York: Macmillan/St.Martin's Press.
———. 2005. The Ousiders: The European Neighbourhood Policy. *International Affairs* 81(4).
Smith, Michael E. 1998. Rules, Transgovernmentalism and the Expansion of European Political Cooperation. In *European Integration and Supranational Governance*, edited by W. Sandholtz and A. Stone Sweet. Oxford: Oxford University Press.
———. 2004. Institutionalization, Policy Adaptation and European Foreign Policy Cooperation. *European Journal of International Relations* 10 (1).
Smith, Steve. 1989. Strategic Aspects of Atlantic Relations in the Reagan Era. In *Atlantic Relations: Beyond the Reagan Era*, edited by S. Gill. Brighton: Wheatsheaf.
Smith, Steven K. and Douglas A. Wertman. 1992. *US-West European Relations during the Reagan Years. The Perspective of West European Publics*. London: Macmillan.
Sobel, Lester A. 1974. *Energy Crisis*. New York: Facts on File.
———. 1975. *Political Terrorism*. New York: Facts on File.
Soetendorp, Ben. 1999. *Foreign Policy in the European Union*. London/New York: Longman.
Soutou, Georges-Henri. 1996. *L'alliance incertaine. Les rapports politico-stratégiques franco-allemands, 1954–1996*. Paris: Fayard.
Spector, Malcolm and John I. Kitsuse. 1977. *Constructing Social Problems*. Menlo Park, CA: Cummings Publisher.
Spiegel, Steven. 1985. *The Other Arab-Israeli Conflict: Making America's Middle East Policy, from Truman to Reagan*. Chicago: University of Chicago Press.
———. 1992. *Conflict Management in the Middle East*. London: Pinter.
Stortoni-Wortmann, Luciana. 2000. The Police Response to Terrorism in Italy from 1969 to 1983. In *European Democracies against Terrorism. Governmental Policies and Intergovernmental Cooperation*, edited by F. Reinares. Dartmouth: Ashgate.

Story, Jonathan. 1995. Spain's External Relations Redefined: 1975–89. In *Democratic Spain. Reshaping External Relations in a Changing World*, edited by R. Gillespie, F. Rodrigo and J. Story. London/New York: Routledge.

Surel, Yves. 2000. The Role of Cognitive and Normative Frames in Policy-Making. *Journal of European Public Policy* 7 (4).

Swinbank, Alan and Christopher Ritson. 1988. The Common Agricultural Policy, Customs Unions and the Mediterranean Basin. *Journal of Common Market Studies* 28 (2).

Szyliowicz, Joseph S. 1975. The Embargo and U.S. Foreign Policy. In *The Energy Crisis and U.S. Foreign Policy*, edited by J. S. Szyliowicz and B. E. O'Neill. New York/Washington/London: Praeger.

Tanner, Fred. 1996. An Emerging Security Agenda for the Mediterranean. *Mediterranean Politics* 1 (3).

Thomson, Robert and Madeleine O. Hosli. 2006. Explaining Legislative Decision Making in the European Union. In *The European Union Decides*, edited by R. Thomson, F. N. Stokeman, C. H. Achen, and T. König. Cambridge: Cambridge University Press.

Thränhardt, Dietrich. 1999. Germany's Immigration Policies and Politics. In *Mechanisms of Immigration Control. A Comparative Analysis of European Regulation Policies*, edited by G. Brochmann and T. Hammer. Oxford/New York: Berg.

Tibi, Bassam. 1998. *The Challenge of Fundamentalism. Political Islam and the New World Disorder*. Berkeley/Los Angeles/London: University of California Press.

Tovias, Alfred. 1977. *Tariff Preferences in Mediterranean Diplomacy*. London: Macmillan.

———. 1995. Spain in the European Community. In *Democratic Spain. Reshaping External Relations in a Changing World*, edited by R. Gillespie, F. Rodrigo, and J. Story. London/New York: Routledge.

———. 1996. The EU's Mediterranean Politics under Pressure. In *Mediterranean Politics*, edited by R. Gillespie. London: Pinter.

———. 1998. Spain's Input in Shaping the EU's Mediterranean Policies, 1986–96. *Spain and the Mediterranean since 1898* 13 (1–2).

Tovias, Alfred, and Mehmet Ugur. 2004. Can the EU Anchor Policy Reform in Third Countries? An Analysis of the Euro-Med Partnership. *European Union Politics* 5 (4).

Trebous, Madeleine. 1970. *Migrations et Développement, le cas de l'Algérie*. Paris: Etudes du Centre de Développement de l'OCDE.

Tsardanidis, Charalambos and Stefano Guerra. 2000. The EU Mediterranean States, the Migration Issue and the "Threat" from the South. In *Eldorado or Fortress? Migration in Southern Europe*, edited by R. King, G. Lazaridis, and C. Tsardanidis. London/New York: Macmillan/St.Martin's Press.

Tsebelis, George. 1994. The Power of the European Parliament as a Conditional Agenda Setter. *American Political Science Review* 88 (1).

Tsoukalis, Loukas. 1977. The EEC and the Mediterranean: is 'Global' Policy a Misnomer? *International Affairs* 53 (3).
———. 1981. *The European Community and Its Mediterranean Enlargement.* London/Boston/Sydney: George Allen & Unwin.
Vandewalle, Dirk. 1997. Islam in Algeria: Religion, Culture, and Opposition in a Rentier State. In *Political Islam. Revolution, Radicalism, or Reform?* edited by J. L. Esposito. Boulder/London: Lynne Rienner Publishers.
Vaquer i Fanés, Jordi. 2003. The Domestic Dimension of the EU External Policies: The Case of the EU-Morocco 2000–02 Fisheries Negotiations. *Mediterranean Politics* 8 (1).
Venturini, Alessandra. 1994. *Changing Patterns of Labour Emigration in Southern Europe.* Bergamo: Università degli Studi di Bergamo, Dipartimento di Scienze Economiche.
Vertzberger, Yaacov Y. 1990. *The World in Their Minds: Information Processing, Cognition, and Perception in Foreign Policy Decision Making.* Palo Alto: Stanford University Press.
Wæver, Ole. 1995. Identity, Integration and Security. Solving the Sovereignty Puzzle in the E.U. studies. *Journal of International Affairs* 48 (2).
Wæver, Ole, Berry Buzan, Morten Kelstrup, and Pierre Lemaitre. 1993. *Identity, Migration and the New Security Agenda in Europe.* London: Pinter Publishers Ltd.
Walker, Neil. 1998. The New Frontiers of European Policing. In *The Frontiers of Europe*, edited by M. Anderson and E. Bort. London/Washington: Pinter.
Wallace, William. 2003. Looking after the Neighbourhood: Responsibilities for the EU-25. In *Policy Papers N.4*: Groupement d'Etudes et de Recherches Notre Europe.
Wallace, William and David Allen. 1977. Political Cooperation: Procedure as Substitute for Policy. In *Policy-Making in the European Communities*, edited by H. Wallace, W. Wallace, and C. Webb. London/New York/Sydney/Toronto: John Wiley & Sons.
Walt, Stephen M. 1985. Alliance Formation and the Balance of World Power. *International* 9 (4).
Waltz, Kenneth. 1979. *Theory of International Politics.* New York: Columbia University Press.
Ward, Stuard. 1997. Anglo-Commonwealth Relations and the EEC Membership: The Problem of the old Dominions. In *Britain's Failure to Enter the European Community 1961–63. The Enlargement Negotiations and Crises in European Atlantic and Commonwealth Relations*, edited by G. Wilkes. London/Portland, OR: Frank Cass.
Waterbury, John. 1979. Les implications politiques et diplomatiques du dialogue international. In *Le Dialogue Euro-Arabe*, edited by J. Bourrinet. Paris: Economica.
Weil, Gordon L. 1970. *A Foreign Policy for Europe?* Bruges: College of Europe.
Weintraub, Jeff. 1997. The Theory and Politics of the Public/Private Distinction. In *Public and Private in Thought and Practice. Perspectives on a*

Grand Dichotomy, edited by J. Weintraub and K. Kumar. Chicago/London: University of Chicago Press.

Weldes, Jutta. 1996. Constructing National Interests. *European Journal of International Relations* 2 (3).

Wendt, Alexander. 1987. The Agent-Structure Problem in International Relations Theory. *International Organization* 41 (3).

———. 1999. *Social Theory of International Politics*. Cambridge: Cambridge University Press.

White, Brian. 1999. The European Challenge to Foreign Policy Analysis. *European Journal of International Relations* 5 (1).

Whitman, Richard G. 1999. Securing Europe's Southern Flank? A Comparison of NATO, EU and WEU Policies and Objectives. In NATO Individual Research Fellowships 1997–1999. www.nato.int.

Wilkes, George. 1997. Introduction. In *Britain's Failure to Enter the European Community 1961–63. The Enlargement Negotiations and Crises in European Atlantic and Commonwealth Relations*, edited by G. Wilkes. London/Portland, OR: Frank Cass.

Wilkinson, Paul. 2001. *Terrorism versus Democracy: The Liberal State Response*. London/Portland, OR: Frank Cass.

Williams, Allan M. 1991. *The European Community. The Contradictions of Integration*. Oxford, UK/Cambridge, MA: Blackwell.

Williams, Michael C. 2001. The Discipline of the Democratic Peace. Kant, Liberalism and the Social Construction of Security Communities. *European Journal of International Relations* 7 (4).

Williamson, Oliver E. 1975. *Markets and Hierarchies*. New York: Free Press.

———. 1990. A Comparison of Alternative Approaches to Economic Organization. *Journal of Institutional and Theoretical Economics* 146:61–71.

Wolfers, Arnold. 1962. *Discord and Collaboration: Essays on International Politics*. Baltimore: Johns Hopkins University Press.

World Bank. 1981. *Morocco. Economic and Social Development Report*. Washington, DC: World Bank.

Xenakis, Dimitris K. and Dimitris N. Chryssochoou. 2001. *The Emerging Euro-Mediterranean System*. Manchester: Manchester University Press.

Yannopoulos, George N. 1976. Migrant Labour and Economic Growth: The Post-war Experience of the EEC Countries. In *The EEC and the Mediterranean Countries*, edited by A. Shlaim and G. N. Yannopoulos. Cambridge: Cambridge University Press.

———. 1989. The Management of Trade-Induced Structural Adjustment: An Evaluation of the EC's Integrated Mediterranean Porgrammes. *Journal of Common Market Studies* 26 (4).

Yapp, M. E. 1996. *The Near East since the First World War. A History to 1995*. 2nd ed. London/New York: Longman.

Young, John and John Kent. 2003. *International Relations since 1945: A Global History*. Oxford: Oxford University Press.

Young, Oran R. 1999. Comment on Andrew Moravcsik, "A New Statecraft? Supranational Entrepreneurs and International Cooperation." *International Organization* 53 (4).

Youngs, Richard. 2001. *The European Union and the Promotion of Democracy*. Oxford: Oxford University Press.

Zaharidis, Nikolaos. 1999. Ambiguity, Time, and Multiple Streams. In *Theories of the Policy Process*, edited by P. A. Sabatier. Boulder, CO: Westview Press.

Zielonka, Jan. 1998. *Explaining Euro-Paralysis. Why Europe Is Unable to Act in International Politics*. London/New York: Macmillan/St.Martin's Press.

Index

9/11
  intelligence preceding, 21
  EMP agenda and, 170–71
African, Caribbean, and Pacific (ACP) countries, 167, 168
Algeria, *197, 199, 207, 208, 211, 213*
  5 + 5 meetings and, 158
  cancellation of elections, 141–43, 161
  Cooperation Agreement and, 95
  demilitarization of Mediterranean and, 67
  economy, 119
  EEC and, 54–55, 94–95, 103
  EMP and, 170
  Euro-Mediterranean Association Agreement and, 173
  France and, 47, 50, 87, 141
  gas and, 153
  Islamic fundamentalism and, 141–43
  migration and, 138–39
  nationalization of foreign assets and, 74–75
  oil and, 75–76, 77–78
  Spain and, 153
  trade and, 55, 75–76, 162
  USSR and, 66
Arab-Israeli conflict
  Big Four Talks and, 87, 89
  demilitarization of Mediterranean and, 67
  Euro-Arab Dialogue and, 108
  European attitudes toward, 108
  European security and, 64, 80
  Jordan and, *193*
  Kissinger and, 80–83
  oil trade and, 77, 78–79
  terrorism and, 69–72, 143
  U.S. and, 116, 145–47
  USSR and, 92
  Venice Declaration and, 115–16
  Working Group on the Middle East and, 93
  Yom Kippur war (1973), 65, 67, 82
  See also oil shock
Arab-Israeli peace process
  Commission and, 147
  divergences between U.S. and Europe, 145–48
  EMP and, 163–68, 174, 180
  Madrid Conference, 145–46, 154
  Maghreb countries and, 163–64
  marginalization of Europe, 145, 164, 178
Arab League, 101–102, 104, 108
Arab nationalism, 46–47
Association Agreements. *See specific countries*; Euro-Mediterranean Association Agreements

Barcelona Conference (1995), 147, 169–70
Barcelona Declaration (1995), 167, 169–70, 172, *214*

Belgium
  foreign population in, *208, 209*
  France and, 85, 99
  Israel and, *201*
  Negotiations on the GMP and, 92–94, 99, 101
  reform of armed forces, 133
  Spain and, 50, 92, 100
  terrorism and, 72
Big Four Talks, 82, 87, 89
Black September (1970), 71
Brandt, Willy, 83, 89, 92, 102
CAP. *See* Common Agricultural Policy
Central and Eastern European countries (CEECs), 148–51, 155
CET. *See* Common External Tariff
Charter for Peace and Stability, 171, *214*
Claes, Willy, 142
cognitive interaction, 35–39
cognitive uncertainty, 19–25
cold war, 45–52, 66–68, 85, 89
  bilateral agreements during, 45
  effect on policy innovation, 45, 60
  effect on policy window, 35, 45, 48–49, 52, 80, 120–23, 126–27
  end of the cold war and desecuritization, 132–34
  end of the cold war and EFP making, 120
  Greece and, 45, 59
  Mediterranean and, 45–52
  second, 114–20
  Turkey and, 45, 59
Commission. *See* European Commission
Committee of Permanent Representatives (COREPER), 13, 95, 96–97, 99
  France and, 96, 97
  Netherlands and, 97
  UK and, 99
Common Agricultural Policy (CAP), 58, 100, 122

Common External Tariff (CET), 57–59, 84
Common Foreign and Security Policy (CFSP), 2, 14, 150, 164, 175, 177
Common Market, 51, 56, 84, 171
Common Strategy for the Mediterranean (2000), 171
Conference on Security and Cooperation in the Mediterranean (CSCM), 157, 158–63, 167
COREPER. *See* Committee of Permanent Representatives
Cyprus
  Association Agreement (1973), 47, 48, 49, 53, 54–55, 59, 105
  Common External Tariff and, 57
  conflict, *196*
  EU membership, 149, 173, *193*
  MEDA and, *215*
  Mediterranean détente and, 67
  trade and, 76, 122
  U.K. and, 67, 68

détente
  containment of USSR and, 81
  European economy and, 48, 99
  importance of, 48–49
  in the Mediterraneann, 66–68
  international politics and, 47, 64
  Pompidou and, 89
  Southern enlargement and, 91
  Soviet invasion of Afghanistan and, 112–15
Dialoguee 5 + 5, 158

EAD. *See* Euro-Arab Dialogue
Economic and Social Committee, 140
EEC. *See* European Economic Community
Egypt, *208, 213*
  Arab League and, 104
  Cooperation Agreement and, 105
  economy, 119
  EEC and, 48, 54–55
  ENP and, 176

Euro-Mediterranean Association Agreement and, 173
  nationalization of foreign assets and, 74
  oil and, 77
  Preferential Agreement (1973), 49, 53
  trade and, 57, 153
  USSR and, 66, 67
entrepreneurship, 28–34
  entrepreneurial 'believers,' 3, 9, 28–30, 33, 65
  entrepreneurial 'brokers,' 3, 9, 17, 28–34, 35, 37
  Commission and, 30–31, 112–13, 123–25, 157, 186–88. *See also* Commission, entrepreneurship
  France and, 86–91, 101, 102
  Spain and, 151–57
  See also policy entrepreneurship
EPC Working Group on the Middle East, 93
Euro-Arab Dialogue (EAD), 63–65, 91, 101–104, 108–109, 170
  France and, 102, 104
  intergovernmentalism and, 179
  launch of, 63–65, *206*
  oil shock and, 65
  Working Group on the Middle East and, 93
EUROFOR, 134
EUROMARFOR, 134
Euro-Mediterranean Association Agreements, 172, 173
  See also specific countries
Euro-Mediterranean Partnership (EMP)
  agenda, 169, 171, 180
  aid and, 150, 168–69
  Arab-Israeli relations and, 163–68
  democratisation and, 170
  development of, 129–30, 155, 157, 167–69, 185
  economic liberalization, 171
  entrepreneurship and, 155–57
  human rights and, 170
  institutional structure of, 168–69
  RMP and, 129, 155–57, 167
  Second Intifada and, 171
  security and, 171, 174–75
  Spain and, 158–63
  trade and, 171–72, 179–80
  U.S. and, 158
  vs. ENP, 176
  vs. GMP, 179
  See also specific countries and aspects
European Commission
  adjustments to Agreements and, 94–95
  CEECs and, 148–50
  cold war and, 49–52, 60
  Cooperation Agreements and, 107
  COREPER and, 95, 99–100
  CSCM and, 159–61
  delegation of powers to, 13
  EEC agreements with Mediterranean countries and, 49–52, 52–53, 55
  EMP and, 129–31, 157–59, 163–66, 169–70, 172, 176
  ENP and, 175–78
  entrepreneurship, 17, 38–39, 151, 155–57: as entrepreneurial "believer," 30–31; as entrepreneurial broker, 31; attempts at, 112–13, 123–25, 177–78; evaluation of, 186–88; lack of, 49–50
  EU enlargement and, 148–50
  Euro-Arab Dialogue and, 86, 102, 104, 108–109
  Euro-Maghreb Partnership and, 162–63
  free trade and, 147
  GMP and, 64, 91–95, 96–101, 107, 110
  Italy and, 151
  Maghreb countries and, 96–97, 161–63
  migration and, 140
  Morocco and, 161

European Commission—*continued*
  oil shock and, 78
  POCO and, 14
  RMP and, 155–56, 157, 161, 175, 178, 179
  Southern enlargement and, 126–27
  Spain and, 130–31, 159–61, 182
European Economic Community (EEC), 6, 43–52, 181
  agreements with Mediterranean nonmember countries, 52–60
  balance between Northern and Southern European countries, 84–85, 100
  Cooperation Agreements and, 105–106
  Euro-Arab Dialogue and, 103–104, 107–108
  France and, 54
  Israel and, *196–97*
  militarization and, 66–73
  Portugal and, *197*
  trade with Arab countries and, 73–80
European Free Trade Association (EFTA), 76, *197, 204*
European integration, contemporary analytical approaches to, 10–19
European Initiative for Democracy and Human Rights (EIDHR), *215*
European Neighbourhood Policy (ENP)
  Action Plans, 176–77
  development of, 175, 179
  EMP and, 129–31
  enlargement of, 176
  entrepreneurship and, 177, 187
  Mediterranean countries and, 175–78
  Middle East and, 180
  RMP and, 178
  tensions within, 176–77
  vs. EMP, 176
European Parliament
  GMP and, 64, 91–92, 96, 110, 150, 165
  EMP and, 150, 174
  ENP and, 177
  Israel and, *212*
  migration and, 140
  Morocco and, 161–62, *212–13*
  Southern enlargement and, 123
European Political Cooperation (EPC)
  economic development in the Mediterranean and, 100
  Euro-Arab Dialogue and, 63–64, 86, 101–104
  France and, 87, 90, 92, 109
  Italy and, 92
  oil and, 78
  Single European Act (SEA) and, 112–13
  terrorism and, 73
  Working Group on the Middle East, 93
  Working Group "Problems of the Mediterranean," 78, 92–94
European Union (EU) enlargement
  Eastern, 145, 148, 149–50
  Northern, 84–85
  Southern, 148–49

framing. *See* cognitive interaction
France
  5 + 5 meetings and, 158
  Algeria and, 47, 50, 87, 141
  arms deals, 67, 87, 89, 102, 141–42, *201*
  Big Four Talks and, 82
  CAP and, 58
  CSCM and, 158
  EMP and, 157, 160–61, 164–67
  "empty chair" crisis, 54
  entrepreneurship, 52, 63–65, 86–91, 101–102, 109–10, 151, 160–61, 164–67
  EPC and, 87, 90, 92, 109
  Euro-Arab Dialogue and, 86, 103–104
  foreign policy towards Maghreb countries, 47–48, 87–89, 96
  GMP and, 64, 65, 86, 90, 95–96, 99–100

Israel and, 50, 53, 87, 96–97, *208*
migration and, 135–40
Morocco and, 50, 88, 161–62, *214*
Ostpolitik and, 85–86
reform of armed forces, 133
regionalism, 84–85
Southern enlargement and, 121, 149
Spain and, 48, 87–89, 130, 148, 161, 164–66, 178–79
terrorism and, 72, 143
U.S. and, 84, 103–4
Working Group "Problems of the Mediterranean" and, 93

General Agreement on Tariffs and Trade (GATT), 47–48, 57, 59, 176
Germany, 149, 164, 166
  CEECs and, 148
  Cold War and, 26, 48, 50, 56, 71–73, 78, 115
  CSCM and, 158
  economy, 48, 56
  Euro-Arab Dialogue and, 103–104
  GMP and, 91, 92–93
  Israel and, 50, 81
  migration and, 135–37, 139–40
  oil and, 77–78
  Ostpolitik and, 83–86, 87, 89, 109
  reform of armed forces, 133
  terrorism and, 71–73
  U.S. and, 99
Global Mediterranean Policy (GMP)
  Agreements under the GMP, 104–109
  EMP and, 129–31, 156, 168–74, 179
  establishment of, 63–65, 84, 98–102, 109–10, 179, 101
  Euro-Arab Dialogue and, 102, 104–109, 125–26, 170
  framing of, 95–101
  France and, 64, 65, 86, 90, 99–100
  free trade and, 171
  Italy and, 99–100
  Middle East and, 83

"pyramid of privileges" created by, 44
region building and, 164, 181
reciprocity in concessions, 57, 59, 99–100, 106, *197*
RMP and, 155, 168–71
Southern enlargement and, 84, 124–25
specification of content, 98
U.K. and, 98–99
U.S. criticism of, 98
Greece
  aid provisions and, 56
  Association Agreement (1962), 49, 53, 56, 105
  Cold War and, 45–48
  EEC and, 44, 49–51, 52, 125–26
  ENP and, 176
  financial aid and, 100
  reform of armed forces and, 133
  Southern enlargement and, 111–12, 120–23
  trade and, 57–60
  U.S. and, 67
  worker mobility and, 56
Gulf War, 141, 145–46, 159, 161–62

ideational intergovernmentalism, 6, 10, 15, 32, 40, 41
INTERREG, 177
Islamic fundamentalism, 130–32, 141–44, 153, 162, 178, 182, 184
Israel, *208, 210, 214*
  Action Plan, 176
  agricultural trade, 51
  arms deals and *200, 201*
  Big Four Talks and, 82
  CET and, 57, 59
  EEC agreements with, 44, 46–48, 49, 52 54
  EEC and, 46, 52–54, *196–97, 208*
  Euro-Mediterranean Association Agreement and, 173
  European criticisms of, 81, 93, *212*
  financial aid to, *215*
  France and, 50, 87, 96–97, *208*

Israel—*continued*
  Germany and, 48, 50, 96
  Kissinger and, 81
  Morocco and, *213*
  Netherlands and, 96
  Nonpreferential Agreement (1964), 49, 53
  Preferential Agreement (1970), 49, 53
  Spain and, 50, 96, 100–101, 152, 153–54, 182, *196, 204*
  trade and, 96–97, 119, 153, *204, 206*
  U.S. and, 66–67, 81–82, 115–17, 163–64
  Working Group on the Middle East and, 93
  Yom Kippur war (1973) and, 82
  See also Arab-Israeli conflict; Arab-Israeli peace process
Italy
  Algeria and, 54, 142
  cold war and, 68
  CSCM and, 157, 158, 160
  EEC and, 93–94
  EMP and, 157, 158, 167
  ENP and, 179
  entrepreneurial efforts: against a Mediterranean initiative, 48–52; in favour of a Mediterranean initiative, 92–93, 130, 151, 157, 158, 160
  France and, 85, 90
  GMP and, 64, 91–92, 96, 97, 99–101, 110
  migration and, 20, 22, 135, 139
  oil and, 76, 79
  reform of armed forces and, 133
  Southern enlargement and, 149, 166
  Spain and, 167, 178, 182
  terrorism and, 71–72
  trade and, 48, 49–51, 60–61, 76, 121
  U.S. and, 103

Jordan, *197, 208*
  Action Plan, 176
  arms sales and, 87, 153
  Cooperation Agreement, 105
  EEC and, 55, 60
  Euro-Mediterranean Association Agreement and, 173
  France and, 87
  Palestinians and, 145
  terrorism and, 71
  trade and, 76
  U.S. and, 67

Kissinger, Henry, 80–83

Lebanon
  Action Plan, 176
  aid to, 56
  Cooperation Agreement, 49, 53
  Euro-Mediterranean Association Agreement and, 173
  Germany and, 135
  Nonpreferential Agreement (1968), 49, 53
  Preferential Agreement (not ratified), 49, 53, 55
  trade and, 57, 76
  U.S. and, 67, 116
Liberal intergovernmentalism, 11, 17, 29, 32, 41, 113, 120, 189
  constructivism and, 189, 191
  entrepreneurship and, 17, 29, 30, 31–32, 39, 110, 186
  EFP and, 174, 184, 188
  EMP and, 174
  EPC and, 86
  GMP and, 65, 179
Libya, 78
  5 + 5 meetings and, 158
  arms sales to, 67, 89
  demilitarization of Mediterranean and, 67
  France and, 67, 89, *201*
  marginalization of, 174, *208*
  oil and, 75, 77–78, 92
  Spain and, 88
  trade and, 55, 60
  USSR and, 66

Maastricht Treaty, 140, 147, 170, *213*
Machrek countries, 100, 106, 153, 165
Maghreb countriess, 96–97, 150
   Arab-Israeli peace process and, 163–64
   CSCM and, 157
   financial aid to, 100
   free trade and, 106, 161–63
   GMP and, 106
   migration and, 138, 140
   proposal for Euro-Maghreb partnership, 161–62
   RMP and, 129, 156
   Spain and, 149, 152, 157, *211–12*
Malta
   5 + 5 meetings and, 158
   Association Agreement (1971), 49, 53, 105
   EU membership, 149, 173, *193*
   Germany and, 48
   negotiations with EEC, 54–55, 56
   trade and, 57, 76
   UK and, 67
MEDA, 172–74, 176–77, *210, 215*
Middle East
   Maghreb countries and, 163–64
   terrorism and, 68–73
   relations between Europe and the U.S. on, 80–83, 115, 145, 148
   EPC Working Group on, 93
   See also specific countries; Arab-Israeli conflict, Arab-Israeli peace process
Mitterrand, Francois, 149, 158, 161
Morocco
   5 + 5 meetings and, 158
   Action Plan, 176
   Association Agreement (1969), 49, 51, 53, 54–55, 57–59
   Cooperation Agreement, 105
   EEC and, 48, 54–55
   EMP and, 170
   ENP and, 176
   EP and, 161–62, *212–13*
   Euro-Mediterranean Association Agreement, 173
   Fisheries agreement, 166
   France and, 50, 88
   human rights' record, *212–13*
   Mediterranean security and, 134
   migration and, 135, 139
   nationalization of foreign assets and, 74–76, 94–95
   Spain, 149, 153, 166
   trade and, 59, 122, 161–63
   USSR and, 66

neofunctionalism, 11, 14, 39, 164, 187–91
   supranational/neofunctionalist approaches, 30–31, 39, 112–13, 127, 155, 179, 187, 190–91
Netherlands
   CSCM and, 158
   EEC and, 85
   Euro-Arab Dialogue and, 103
   GMP and, 101–103
   Israel and, 81, 102
   Middle East and, 92–93, 96
   reform of armed forces and, 133
   oil and, 77–79, 92
   Spain and, 50
   terrorism and, 77
   trade and, 166
Nixon, Richard, 67, 81, 98
North Atlantic Treaty Organization (NATO)
   Cold War and, 115
   EEC association agreements and, 46
   France and, 90
   Islamic fundamentalism and, 141
   Israel and, 82
   reorganization of, 133, 142
   Spain and, 152, 154, *211*
   Strategic Concept, 142

oil
   EEC energy policy and, 106
   diplomacy and, 81, 92, 102–103, 126, 144
   drop in price of, 117, 118

oil—*continued*
  Euro-Arab Dialogue and, 102–104, 108
  Libya and, 55
  nationalization and, 74–78
  security and, 66, 102, 109, 117–18, 126
  terrorism and, 71, 109, 131
  See also oil shock
oil shock, 64–65, 73–75, 99, 101–103, 117, 185
  disjointed reaction of EEC member states, 78–80
  Euro-Arab Dialogue and, 102–103
  U.S. approach to, 83
  See also oil
Organization of Petroleum Exporting Countries (OPEC), 77–78, 83, 102, 117, *199*

Palestine Liberation Organization (PLO), 154
Palestinian Authority, 176, *193, 208*
  Action Plan, 176
  Euro-Mediterranean Interim Association Agreement and, 173, *215*
PHARE, 150, 155
POCO. *See* Political Committee
policy entrepreneurship, 17, 19, 28–34, 178–87
  absence of a policy entrepreneur, 49–52, 60, 112–13, 151
  Commission and, 30–31, 112–13, 123–25, 157, 186–88. *See also* Commission, entrepreneurship
  EMP and, 129, 131
  ENP and, 177–78, 187
  Euro-Arab Dialogue and, 86, 179
  existence of EFP and, 3
  France and, 86–91, 102
  GMP and, 86–91
  qualities for success, *195*
  Spain and, 151–57

  See also entrepreneurship
policy windows
  absence of , 44, 60, 61, 112, 113–14, 121, 123
  cognitive uncertainty and, 19–25
  policy entrepreneurs and, 3–5, 12
Political Committee (POCO), 14, 73, 92, 99, 102–103
politicization, 23–24, 25, 178, 181, 185
  of Arab-European relations, 65, 75
  of cold war and, 47–48
  of economic relations, 73–75
  of Islamic fundamentalism, 141–43, 144, 178
  of migration, 139–40
  of oil, 78
  of terrorism, 69
Pompidou, Georges, 87–90, 97, 102, 109, *201*
Portugal
  CAP and, 122
  EFTA and, 76, 96, *197, 204, 206*
  immigration and, *208*
  Mediterranean Forum and, 158, *213*
  reform of armed forces, 133
  oil and, *199*
  preaccession aid, 122–23, 125
  regime change and, 121
  Southern enlargement and, 51, 111–12, 120–23, 125–26, *193*
  U.S. and, *200*

Reagan, Ronald, 114, 116
reciprocity in economic concessions, 57, 59, 99–100, 106, *197*
Regional Economic Development Working Group (REDWG), 145
Renovated Mediterranean Policy (RMP), 164, 167, 168–70
  Commission and, 155–57, 161, 175, 178, 179
  EC and, 155–57
  entrepreneurship in, 156–57
  launch of, 129

RMP. *See* Renovated Mediterranean Policy
Rossi Report, 91–92

Schumann, Maurice, 87–90, 96, *201, 202*
Sixth Fleet (U.S.), 68, 133, 158
Southern enlargement, 51, 111–13, 125, 126–27, 129, 167, 179, *193, 207*
    negative effects on Mediterranean, 120–23
Soviet Union (USSR)
    Algeria and, 66
    Arab-Israeli conflict and, 92
    Cold War and, 45–48, 66–68
    CSCM and, 158
    effects of collapse, 132–34, 136, 142
    Egypt and, 66, 67
    Germany and, 84
    invasion of Afghanistan, 114–17
    Libya and, 66, 89
    Morocco and, 66
    Middle East and, 81
    Tunisia and, 66
Spain
    Belgium and, 92, 96, 100
    CEECs and, 148–49
    CSCM and, 158–63
    EEC and, 50–51, 53–54, 145
    EMP and, 130–31, 157–58, 178–80, 182
    entrepreneurship, 151, 155, 156, 157–68
    foreign policy, 151–54
    France and, 48, 87–89
    Franco, 88, 105, 121, 152, 178
    Germany and, 92–93
    GMP and, 91–93
    Israel and, 96–97, 101
    Maghreb countries and, 153–54
    migration and, 20, 22, 135, 139, 142
    Morocco and, *214*

Preferential Agreement (1970), 49, 53
reform of armed forces and, 133
Southern enlargement and, 111–12, 120–23, 125–26
trade and, 57
U.S. and, 67
Strategic Defense Initiative (SDI), 114–15
Syria
    Arab-Israeli conflict and, 145
    Cooperation Agreement, 105
    economy, 119
    Euro-Mediterranean Association Agreement and, 173
    trade and, 55, 76
    USSR and, 66

TACIS, 150
terrorism, 23, 66, 68–73, 80, 109, 116, 119, 130, 131, 142, 143–44, 153, 166, 169, 170, 171, 185
Tunisia, *201, 207, 213*
    5 + 5 meeting and, 158
    Action Plan, 176
    Association Agreement (1969), 49, 53
    Barcelona Declaration and, 170
    CAP and, 58,
    Cooperation Agreement and, 94, 105, 153
    economy, 119
    EEC and, 54–55
    Euro-Arab Dialogue and, 103
    Euro-Mediterranean Association Agreement and, 173
    financial aid to, 88, 153
    France and, 75, 87–88, 102
    GMP and, 49, 53, 94, 95
    Italy and, *203*
    migration and, 138
    nationalization of foreign assets and, 74–75
    security and, 138, 141
    Southern enlargement and, 122

Tunisia—*continued*
  Spain and, 153
  trade and, 153, 162–63, 166
  U.S. and, 67
  USSR and, 66
Turkey
  accession negotiations and, 53
  aid to, 100
  arms deals, 153
  Association Agreement (1964), 44, 49–50, 49–50, 60, 52–53, 105, 173: staged approach, 53, 56–59
  cold war and, 45, 46–48
  customs union, 56, 57, 59, 173
  economic issues, 119
  EMP and, 170
  GMP and, 91, 107
  migration and, 135, 137, 139
  trade and, 122
  U.S. and, 67

United Kingdom
  accession to EEC, 83–86, 109
  Commonwealth relations, 84, *200*
  EEC enlargement and, 84–85
  EPC Working Group "Problems of the Mediterranean" and, 93
  global approach to trade, 84–85
  Israel and, *200*
  Libya and, *198*
  oil shock and, 102
  reform of armed forces, 133
  terrorism and, 71, 73
  U.S. and, 45, 98–99
United States
  9/11 and, 21
  Arab-Israeli conflict and, 116, 145–47
  Arab-Israeli peace process, 145–48
  cold war and, 45–46, 48, 114–17
  divergencies with Europe, 25, 26, 131, 145–48
  Euro-Arab Dialogue and, 103–104, 110
  France and, 84, 103–104
  Germany and, 99
  GMP and, 98–99
  Greece and, 67
  Iraq and, 141
  Israel and, 66–67, 81–82, 115–17, 163–64
  Middle East and, 80–83, 109
  Portugal and, 200
  reaction to oil shock, 83
  Spain and, 67
  Transatlantic Dialogue and, 147
  Truman doctrine, 45
  Tunisia and, 67
USSR. *See* Soviet Union

Venice Declaration (1980), 93, 113, 115–16, 126

Yom Kippur war (1973), 65, 67, 82